Language Use in the Two-Way Classroom

PEFC

PEFC/16-33-111

CATG-PEFC-052

www.pefc.org

BILINGUAL EDUCATION & BILINGUALISM
Series Editors: **Nancy H. Hornberger** *(University of Pennsylvania, USA)* and Colin Baker *(Bangor University, Wales, UK)*

Bilingual Education and Bilingualism is an international, multidisciplinary series publishing research on the philosophy, politics, policy, provision and practice of language planning, global English, indigenous and minority language education, multilingualism, multiculturalism, biliteracy, bilingualism and bilingual education. The series aims to mirror current debates and discussions.

Full details of all the books in this series and of all our other publications can be found on http://www.multilingual-matters.com, or by writing to Multilingual Matters, St Nicholas House, 31-34 High Street, Bristol BS1 2AW, UK.

BILINGUAL EDUCATION & BILINGUALISM
Series Editors: Nancy H. Hornberger *(University of Pennsylvania, USA)* and Colin Baker *(Bangor University, Wales, UK)*

Language Use in the Two-Way Classroom
Lessons from a Spanish-English Bilingual Kindergarten

Renée DePalma

MULTILINGUAL MATTERS
Bristol • Buffalo • Toronto

Library of Congress Cataloging in Publication Data
A catalog record for this book is available from the Library of Congress.
DePalma, Renée.
Language Use in the Two-Way Classroom: Lessons from a Spanish-English Bilingual
Kindergarten/Renée DePalma.
Bilingual Education & Bilingualism: 76
Includes bibliographical references.
1. Education, Bilingual–United States. 2. Kindergarten–United States. 3. Spanish
language–Study and teaching (Early childhood)–United States. I. Title.
LC3731.D47 2010
370.117′5–dc22 2010021281

British Library Cataloguing in Publication Data
A catalogue entry for this book is available from the British Library.

ISBN-13: 978-1-84769-301-3 (hbk)
ISBN-13: 978-1-84769-300-6 (pbk)

Multilingual Matters
UK: St Nicholas House, 31-34 High Street, Bristol BS1 2AW, UK.
USA: UTP, 2250 Military Road, Tonawanda, NY 14150, USA.
Canada: UTP, 5201 Dufferin Street, North York, Ontario M3H 5T8, Canada.

The policy of Multilingual Matters/Channel View Publications is to use papers that
are natural, renewable and recyclable products, made from wood grown in sustainable
forests. In the manufacturing process of our books, and to further support our policy,
preference is given to printers that have FSC and PEFC Chain of Custody certification.
The FSC and/or PEFC logos will appear on those books where full certification has been
granted to the printer concerned.

Typeset by Datapage International Ltd.
Printed and bound in Great Britain by the MPG Books Group Ltd.

Contents

Chapter 1

The Promise and Realities of Two-Way Instruction

Vignette: A Moment of Success and a Moment of Failure

It is a sunny spring morning in Señora Soto's Kindergarten classroom and I am sitting cross-legged on the floor, notebook in hand, trying to extract meaningful field notes from the din and chaos of children playing together in the Housekeeping and Blocks Centers. It is official Spanish time, the time of day when children, regardless of whether they speak Spanish or English at home, are expected to speak with the teacher and with each other only in Spanish. This rule is strictly enforced by Sra. Soto, who is a native Spanish speaker herself and committed to the goals of this two-way immersion (TWI) Kindergarten as she sees them: to make sure English speakers learn Spanish, to make sure Spanish speakers learn English without losing the language their families brought to the USA, and to make sure all children value Spanish and those who speak it. In the mornings, she is Sra. Soto and we speak Spanish, in the afternoons we speak English with her English-speaking alter ego, Mrs. Soto.

I can barely hear Sra. Soto chatting with a small group of children who are working on a puzzle at a table on the other side of the classroom. They are speaking in Spanish, for the most part. I'm impressed, since some of these children only speak English at home. Another boy, despite being a native Spanish speaker, had categorically refused at the start of the year to speak Spanish in this classroom. Laughter erupts from the table; obviously, they are having fun. I realize I have been distracted from documenting the mostly English interactions going on in the House-keeping Center.

Rashid, an African-American child who has been learning Spanish in this TWI classroom for about seven months now, approaches me and whispers in English, 'Why was Sra. Soto laughing?' Still trying to regain concentration on the nearby Housekeeping play, I shake my head and shrug my shoulders. Then, forgetting myself, I respond to his English question with my own, equally transgressive, English question, 'Why are you speaking to me in English?' Rashid replies, still whispering, 'Because

I don't know Spanish'. When I glance (involuntarily?) over at Sra. Soto, Rashid seems to interpret this as a plan to turn him in. He smiles slyly, cocking his head to one side and touching my arm. He says, still in English, 'No no no. Don't tell her. I was only tricking you'. He walks off, looking back at me and still smiling.

This brief vignette illustrates some of the promise but also the reality of trying to teach a minority language such as Spanish in the USA. Over the course of the first seven months of this brand-new Spanish-English TWI Kindergarten program, Sra. Soto was able to help some English-speaking children learn some basic Spanish. She managed to convince some reluctant Spanish speakers to keep speaking the home language that they shared with her in the face of enormous social pressure to speak English, and only English, in this country[1] (Alba, 2007; Suarez, 2002; Wong-Fillmore, 1991). Furthermore, the classroom had a generally friendly and lively atmosphere: children played together with dolls in the Housekeeping Center, they laughed together with the teacher as they put together a puzzle. Overall, this classroom seemed a cheerful, welcoming place. Sra. Soto was strict at times, and was also a warm, caring and imaginative teacher.

Nevertheless, the vignette also illustrates the realities that make TWI teaching a particular challenge. Rashid and I, both native English speakers, knowingly violated the important official Spanish time rule. Both of us were able to speak Spanish, although neither of us was an especially confident speaker at the time. We were probably both up to the challenge of expressing our simple questions in comprehensible Spanish, but we didn't. And we both clearly understood that Spanish was to be spoken, since the division of the day into official Spanish time (mornings) and official English time (afternoons) had been clearly and consistently signaled and enforced since the beginning of the school year in September. We had both witnessed Sra. Soto painstakingly explaining something with repetitions, gestures and pantomime to a child rather than using the child's stronger language, and we had both witnessed children carefully and awkwardly stringing together two or three Spanish words rather than resort to fluent English. Rashid himself had done that. Yet, there was something about two people who share fluency in the same language, safe in the knowledge that we were momentarily alone, that nudged us into speaking English during Spanish time.

Looking back on this vignette, actually, I am appalled. I had chosen to conduct this study because I strongly advocate programs designed to develop and maintain heritage languages like Spanish in the USA, and my own experience of learning Spanish only served to support my conviction that language development requires persistent use of the target language. I find my momentary collusion with Rashid to undermine the classroom 'Spanish-only' rule, a rule I advocated myself, distressing. What was behind this lapse, was it familiarity, laziness, distraction, self-consciousness, a reluctance to code-switch, some peculiar English-speaker solidarity or maybe a little of each? Whatever moved Rashid and me at the time, I am pretty sure these same forces and more were constantly at work in this classroom against the use of Spanish. My observations throughout the school year also made me notice something I had not anticipated: children's interactions often did not require any language at all. Over and over, I witnessed children share classroom tasks and play together happily without saying much at all, and the activity unfolded perfectly well without the linguistic interactions so fundamental to the TWI model.

This book, then, is a critical analysis of the TWI model. It is critical in the sense that I closely examine and interrogate some assumptions about language learning and classroom design that underpin the model. Nevertheless, this is meant to be a constructive criticism. I support these programs wholeheartedly and hope they continue to proliferate in the USA and internationally. There is plenty of evidence that they are effective; overall, children do learn English and another language, usually Spanish, while continuing to achieve academically (Collier & Thomas, 2004; E.R. Howard *et al.*, 2003a; Lindholm-Leary, 2005; Lindholm-Leary & Borsato, 2002). Yet, I believe we need to understand better *how* they work. My goal is to provide some insights that will help improve TWI instruction. Using an extended ethnographic study of one Kindergarten classroom, my hope is that by closely examining this teacher's accomplishments and challenges, I can help teachers better understand the complexities of children's linguistic (and non-linguistic) interactions and the ways that teaching design can help or hinder language use and development.

What is Two-Way Immersion Instruction?

Language is learned and maintained through interaction, in practice rather than as a separate entity to be studied; 'the co-construction of linguistic knowledge in dialogue is language learning in progress' (Swain & Lapkin, 1998: 321). TWI programs are designed based on this theory. Rather than teaching languages directly, language is used as a medium of instruction and speakers are expected to interact with each other as part of the learning process (Christian, 1994; De Jong, 2002).

Children who speak a majority language, or the language that is dominant in the community, are grouped with children who speak a minority language, and all receive instruction in both languages. Occasionally, the term 'dual language' is used to refer to this program design, but can be confusing because it can sometimes refer to a single language immersion model (see Thomas & Collier, 2003 for this distinction). In single immersion programs, children all speak the same language and are all immersed in a common second language, such as French for English-speaking Canadians (Lazaruk, 2007) or English for Chinese speakers in China (Knell *et al.*, 2007). In TWI programs, by contrast, all children are native speakers of one of the two immersion languages and are expected to act as language resources to help each other learn.

Other bilingual models include transitional bilingual education (TBE), where the student's first language is used only long enough to make learning comprehensible in the early years and developmental bilingual education (DBE), where the student's first language is used along with English as long as possible to ensure that the student develops proficiency in both languages (Center for Research on Education Diversity & Excellence, 2001). For English speakers in the USA, there are both total immersion programs, where a foreign language is used exclusively for instruction in the early years and partial immersion, where instruction is divided between English and the foreign language (Lenker & Rhodes, 2007). Like DBE, TWI programs are expected to help children develop full bilingualism, but TWI differs from all these in that both English speakers and English learners are served at once.

The TWI model design suggests a set of implicit understandings of language acquisition; how these manifest in particular teaching practices and interact with other teaching philosophies is explored in more detail in Chapter 3. Language immersion programs in general are based on the assumption that the most effective language learning occurs through meaningful linguistic interactions in the context of natural communication in the second language, through everyday activities that require language use to achieve the communicative task (Lafford & Salaberry, 2003). In this sense, there is less conscious focus on the language than on the communicative goals, and some linguists distinguish unconscious language *acquisition* from conscious language *learning* (Krashen, 1985). The language takes on the role of a means to an end rather than the goal of learning itself, a goal whose own means traditionally have taken the form of grammar exercises and memorization of vocabulary.

Providing sufficient, comprehensible yet challenging language input is considered to be one of the basic principles of immersion education in general, and TWI in particular, which implies that languages be clearly separated and that each be used as an exclusive medium of instruction (E.R. Howard *et al.*, 2007). This means that in the early years, monolingual children will need considerable support to enhance comprehension of the language with which they are not familiar. In a total immersion setting, language can be made comprehensible initially through the use of repetition and references to the immediate context (Krashen, 1985) as well as by using formulaic language that children tend to remember in chunks before they are able to parse it (Ellis, 2008). Specific activities might include providing opportunities for children to participate in unison in songs and chants so that they can savor the sound and feel of a new language without risking exposure of language imperfections (Fassler, 2003), employing activities and games that combine physical movements with their descriptions (Asher, 1984) and using multiple linguistic and extra-linguistic cues (Peregoy & Boyle, 1999).

These strategies provide an alternative to the traditional transmission approach to language instruction that has been referred to as sheltered instruction (E.R. Howard *et al.*, 2007). Sheltered instruction strategies in TWI programs must be carefully distinguished from the so-called sheltered English immersion or structured English immersion (SEI) programs mandated for children with limited English proficiency under California's Proposition 227, as these are based on deficit views of bilingualism and foster transition (second/majority language acquisition at the expense of first/minority language loss) rather than bilingual enrichment (Mora *et al.*, 2001). TWI programs are based on a holistic understanding of a bilingual person as having a unique and complex multilinguistic profile rather than on fractional bilingualism, or the expectation that a bilingual person is the sum of two complete or incomplete monolinguals (Baker, 2006).

The TWI program is also based on research suggesting that extended instruction in one's native language is necessary to achieve long-term academic competence and has a positive effect on second language acquisition (Collins, 2007). Successful English acquisition in children enrolled in TWI programs that offer more instruction time in Spanish than in English supports this interpretation (Quintanar-Sarellana, 2004; Smith & Arnot-Hopffer, 1998). Language interaction between children from different language backgrounds and between the teacher and students is also considered to be more effective than more traditional transmission models of teaching, as this not only provides native language modeling, but also fosters creativity and dialogic engagement (E.R. Howard *et al.*, 2007). In this approach, 'students are not perceived as individuals with empty minds who will learn a language... (rather)... both teachers and students critically perceive their realities and create knowledge within dialogue' (Moraes, 1996: 105).

There are two main approaches to language use in TWI programs. In the 50:50 model, English and the minority language are used for equal amounts of time throughout all grades. In the 90:10 model, the minority language is used almost exclusively in the first year or so of schooling and English is gradually added until the languages are used equally, as in the later years of the 50:50 model. There are three main ways to organize language distribution: by time block (e.g. half-day, alternating days, alternating weeks), by subject area (e.g. math and science in one language, other subjects in the other) and by teacher. In this last version, a teacher may have one group of children for the morning and another for the afternoon, but she/he always uses the same language. It is recommended that Languages Arts is taught in both languages (E.R. Howard & Christian, 2002). The separation of language by teacher (one who uses only English and one who uses only Spanish) can be quite effective in terms of maintaining strict separation of languages, but does require teachers to work well as a team (Morison, 1990). An example of separation by content area is the '50–50 Content Model', developed for schools in the Rio Grande border area where there is a high percentage of minority language speakers; the languages are separated by content area (math in English, science and social studies in Spanish, etc.) (Gómez *et al.*, 2005).

In the study described in this book, the classroom assumed the 50:50 model (although there was some adjustment, which will be discussed further in Chapter 4). Languages were distributed by time block (Spanish in the morning, English in the afternoon). In this self-contained classroom, there was one teacher who taught in both languages.

In the USA, where English is the majority language, Spanish is by far the most common minority language of instruction, with 320 of the 346 TWI programs offering Spanish as the minority language of instruction (Center for Applied Linguistics, 2009). The earliest example was the Coral Way Elementary school, which adopted the model in 1963 largely in response to a growing Cuban immigrant community and the increasing interest in multilingualism in Florida (Pellerano *et al.*, 1998). In the classroom described in this book, Spanish and English were used as languages of instruction, therefore I will focus here on Spanish-English TWI programs in the US context, where English is the majority language and Spanish is a minority language. However, it is important to keep in mind that other minority languages, such as Korean and Navajo, are also supported through TWI programs in the USA. It is also important to keep in mind that language status is socially constructed, and that Spanish is actually the majority language in other sociopolitical contexts, such as the Valencian and Basque regions of Spain (Blas-Arroyo, 2002; Sagasta-Errasti, 2003), in Mexico (Terborg *et al.*, 2007) and in Guatemala (Arriaza & Arias, 1998).

The ideal and the reality of two-way immersion instruction

Fundamental to the philosophy of TWI instruction is that it is an efficient and culturally sensitive way to meet the linguistic and academic needs of both English-speaking and Spanish-speaking children (Bickle *et al.*, 2004; Lindholm-Leary, 2001). For English speakers, the most obvious benefit is learning a second language in a country where foreign language fluency is unfortunately rare (Oxford, 1998). Monolingual English-speaking children are immersed in a foreign language at a young age, when intensive language learning is most effective and beneficial (Bialystok, 2006; Foreman, 2002). Other, less obvious benefits cited for English speakers have included confidence in their ability to learn languages, competence in their own native language, raising self-esteem (learning to take risks in the learning process), an understanding of the objective nature of language and appreciation for another culture (Walker & Tedick, 2000).

Taking a cue from other countries, the USA might benefit from beginning foreign language instruction earlier, teaching academic content in the target language and taking advantage of our multicultural heritage by supporting the teaching of immigrant and indigenous languages (Pufahl *et al.*, 2001; The Associated Press, 2005). TWI programs incorporate all these characteristics, which explains why many English-speaking parents see TWI programs as an excellent option for their children to learn a second language (Lindholm-Leary, 2001; Shannon & Milian, 2002). President Obama has suggested that the US shift its focus from that of an English-only orientation to one that recognizes bilingualism as a goal for everyone, immigrants and English speakers alike, 'Instead of worrying about whether immigrants can learn English – they'll learn English – ...you need to worry about whether your children can become bilingual'[2] (Miller, 2008).

As for Spanish speakers, studies have demonstrated that they reap academic and social as well as linguistic benefits from native language maintenance along with English instruction. Native language instruction has been shown to enhance the academic achievement of Spanish speakers. Thomas and Collier's (1997) landmark comparison study of over 700,000 English language learners' student records over the course of eight years demonstrates that native language instruction, along with some English instruction, was the highest long-term predictor of English achievement, as measured by English reading achievement tests. Students in TWI programs outperformed students in traditional bilingual programs and ESL programs on 11th grade English reading achievement tests. Further, students in TWI programs were less likely to drop out of school than those in traditional (transitional) bilingual programs and ESL programs (Thomas & Collier, 1997). In a study focusing on a TWI school in Cambridge, Massachusetts, native Spanish-speaking students in the Amigos school were found to outscore Spanish-speaking controls (who attended a local transitional bilingual school) in both English and math achievement tests (Cazabon *et al.*, 1998). Students in the Monteverde K-8 TWI school in California enjoy similar academic and linguistic achievement, with an overall ranking on state achievement tests of 7 on a scale of 1 to 10, as well as strong English and Spanish proficiency scores (Quintanar-Sarellana, 2004).

Spanish language maintenance for Spanish speakers has important implications both for the immediate benefit of the student and for longer-term benefits to the family and community. Former US Secretary of Education, Richard Riley, a supporter of TWI programs, characterized Spanish as an asset that must be cultivated for Spanish-speaking immigrants, 'If we see to it that immigrants and their children can speak only English and nothing more—then we will have missed one of the greatest opportunities of this new century, namely, to take advantage of the invaluable asset that helps define a culture' (Riley, 2000). In fact, the majority of Latinos living in the USA were born there; only 39.1% were born outside the USA (National Council of La Raza, 2001). This suggests that while, as for all immigrant groups, learning English is a priority for Latinos, another real concern for Latinos is maintaining Spanish fluency among children who are born in the USA or immigrate early in their lives.

Although Riley's term 'immigrant' excludes Puerto Rican children living in US states, their language and cultural experiences parallel those of immigrants in many ways. It is also important to keep in mind that the immigrant experience varies widely, even among immigrant groups from different Spanish-speaking countries (Suarez-Orozco, 1987). Nevertheless, the unfortunate common tendency for heritage language loss across generations that Riley alludes to is borne out by research (Rumbaut *et al.*, 2006; Wong-Fillmore, 2000). For some Latinos, it is not so much a question of Spanish maintenance but actually learning Spanish as a second language. Some second- and third-generation Latinos who have lost proficiency in Spanish later attempt to reclaim their heritage language, either for themselves or for their children (Olvera, 2004). Some English-speaking Latino parents enroll their children in TWI programs not only to maintain their heritage language, but also to foster their social and cultural integration with other Spanish speakers (Lindholm-Leary, 2001).

Another argument presented for TWI programs is based on increasing conditions of segregation experienced by Latino people in the USA. Even among critics of traditional bilingual education, who argue that placing Latino students in bilingual classrooms exacerbates their segregation, some have argued that TWI programs can meet the linguistic needs of these students while integrating them with their Anglo counterparts (Donato, 1993). Immigrant children not only tend to be segregated from their English-speaking peers and thus miss the opportunity for interaction with them, but their experience of English in school tends to be limited to 'bits and pieces of artificial-sounding language used in drills in their ESL classes' (Valdés, 2001: 13). It may be that TWI programs are the best option for avoiding the linguistic isolation that minority language speakers experience, while at the same time providing an opportunity for developing cross-cultural understandings (Alanís, 2007).

Profiles of different yet successful TWI programs show that the program is feasible under a variety of local conditions (Christian *et al.*, 1997; E.R. Howard *et al.*, 2003c). Nevertheless, the potential benefits to both English and Spanish speakers are based on an ideal that is difficult to achieve in actual practice. The TWI program is designed to enable a reciprocal learning and teaching relationship between speakers of minority and majority languages (Christian, 1994; Thomas & Collier, 2003). This reciprocity assumes symmetry in terms of both instructional time and native speaker proficiencies, so that speakers of both languages have ample opportunity to be 'immersed' in their target language (Christian & Genesee, 2001). In this sense, the TWI program design relies on a significant immersion in both languages, the minority as well as the majority language. Strict language separation is considered a defining feature of TWI programs, and language separation should be clearly signaled by time, day, instructor, the posting of signs indicating the current language of instruction, physical separation of literature and classroom displays, the use of different colored markers or crayons, separate notebooks for languages, etc. (Torres-Guzmán, 2007).

Nevertheless, some studies indicate that this ideal of symmetrical immersion is not achieved in real schools and classrooms, and that instead the majority language tends to be over-represented (Amrein & Peña, 2000; Collins, 1998; Hayes, 2004; Shannon, 1995; Valdés, 1997). One survey of TWI teachers found that actual implementation tended to fall short of the program definition in terms of the use of minority language for instruction and the percentage of minority language speakers, suggesting that local decisions are made under the influence of prevailing social values that include mastery of English at the expense of Spanish mastery for language minority speakers (Torres-Guzmán *et al.*, 2005). The degree of (in)congruence between the theoretical model of TWI and its implementation is determined by local values (such as language prestige) and assumptions (such as expectations for children of different language and cultural backgrounds) (Mora *et al.*, 2001). The high status of the native English speakers, both because they speak the higher status language and because they tend to come from higher socioeconomic status backgrounds, favors the presence of English, as does the increasing pressure to perform well on standardized tests of English language proficiency in early grades (E.R. Howard *et al.*, 2003c). The ways in which the use and quality of Spanish was undermined in this particular classroom are explored in more detail in Chapter 4.

Plan of the Book

Chapter 2 invites readers to consider the ways in which curriculum design and instruction influence the effectiveness of TWI classrooms. I provide a literature review of classroom-based studies that look at what actually happens in TWI classrooms and how teaching techniques shape these classroom processes. I also explain the context, methodology and philosophy behind the research described in this book.

Chapter 3 describes Sra. Soto's teaching philosophies as conveyed to me through our formal and informal interviews. This is based on the under- standing that no teacher has a single overarching and consistent teaching philosophy, but rather a collection of teaching philosophies that are not necessarily complete or coherent. I situate these philosophies within the academic literature on teaching and learning. I develop a professional portrait of Sra. Soto that demonstrates how her personal history, training, teaching experience and values all contribute to her teaching philosophies. By making connections between interviews and classroom observations,

I examine how Sra. Soto's philosophies contributed to her classroom design and teaching practice, both in general terms and more specifically in terms of language learning.

Chapter 4 examines the reality of language asymmetry which threatens the ideal TWI design that is based on a reciprocal learning and teaching relationship between speakers of minority and majority languages. I look at the ways in which social factors (such as children's earlier educational experiences and attitudes toward Spanish) and institutional factors (such as the exclusive use of English for announcements and school assemblies) skewed the classroom language balance in favor of English. I analyze Sra. Soto's systematic pedagogical strategies aimed at fostering Spanish use.

Chapters 5–8 analyze some of the different activity structures in the classroom, focusing on repetitive routines and rituals, Language Arts, group work at tables and Housekeeping and Blocks Centers. Classroom activity structures determine the nature of the activity, the norms of legitimate participation and the nature of relationships and interactions among participants. I elaborate how the expectations for speaking and behaving in these four different kinds of activities can provide different kinds of support and challenges for language learning.

Chapter 5 focuses on how certain daily rituals can provide a framework of familiarity and repetition that inspires confidence in reluctant language learners. These classroom rituals form a sort of bridge between separate curricular activities, guiding children through the change from one activity to another while maintaining some sense of continuity. Procedural instructions, clean-up times, and chants and songs quickly became familiar and comprehensible to the children through repetition and routine.

Chapter 6 focuses on Language Arts, a classroom activity in which the teacher leads the class in activities specifically focusing on language in use. I look at ways that this teacher supported comprehension and engaged children's attention and participation in the narratives that were woven by the teacher in the teacher-centered but highly participatory activity of Story time.

Chapter 7 focuses on Tables time, a classroom activity in which children worked in groups (at assigned tables) on individual projects. I describe the opportunities for language learning that emerged from this strongly task-oriented activity structure, emphasizing Sra. Soto's strategies for maintaining children's attention and enhancing comprehension, as well as her responses to problems that arose during task completion.

Chapter 8 focuses on play Centers, the least structured classroom activity. In the Housekeeping and Blocks play Centers, children were expected to play with the toys provided in the absence of the teacher, but with the purpose of encouraging conversation in the target language toward the broader goal of language development. I describe how Sra. Soto carefully designed the physical environment to afford conversation, as well as some of her intervention strategies aimed at encouraging the children to produce more target language conversation. Since Sra. Soto described these Centers as her least successful classroom activities, I analyze the classroom interactions in order to explain this phenomenon.

Chapter 9 reviews the observations and interpretations from the previous chapters and proposes a series of implications for practice. I consider the implications for program design as well as classroom design and teaching methodology. In particular, I emphasize that a TWI classroom can not only be an effective environment for language learning, but also a site for maintaining and revitalizing minority languages. Nevertheless, we need to analyze carefully the complex ways in which power-laden dynamics among languages, teachers, children and the institution of schooling operate in order to meet the linguistic and social goals of the program.

Finally, throughout the book I will present brief excerpts from my classroom observations. These excerpts will consist of brief narrations of the incident and/or direct quotes from the participants. They will be separated from the main text and written in the present tense, with the following formatting conventions:

(1) English translations will appear in italics and parentheses (*like this*).
(2) Physical description and commentary will appear in block parenthesis [like this].
(3) In order to remind readers of the children's designated home languages,[3] (English) or (Spanish) appears in parentheses after the child's name.

Here's an example, taken from an encounter I had with Kathleen one day while I was videotaping her playing with two other girls in the Housekeeping Center:

Kathleen (English): [Enters Housekeeping, removes my microphone from the chair and places it on the bookshelf behind her] Señora, está aquí. ¡Señora! (*Ma'am, It's here. Ma'am!*)
Researcher: No no no no. ¿Por qué? (*No no no no. Why?*)

Kathleen (English): Porque me quiero sentar aquí. (*Because I want to sit here*)
Researcher: [Picks up the microphone and moves it to the toy chest] ¿Aquí? (*Here?*)
Kathleen (English): [Nods affirmation]

Notes

1. There is legal as well as social pressure. In 1998, California passed Proposition 227, which required public schools to teach Limited English Proficient (LEP) students only in English, in principle eliminating bilingual education. For more information, see http://primary98.sos.ca.gov/VoterGuide/Propositions/227.htm.
2. This quote was excerpted from a video recording of a campaign event in Powder Springs, Georgia. On WWW at http://www.youtube.com/watch?v=BZprtPat1Vk&feature=fvw.
3. It is useful to keep in mind that these do not necessarily reflect actual proficiency and preference; this is discussed more fully in Chapter 4.

Chapter 2

The Pragmatics of Two-Way Immersion Instruction: A Closer Look at What Really Happens

Beyond Recipe Approaches

I have argued elsewhere (Hayes, 2005: 2) that **two-way immersion** (TWI) program design might seem like a recipe (take one part speakers of language A, one part speakers of language B, stir and simmer). This is because the program is defined by the presence of roughly equal numbers of speakers of each language[1] and the use of both languages for instruction, as this definition from the Center for Applied Linguistics (CAL) website exemplifies:

> **Two-way immersion** is a distinctive form of dual language education in which native English speakers and native speakers of another language are integrated for academic content instruction through both English and the partner language. The structure of these programs varies, but they all integrate the two groups of students for most instruction and provide at least 50% of instruction in the partner language at all grade levels. (On WWW at http://www.cal.org/twi/)

While there have been recommendations for instructional approaches (E.R. Howard *et al.*, 2007), the 'defining criteria' (E.R. Howard & Christian, 2002), 'curriculum and instruction' (Sugarman & Howard, 2001) and 'important characteristics' (E.R. Howard *et al.*, 2003b: 7) of the TWI model tend to be defined structurally in terms of percentages of language use and speakers. This critique is not to undermine the CAL definition; CAL provides a valuable and comprehensive database of research and information on TWI programs on their website. Nevertheless, I wish to highlight the need for program designers and teachers to look beyond the defined surface structure and consider how existing assumptions about teaching and learning might need to be adapted. In this book, the teacher's pedagogical assumptions and values are described in Chapter 3, and ways in which these were manifested in various aspects of her curriculum and instruction are described in Chapters 4–8. In conjunction with teacher interviews, my classroom observations revealed how some pedagogical assumptions surpassed others in supporting the fundamental principles underpinning TWI program design.

The apparently simple recipe-like equation (roughly equal numbers of language speakers) implied by the structural definition of TWI is actually built on a complex process of language interactions in which native-speaking children of both languages essentially teach each other their languages; 'both student groups receive accelerated instructional benefits from their other language peers' (Thomas & Collier, 2003: 62). Of course, the teacher is an important source of learning as well, but the special benefit of TWI is the presence of peers as additional language resources (Christian, 1996) or models (Cziko, 1992) for the children. The interactions among children, particularly across the two languages, are essential to the success of these programs in promoting bilingual development (Lindholm, 1990).

A key role of the TWI teacher is directing and guiding these interactions, which suggests that she/he needs to be skillful at designing a classroom environment where children will not only be allowed to, but want to, engage with each other in dialogue. The TWI teacher not only needs to keep children talking, but also to keep them talking in both languages. This might be harder than it sounds. The institution of schooling has some time-honored traditions that are difficult to ignore: students should listen to the teacher rather than talking with each other, the teacher possesses knowledge that students absorb by focusing attention on the teacher, and success is measured in terms of individual achievement rather than collective endeavor (Stigler & Hiebert, 1998; Tobin *et al.*, 1989; Varenne & McDermott, 1998; Windschitl, 1999).

In short, even for teachers who explicitly advocate what can seem like rather chaotic, noisy classrooms where children share responsibility for teaching each other through linguistic interactions, the culture of schooling itself can make these kinds of practices difficult to sustain (DePalma, 2006). Without a closer look into what actually happens in TWI classrooms, the full potential of these programs may not always be reached. Ethnographic studies like this one, where classroom processes are directly observed over an extended period of time, provide insight into exactly *how* the TWI recipe for success works as well as what processes might counteract this success. This kind of research can help us determine what kinds of teaching methodologies might work best and provide guidance in designing successful programs.

Classroom-based Research: Not just Whether, but how Two-Way Immersion Works

There are a variety of research methods that can help evaluate classroom practice and program design, many of which have been used to investigate TWI programs. DeJong (2002: 15) describes the recursive relationship between measured achievement and program design, 'the Barbieri TWBE program uses achievement data to reflect on practices and how these practices relate to theory and outcomes'. In this particular school, the children's scores on achievement tests reflect patterns that can inform curriculum design. For example, based on these achievement patterns, the decision was made to separate the children by language for initial literacy instruction in their native languages. While this example demonstrates an effort to direct program design based on program evaluation, the program evaluation is indirect, based on student achievement scores rather than on any direct investigation of classroom practices and dynamics.

Other program evaluation methods circumvent test scores altogether, based on an assumption 'that successful bilingual programs can only be fully understood from a variety of points of view beyond standardized testing' (Smith *et al.*, 2002: 2). In a study of a TWI school in Arizona, these authors, all having participated in the school as either parents or teachers, chose to use participant observation, interviews with teachers, parents and students, and analysis of the written work of the students. Most of the data reported come from interviews, thereby capturing the philosophies and attitudes of the parents, teachers and children. There is only one piece of observational data reported, an example of a literature discussion group in which the teacher leads the discussion in Spanish and the children respond in English or Spanish, illustrating the children's ability to understand Spanish and the teacher's willingness to accept not only contributions in English, but also contributions bringing in children's personal opinions and relevant experiences outside the class (Smith *et al.*, 2002). While the classroom observation component in this study does allow a glimpse into the classroom practice, a more systematic analysis, involving more observational data with triangulated interview data might have provided a more comprehensive insight.

Senesak's (2002: 1) paper examining the Inter-American Magnet School in Chicago, one of the oldest TWI program in the USA (founded in 1975) is intended to provide guidance for program design, 'Given the variability in program design and delivery of such programs, it is useful to examine individual programs to identify factors that may contribute to the effectiveness of this model'. This study is comprehensive, consisting of data collected over a 10-year period from 1991 to 2001, including classroom observations and interviews as well as proficiency test scores of the students. However, the classroom practices are described very generally, more in terms of overall curriculum than in terms of what actually happens in the classroom, and as such are more descriptive than analytical. For example, the program is characterized by 'pedagogical approaches and strategies that are student-centered, fostering interaction and active engagement in learning' (Senesak, 2002: 15). These pedagogical strategies included children researching topics that tied cultural information about indigenous American civilizations with Chicago standards in math, science and Language Arts. Children were assigned a topic and asked to prepare the investigation by writing research questions based on what they already knew and what they wanted to know, and activities included a trip to a museum and a writing workshop, in which children 'created informational and fictional books about some aspect of Mayan culture' (Senesak, 2002: 9). While comprehensive in scope, this sweeping description does not permit analysis of specific classroom practices and instructional strategies.

Freeman provides a comprehensive school-wide view in her study of the Oyster Bilingual School in Washington, DC. Based on extensive classroom observation and interviews with students and teachers, she provides a compelling explanation of how the school develops a culture in opposition to the broader societal culture, an alternative space where Spanish language and Spanish-speaking cultures are valued (Freeman, 1998). Nevertheless, while Freeman allows glimpses within the classroom, her emphasis is on the school-wide culture rather than on particular classroom practices.

On the other hand, some studies that focus on classrooms have provided useful insight into how bilingual language acquisition might be facilitated through certain classroom practices. Legarreta's (1977) quantitative analysis of classroom language suggests that variations in the program model significantly affected children's relative use of Spanish and English. She measured the percentage of Spanish and English used by teachers and children in the concurrent approach (in which the two languages are used simultaneously) compared with the 'alternate days' approach, in which the languages are separate by day. She found that teachers' speech on average favored English considerably

(72%) in the concurrent approach, while teachers in the alternate days approach divided their speech more equally between Spanish and English. Spanish-speaking children's use of language closely mirrored teachers' language choices, suggesting that an alternate day approach is more successful in fostering equity between the languages and providing a balanced language environment, which is the goal of the program design (Legarreta, 1977).

This was one aspect of classroom practice commented on by Freeman in the school-wide study cited above. The Oyster School in Washington, DC, the subject of Freeman's study, employs an unusual version of language allocation in which each classroom has two teachers present at all times, one designated Spanish dominant and one designated English dominant. Freeman (1998) found that teachers spent considerably more time speaking in English than in Spanish.[2] These findings suggest that careful separation and non-redundancy across languages is an important aspect of the program model.

Ethnographic studies of classroom activities can provide valuable insight into how children learn, particularly when long-term observation is used. Kuhlman's (1993) study of interactive journal writing in a TWI first grade demonstrated that the children's second language skills emerged in very different ways, following different growth trajectories. This suggests that a flexible approach to language learning, such as a workshop approach characterized by this journal-writing project, allows children to develop in ways that may not be available in a more rigid setting. Further, the interactive nature of the writing seemed to foster a progression from initial personal orientation in the writing toward increased audience orientation (Kuhlman, 1993). Similar patterns emerged in Riojas-Clark's (1995) study of writing in a TWI Kindergarten; children's development in both languages followed unpredictable and diverse trajectories.

Potowski's study of Spanish language use in a TWI school is one of the most thorough classroom ethnographies available to date; she spent two years with the same cohort of students, first when they were fifth-graders and then when they were eighth-graders. Using quantitative analysis of language use, language proficiency measures and classroom observations, she concluded that while students developed a reasonable level of Spanish proficiency, this tended to be considerably lower than their English proficiencies. While most of them developed positive attitudes toward Spanish, getting them to actually use Spanish, even during official Spanish time, remained a challenge (Potowski, 2004).

Pérez's (2004) ethnographic study of a TWI program consisting of 14 classrooms in two schools over the course of six years provides a complex global perspective on program development, from conceptualization and design through to processes of revision and renewal. This comprehensive focus, which includes close-up glimpses of classroom practice and children's literacy production alongside broader analyses of how attitudes developed over time, provides a connection between macro-processes at the level of community and political context and the micro-processes of decisions affecting everyday classroom practice.

Ethnographic studies that focus on specific teaching strategies provide a useful analysis of the effectiveness of these strategies. Peregoy and Boyle (1999) examined strategies employed by a Kindergarten teacher during Spanish time to ensure English-speakers' comprehension. They describe 'multiple-embedded scaffolds', routines and redundant practices that provided the children with cues for comprehension that gradually diminished as the children's comprehension level increased (Peregoy & Boyle, 1999). In an earlier study, Peregoy (1991: 474) described the role of children's play in providing 'opportunities for spontaneous, natural second language acquisition through social interactions based on play'. However, the only example, that of an English-speaking child gaining entry into the pretend play of four Spanish-speaking girls, includes no Spanish speech on the part of the English-speaking girl, and only one brief comment on the part of a Spanish-speaking girl, who comments '*Ella tiene hambre*' (she's hungry) (Peregoy, 1991). In fact, this segment suggests that, contrary to Peregoy's claim that English speakers spontaneously practice Spanish during play, English speakers can manage to engage in play without using Spanish, a potential challenge that I will explore further in Chapter 8.

In another study of the language generated during free play, in this case in a pre-Kindergarten TWI classroom, children's play language is described as rich in characteristics associated with verbal literacy, including logical reasoning, story sequencing and descriptive language. This study, in contrast to Peregoy's, provides examples of children's pretend play narratives, which are, in fact, relatively complex, with children constructing multiple-turn detailed sentences relating to a single theme (Riojas-Cortéz, 2001). However, despite their Mexican heritage, the majority of children in this study were English dominant (11 out of 12) and these play episodes were apparently completely in English (at least there is no mention that they are transcribed from Spanish). Therefore, this may not be a characteristic example of children interacting across languages, or even speaking a language in which they are all less than proficient. Further, the teacher is not depicted in the study, making it difficult to analyze the relationship between her classroom practices and the children's participation. These two aspects, children interacting in a language in which many of them were not comfortable and the teacher's techniques to foster these interactions, comprised the main focus of my study.

This Study: A Two-Way Immersion Kindergarten Classroom

The study is based on an ecological perspective, which strongly implicates the researcher as an inseparable part of the reality studied. This requires not only an explicit description of the researcher's role and participation in the classroom, but also an explicit analysis of the researcher's thoughts and the ways in which they changed as a result of participation:

> The educational researcher must, in some way, find ways in which to represent not only the conclusion of inquiry, but, as well, the path of thinking and inquiry that has led to these conclusions. This does not mean merely reporting a set of methodologies that were followed. It means showing the *connections* between the researcher and the subject of inquiry. (Sumara & Carson, 1997: xvi)

In order to retrace this path of inquiry and to make explicit the ways in which my own ways of thinking shaped this study and vice versa, I will begin by reviewing my initial purpose as stated in my research proposal: *The purpose of my research is to investigate how social interaction contributes to language development in a two-way bilingual Kindergarten classroom.* Once I actually started the research, I began to note patterns in the data that, in connection with my own interests and perspectives, shaped the particular focus of the study. Honest and effective researchers should make explicit their pre-existing theoretical frameworks, which inevitably help shape theory production in every new study. It was impossible for me to engage in this research project without bringing my own theoretical and value-laden framework(s) to bear; my researcher's mind was anything but a blank slate (Bigus *et al.*, 1994).

There were three main foci that emerged in the early stages of the study:

(1)   An exclusive focus on Spanish time

A few weeks into the study, I decided to focus exclusively on the official Spanish time in the classroom, as my initial observations revealed that even the Spanish speakers tended to speak quite a lot of English during official Spanish time. It became apparent to me that enforcing

Spanish use during Spanish time would be one of Sra. Soto's greatest challenges. Even in early interviews and discussions, Sra. Soto began to comment that children, including Spanish speakers, tended to speak to each other in English, even during Spanish time, as exemplified by a quote from our first interview:

> They are supposed to be speaking Spanish. The problem is the language of outside, and you knew this, both of us will realize this, the dominant language of the populace out there is English. And our Hispanic kids really do not see the benefit and or value of their Spanish language.

My initial observations coincided with this statement as well as the views of other TWI teachers who identified 'promoting Spanish language use among all students' as a linguistic challenge (E.R. Howard & Loeb, 1998).

Similar to trends described in the research literature (see Chapter 4 for a review of this literature), many of the Spanish speakers in this classroom were actually more English proficient than the TWI model assumes (Spanish speakers, like English speakers, are expected to be dominant in their assigned language). Based on Sra. Soto's initial comments, my initial observations and the support for these early observations found in the literature, I decided to focus my data collection exclusively on the official Spanish time, which took place every day in the morning. My own theoretical understandings of sociolinguistics and my stance toward language politics influenced this decision as well; I am concerned with the maintenance of minority languages in contexts like the USA, where a strongly hegemonic language threatens the vitality of less socially powerful languages (Skutnabb-Kangas, 2007; Suarez, 2002). I believe strongly in the social and linguistic principles behind TWI design, but I consider the tendency of English to assert itself as a stronger presence in TWI classrooms to be of serious concern for their potential to promote the minority language (Amrein & Peña, 2000; Hadi-Tabassum, 2006; Torres-Guzmán *et al.*, 2005). This focus on Spanish use does not imply that English time wouldn't have been interesting as well, but reflected more the particular interests of the teacher and the researcher in this study.

(2)   A focus on classroom design and teacher interpretations

Initially I was planning to focus on children's interactions in terms of their own characteristics and relationships (gender, friendship groups, personality, etc.). Nevertheless, my early discussions with Sra. Soto quickly revealed that she was a highly experienced and analytical teacher who willingly engaged with me in discussions of her teaching approaches and the reasons behind them. As our discussions continued throughout the year, I became more and more interested in Sra. Soto's teaching philosophies and classroom design. To this end, this book is framed from Sra. Soto's perspective, beginning with an analysis of her pedagogical theories, followed by her strategies for creating an artificial Spanish-speaking community during Spanish time and, finally, detailing the different pedagogical strategies she used in different classroom activity types.

This decision was also based on my own conviction that whatever the ideal program design, teachers' understandings of not only the pedagogical underpinnings of the particular program, but also other, potentially conflicting, pedagogical understandings shape what really happens in the classroom. While achieving bilingualism is an important goal of the TWI program, this goal cannot be evaluated without considering the child as a whole person, who will be learning many lessons about themselves and the world around them through their participation in a classroom ecology that has been designed by the teacher. I believe that language acquisition and even linguistic and cultural attitudes cannot be examined outside the broader pedagogical context that examines the full range of messages that might be implicitly available for children within and beyond the classroom. Implicit and explicit pedagogical decisions determine power relationships in the classroom that reflect, challenge or support broader social structures (Hadi-Tabassum, 2005; Valdés, 1997), and implicit aspects of school culture can sometimes short-circuit explicit teaching goals (DePalma, 2006; Hayes, 2005). In short, an analysis of a particular model of language teaching and learning cannot be separated from a broader analysis of teaching and learning in classroom contexts.

(3)   A focus on social production of success and failure

As I discussed with Sra. Soto her perceptions of successful and unsuccessful children (both in terms of academics and language learning), I realized that my own interpretations were guided by a particular understanding of school and school failure. These interpretations are exemplified in the work of Varenne and McDermott, who argue that children perform in school in response to an awareness of being constantly evaluated and sorted. According to Varenne and McDermott's (1998) analysis, the social production of failure is designed into the institution of schooling, endemic to the institutional context. Within this context, the school's function is to sort by ability and the children's job is to manage behavior in such as way as to appear capable, a job that includes masking or downplaying inabilities. In my own earlier work, I have critically analyzed how success and failure is produced in classrooms, not in terms of actual performance or proficiency, but in terms of how children come to be produced as certain kinds of learners in particular classroom activity settings (DePalma, 2006, 2008; Matusov *et al.*, 2007).

Therefore, as I began to focus more on Sra. Soto's interpretations of the failure and success of the children and the relative effectiveness of her strategies, I drew heavily on my own perspective. For this reason, in Chapters 5–8, I have highlighted children who have been produced through the social processes of this classroom as successful in one activity setting yet unsuccessful in others. I also chose to spend more time observing in the Centers, the classroom activity with which Sra. Soto was least satisfied and which I characterized as a site of failure production. My discussions with Sra. Soto and my own theoretical perspective led me to focus on ways in which the children were constructed as successful or unsuccessful students and language learners in the different activity settings of this classroom.

Therefore, while I had prepared an initial set of very general research questions that focused broadly on social interactions among children, these draft research questions were, in turn, shaped and focused throughout the study and can finally more specifically be summarized as:

(1) What patterns of language use emerge among the children during official Spanish time?
(2) How does classroom design influence this language choice and usage?
(3) How do the teacher's assumptions about language development and her philosophies of teaching influence her classroom design?
(4) How is success and failure produced differently in different class-room activity settings?

Research context

The study took place at Larson Elementary School[3] in a small urban area in the Mid-Atlantic region of the USA. Most of the other classrooms in the school were either transitional bilingual (using Spanish as little as necessary to speed children's acquisition of English) or strictly English-only. The year of this study coincided with the district's first TWI program, which in the inaugural year consisted of two Kindergarten classrooms at Larson. The program was planned to expand by one year each year, thereby following this initial cohort throughout their schooling until the TWI option was available to all the six grades contained in this school. Therefore, the Larson TWI program was not school-wide but rather a 'strand within a school' (E.R. Howard & Sugarman, 2001).

The school district included some, but not all, of the urban area in which it was located as well as a portion of a nearby suburban zone, creating an overall mixed urban/suburban catchment area. The city's population is estimated at just over 70,000 and includes a diverse ethnic population, including large numbers of families of European, African-American and Latino heritage. While city neighborhoods are not divided clearly along ethnic lines, there is a predominantly Latino neighborhood just a few blocks south of the school. Around the time of the study, this neighborhood was found to have the highest percentage in the state of household incomes below 200% poverty level. The neighborhood includes a very active and long-standing Latino community center, which has estimated its membership as roughly 85% Latino, 14% African-American and 1% Caucasian. Approximately one third of the Latino population was estimated to have recently arrived from Puerto Rico, another third consists of long-established families of Puerto Rican ancestry, and another third to constitute families of other Latin American origins (this includes Mexico, the Dominican Republic and Guatemala).[4]

I was not able to find systematic reporting of language use in this community, but over the years I spent working with the Latino center I noticed that most of the children I met there were bilingual and many seemed to prefer speaking in English, despite the fact that many parents and other older family members were strongly Spanish dominant. These observations suggest that while the local Latino community provided a stronger Spanish-speaking context than the surrounding suburban or other urban areas, these children also had significant exposure to English even in the local Latino community center, perhaps due in part to the high percentage of families who have been established in the area for several generations.

According to district demographic data produced the year before the TWI program was inaugurated at Larson, about 90 of the 440 children who attended the school were of Latino descent, and it was estimated that at the district level this student population was growing faster than overall enrollment. Larson already housed what the district referred to as its elementary bilingual program, which was of the type referred to in Chapter 1 as transitional bilingual education (TBE). For this reason, there was a relatively high, but by no means majority, number of Spanish-English bilingual teachers, many of whom were also of Latino background. This does not mean, however, that Spanish was spoken to any significant degree in the broader school community; in fact, my experience suggested that the broader school context was strongly English dominant, with many monolingual English-speaking teachers. This majority of monolingual English speakers included the principal, although she enthusiastically fought for the new TWI program to be approved and mentioned to me several times her own desire to learn Spanish.

The new TWI program was meant to eventually replace the existing transitional program. During the year of the study and the first year of the TWI program, the two TWI Kindergarten classes were separate, self-contained classrooms where the same teacher taught both the English and Spanish portion of the curriculum. There were two Kindergarten teachers, both of whom were fluently bilingual Spanish-English speakers who were born and raised in Spanish-speaking countries. I chose to collect my data in the classroom of Sra. Soto, a fluent Spanish-English bilingual, who had taught for several years at Larson before she was selected to teach in the new TWI program. I chose to focus on Sra. Soto's classroom because I had met her the year before while she was teaching a transitional bilingual 3rd grade class at Larson, and our conversations had revealed that she was passionately committed to the cause of Spanish language maintenance for Latino children. Having immigrated to the USA from a Spanish-speaking country as a child, she frequently mentioned to me and to others how important it was for her to have maintained her own Spanish proficiency.

Participation in the TWI program was strictly voluntary and limited to families within the district, and parents were informed of the program goals and structure before committing to their children's participation. Once selected for participation, the children were assigned as Spanish speaking or English speaking without recourse to language testing. According to Sra. Soto, these assignments were based on surnames and parents' reporting of language use in the home and did not always reflect language proficiencies and preferences, a concern that is explored in more detail in Chapter 4.

Of the 21 children in the classroom, 10 were designated as Spanish speakers. Two of these, one child who left early in the year and another who arrived later in the year, were from Mexico; the rest were from Puerto Rican families. Of the 11 children designated as English speaking, five had some Latino heritage but spoke exclusively English outside the classroom context; four were African-American, and none of these had any Latino background. While information on the children's social, family and economic backgrounds was not provided, Sra. Soto gathered information about financial situations, family constitution and dynamics, etc., based on speaking to parents. This information turned out to be more complex than statistics might reflect: family income and composition shifted, parents changed residence and children changed custodial parents during the course of the study. Sra. Soto shared this information and her interpretations of how these factors influenced the child's progress in our formal interviews and casual conversations as well as through written narrative descriptions of each child's progress over the year, which she produced for me as requested toward the end of the year.

Sra. Soto divided each day into two official language periods, Spanish in the morning and English in the afternoon. The official language changed when the children went to lunch at 11:30 am. The school day was also divided into seven major curricular activities. In the morning, during Spanish time, the children had Language Arts (indicated in the official schedule as 'Whole Group Literacy'), Tables time (indicated in Sra. Soto's schedule as 'Small Group Skills Time) and Centers (indicated in her schedule as 'Learning Centers Activities'). Throughout my study, I refer to the names of these activities as above, rather than as written on her schedule, because these are the terms Sra. Soto used in practice, as she spoke with the children and with me. In the afternoon, during English time, the children had English Language Arts (indicated in her schedule as 'Whole Group Literacy English') and Specials. Specials rotated every three days and consisted of 45 minutes of either library, gym or a combined music/art period, all of which took place outside Sra. Soto's classroom with different teachers, and all of which were conducted in English. On completion of the Special of the day, the children then returned to Sra. Soto's classroom for combined math/ science and then social studies in English before dismissal at 3:10 pm.

Therefore, the only content area instruction officially in Spanish was Spanish Language Arts. English Language Arts, along with all other content area instruction, took place during English time. Nevertheless, Sra. Soto discussed topics generally associated with math, science and social studies (e.g. counting, animal habitats and countries) during Spanish Language Arts in the morning. This practice of making connections across the curriculum, and importing these other content area topics into the Spanish Language Arts, will be discussed in more detail in Chapter 3. In Chapter 6, which treats in more detail the Spanish Language Arts activity, this practice is exemplified.

In addition to these officially designated curricular topics, for the purpose of this research I created another category – daily rituals and routines. These familiar daily activities usually occurred as the children switched from one curricular activity to another, for example, when Language Arts ended and children moved from the rug in the front of the room to the tables and prepared for Tables time. These transitional activities included cleaning up, receiving instructions for the next activity and participating in chants and songs. Each type of routine was characterized by a particular classroom dynamic, as will be discussed in more detail in Chapters 5–8.

Gaining entry: My research relationship with the school

I had already established a working relationship with the school before beginning the study, as I was supervising pre-service teachers placed in this school for a practicum associated with their university course in Language Arts teaching methodology. I knew the principal and several of the teachers and, when I heard that the school was proposing a TWI program, I offered to help. I wrote a letter of support to the school board at the principal's request and was invited by the principal to attend the planning meetings, which included the School Board meeting at which the proposal was approved.

Because of my active role in support of the program, and perhaps because I was already working in the school on behalf of my university, developing a research relationship never seemed to be an obstacle. The principal introduced me as the 'program evaluation person' to the parents and teachers during the first PTA meeting I attended, and I was warmly treated as part of the school rather than an outside researcher from the beginning. I was invited to all meetings related to the program, which, aside from the meetings described above, also included a program-planning meeting and two in-service trainings.

The second in-service training consisted of a visit to a TWI program established nearby. This took place in the summer before the program started, and it was on this date that I was informed that Sra. Soto had been selected to teach one of the TWI Kindergarten classrooms. Therefore, although there were several other Larson teachers and the principal present, I decided to focus my attention exclusively on Sra. Soto during this visit. As with all meetings I attended, I recorded field notes, but this visit was especially fruitful as I was able to discuss with Sra. Soto her plans for the classroom and pedagogical theories before the program began.

During this visit, we, the visitors from Larson, divided into small groups or pairs and walked around the school freely. Together, Sra. Soto and I observed three teachers at some length, and her comments and criticisms of these teachers provided valuable insight into her own pedagogical understandings and values (described in detail in Chapter 3). I kept a journal of our visit, in which I recorded my conversations with Sra. Soto as we toured the school together. This journal included Sra. Soto's critical commentary on the teaching practices we observed, as well as more general reflections on teaching and language learning. She also shared with me, on this day, her developing plans for her own TWI classroom. This early relationship with the teacher allowed me to begin to develop an insider perspective even before the classroom existed, and I began the classroom observation with the goal to not only record what was happening, but also more specifically to observe the classroom development in light of Sra. Soto's own views and expectations.

Data collection

At the start of Chapter 1, I describe myself as a Spanish language learner at the time of the study, so it's important to clarify that I never had any trouble understanding what was going on in the classroom, nor did I have any particular trouble transcribing Spanish sections of the data (although I did consult with a Spanish native speaker in case of doubt or ambiguity). Although I am not a native Spanish speaker, I tested my Spanish comprehension before beginning classroom observations by observing a few bilingual classes at the school the year before the study began. These observations were part of my university job as practicum supervisor, but they also assured me that my Spanish competence would be sufficient for these observations.

During the school year, I conducted classroom observations totaling approximately 90 hours on 48 separate days, collecting videotaped and audiotaped data and writing field notes. My standard procedure was to set up the video camera and the tape recorder and sit near the video camera taking handwritten field notes, occasionally changing the location of the camera and tape recorder depending on my observations. The field notes provided an overall schema of the classroom events for each day. The videotapes preserved the action in a way that provided important continuity throughout the project, as later I was able to revisit the videotapes as needed and review exactly what took place on any given day. The audiotapes served to clarify any spoken discourse that was not adequately captured by the other data points.

On most days, I also discussed with Sra. Soto some of my observations and her own observations and reflections. I summarized these discussions in my daily reflection journal, which I recorded into a hand-held tape recorder as I drove home each day in order to capture the day's events and my reflections as soon as possible. I also conducted five formal interviews with the teacher as well as one formal interview with the district's Bilingual Supervisor. Owing to my increasing interest in Sra. Soto's perspectives, two of the teacher interviews were scheduled specifically so that Sra. Soto could watch a segment of my videotape and share her interpretation of the events. Finally, at the end of the year, Sra. Soto wrote for me a brief summary evaluation of each child, describing their development throughout the year and some reflections on what might have affected their progress.

Data coding and analysis

Most observation days yielded multiple data sources, usually including a videotape, audiotape and reflection journal entry. For each day, I typed my handwritten field notes, transcribed my audiotaped journal reflection and reviewed the videotape, writing a reflective summary of the videotape. I produced a summary chart listing for each day the data points available and a brief description of the key events of the day.

Later, after the data collection period, I reviewed the data day by day, transcribing parts of the videotaped and audiotaped data and writing a daily summary note that included my reflections on emerging data trends as well as the partial transcriptions for this day. These summary notes, concurrent with the organization of data into categories, served the purpose of memos, a feature of grounded theory methodology – 'a memo is a note to yourself about some hypothesis you have about a category or property, and particularly about relationships between categories' (Dick, 2000). I transferred these summary data to the computer-based data analysis program *NVivo*, creating and reorganizing categories reflecting the trends emerging from the data. The analysis from this point consisted mainly of reviewing data by category and manipulating these categories, subdividing some and subsuming others into broader categories. The book's final structure reflects some of this analytical structure. Beginning from some of the broader categories, I referenced the original data sources as appropriate, reviewing and expanding transcriptions to include in the text. The vignettes and transcriptions in this book thus reflect a triangulation of the video, audio and field note data available for each segment.

A *post-hoc* coding of conversation

After completing all my observations, I decided to devise a way of measuring conversation levels to check the impression that Sra. Soto and I shared that children did not usually engage in extended conversation in the Housekeeping and Blocks Centers. Therefore, the analysis of conversation in these Centers (Chapter 8) includes both the usual excerpts from observations and discussions with the teacher along with a brief *post-hoc* analysis of what I've termed dialogic density. This analysis emerged after the data collection was finished; I reviewed the video tapes after the study was complete and reflected on both my own and Sra. Soto's interpretations. I noticed that Sra. Soto's participation in the Centers did not usually have the effect that she intended, which was to elicit conversation. To test these impressions, I devised a coding scheme for conversation (see the Appendix for a copy of the actual coding template used). Once again, I reviewed all videotaped segments of the Centers,[5] this time counting the number of utterances in Spanish and English, as well as the number of utterances that were a mix of both languages and utterances for which the language was unclear. The purpose of this analysis was to determine the extent to which the children engaged in conversation in the Centers, as well as the relative frequency of Spanish in these Centers throughout the year.

I also noted the maximum and minimum number of children in the segment, and the length of the segment in seconds, accounting also for the length of time spent in the Center by the teacher and the length of time the Center was occupied by one child or fewer than two children. This was to provide a context for these measures of conversational frequency, since one child cannot be expected to engage in conversation,[6] and also to determine the extent to which, on the whole, the Centers were popular.

I thematically coded Sra. Soto's utterances in the Centers in an attempt to see patterns in terms of what kinds of utterances on the part of the teacher were most successful in eliciting the children's conversation. This coding grew out of my observations that Sra. Soto's participation in the Centers tended to elicit short responses from the children rather than extended conversation.

In Chapter 8, I provide a more detailed explanation of the theoretical basis for the coding categories, but at this point, focusing on methodology, I would like to emphasize that these particular coding decisions grew out of Sra. Soto's concern for conversation and my own observations, as noted in my field notes and journal entries, of the relative scarcity of sustained conversation. It is also important to recognize that this numerical analysis is not to be considered an attempt at providing new data, or the same data in a more objective and thus more 'reliable' form. Some of the data in Chapter 8 are expressed in terms of numbers and percentages, but these numbers and percentages are derived from existing ethnographic data. They are intended as a *post-hoc* analysis, a way to systematically organize my existing data. Their numerical nature does not imply that they are any more objective in nature than the narrative data, or that it is any more possible to separate these data from their ecological whole. All data in this study are based on reflective researcher observation, and therefore are not intended to be transferred out of my interpretive context.

According to Brice Heath, the use of frequency counts can help keep qualitative research honest:

> The constant interplay of rich descriptive materials from field notes and such simple quantitative steps as frequency counts or ratios helps researchers guard against rushing to select the "perfect" example from their qualitative data to illustrate a point. (Heath, 2000: 32)

Silverman makes a similar point:

> It is usually a mistake to count for the sake of counting... (But) simple counting techniques, theoretically derived and ideally based on members' own categories, can offer a means to survey the whole corpus of data usually lost in intensive, qualitative research. Instead of taking the researcher's word for it, the reader has a chance to gain a sense of the flavor of the data as a whole. In turn, researchers are able to test and to revise their generalizations, removing nagging doubts about the accuracy of their impressions about the data. (Silverman, 2000: 185)

It is this mutually linked and supportive relationship described by Silverman that I am hoping to achieve with the introduction of the tabulated data in Chapter 8.

Similarly, Silverman (2000: 180) describes the validating power of analyzing unusual or what he terms 'deviant' cases, stressing that in qualitative analysis, unlike quantitative analysis, all data must be accounted for in the study. It is with this goal in mind that I include in Chapter 8 a narrative analysis of two 'deviant' cases, relatively long conversations that were initiated by Sra. Soto during the children's Center play.

Research philosophy

As mentioned earlier, this study is based on the assumption that an event can only be understood in the context in which it takes place (Carson & Sumara, 1997). Although I was not a school employee and entered the research situation as an outside researcher, I eventually became part of the classroom dynamic. Clearly, I was not, in a traditional sense, a full participant, but neither was I external to the system. I never had the sensation of 'collecting data' in the sense often conjured by the term, that of collecting pieces of information using standardized equipment. Despite my best efforts to carefully plan the data collection and strategically time my classroom visits, I often ended up with the strange sensation that the study seemed to flow around and through me in often unexpected ways. Maykut and Morehouse's (1994: 25) notion of indwelling, where the researcher directly experiences the phenomenon studied (indwelling meaning *to live within*) and at the same time 'removes him/herself from the situation to rethink the meanings of the experience' seems to capture my experience.

In this approach, the human researcher is considered to be, and here Maykut and Morehouse draw on Lincoln and Guba's terminology, *human-as-instrument*, more fully equipped for data collection than any objective, non-human machine because of particular abilities exclusive to humanity:

> Lincoln and Gruber argue that a human instrument is responsive, adaptable, and holistic. Further, a human investigator has knowledge-based experience, possesses an immediacy of the situation, and has the opportunity for clarification and summary on the spot. Finally, a human investigator can explore the atypical or idiosyncratic responses in ways that are not possible for any instrument which is constructed in advance of the beginning of the study. (Maykut & Morehouse, 1994)

In ethnographic research that requires the researcher to interpret what she/he sees, trustworthiness replaces the criterion of objective truth inherent in positivistic approaches, since objectivity assumes the presence of 'objective, nonreactive, and neutral reality' irrelevant to the social world (Mishler, 2000). Trustworthiness is achieved by making the research process as transparent as possible to the reader by providing multiple sources of data and allowing readers to access data directly (Maykut & Morehouse, 1994). In my case, I accompany my own interpretations with extended transcripts and extracts from field notes so that readers may make their own interpretations. 'There are always, in principle, *many* interpretations of a text, a text can always be interpreted at different levels (more or less "deeply"), and interpretations can never be proven' (Gee, 1996: 101). When we use an interpretive framework to analyze meaningful, complex and socially mediated events and discourses, trustworthiness is found in the degree to which our reader can, through maximum access to the data and to the descriptive context, challenge or verify the interpretation.

I mentioned earlier that I became increasingly interested in viewing the emerging data through the teacher's interpretive perspectives, which led to frequent discussions with her about classroom incidents as well as two special interviews where she and I viewed a videotaped segment of the Centers time so I could better understand her perception of the activity and her own intervention strategies. Nevertheless, this does not suggest that we always shared the same interpretations, or that I simply presented an analysis from her point of view. Instead, I took a critically situated perspective on her interpretation. Wainwright criticizes attempts to present a purely insider perspective (sometimes referred to as an emic perspective), which he disparagingly defines as:

> The tendency to adopt an uncritical attitude to the beliefs and consciousness of informants, without considering their epistemological adequacy or their emancipatory potential... (which results in)... a form of voyeuristic relativism where everyone's testimony is accorded equal status, and no attempt is made either to explain or inform the development of consciousness. (Wainwright, 1997)

The alternative approach, an etic perspective, bases interpretation on the interpretive framework and values of the observer, usually rooted in a broader academic community.

Perhaps a more useful and relevant description of the development of my own perspective comes from Berry (as cited in Rogoff *et al.*, 1993), who describes a perspective that draws on both the preconceptions and values of the researcher and the views of the other participants. This perspective is based neither on the uncritical acceptance of the other's view nor a rigid unchanging view of the researcher, but evolves from the *imposed etic*, or naïve view brought to the study by the researcher, as it synthesizes during the process of research with the purely *emic* view of the existing members of the community to form a *derived etic* perspective, or one that maintains the researcher's interpretation but is still faithful to local meanings. In my case, I developed a particular derived etic perspective that reflected critically on the teacher's actions based on an examination of ways in which her actions *seemed to me* to aid or impede the achievement of *her own goals*.

In this study, I wanted to take Sra. Soto's insider perspective into account and, while not completely erasing or disregarding it, offer my own interpretation framed by my own understandings, interests and concerns. My interpretations are, like Sra. Soto's, situated within a particular professional/academic community and shaped by personal values and experiences, suggesting that the tendency to situate emic perspectives as somehow 'inside' culture and etic perspectives as beyond or above the culturally bounded understandings of the research informants is deeply flawed. Inevitably, my own perspective is privileged because I am the researcher and author of this analysis: Sra. Soto speaks only through me and, in so doing, she is inevitably diminished, simplified, objectified and finalized (Bakhtin, 1999). In fact, a great deal of interpretation occurred after the study was over and I was able to finish coding and analyze the data as a whole. Sra. Soto was not able to participate in this later analysis, since she left the school a couple of weeks before the year ended due to a family move (a substitute teacher finished the year).

It might be helpful for readers to take this positioning of researcher/subject into account when reading the following chapter, which describes Sra. Soto's multiple (and, in my opinion, sometimes contradictory) teaching philosophies. It would be a useful exercise in trustworthiness to consider throughout this book how she might respond to my interpretations of her pedagogical actions and explanations. Indeed, I hope to provide enough data in extended quotes and vignettes to allow the reader to engage in his/her own interpretation of my interpretation of the data.

Notes

1. Approximately equal numbers of children are usually assigned as native speakers of one or the other language, although in some programs, particularly in border areas with a well-established bilingual community, roughly one third of the children are identified as bilingual (see, e.g. Gómez *et al.*, 2005; Takahashi-Breines, 2002).
2. My personal experience with this school supports Freeman's observation, as my children attended the school for one year. English teachers may translate Spanish teacher's instructions into English for the benefit of the less bilingual English speakers, but in the long run, this can serve to impede their language acquisition.
3. Teachers, administrators, children and the school are all assigned pseudonyms.
4. I have withheld the sources for this information in the interest of participant anonymity.
5. This analysis excluded certain parts of videos where the data were not clear enough for this type of analysis, for example, portions where the children were out of sight or the sound was unclear. I also excluded a segment where an accident occurred and the teacher stopped the play to lecture the children, because this did not represent a play dynamic.
6. There was an occasion in which one child, alone, spoke briefly with her dolls, but I did not code this as conversation (see Chapter 8 for a more detailed description of my working definition of conversation).

Chapter 3

From Teaching Philosophies to Classroom Design

Sra. Soto was a fluent bilingual English and Spanish speaker. A native of Argentina, she had lived in the USA since late childhood, and told me she had attended an English immersion school in Argentina. I did not select Sra. Soto; I had already decided to collect my data focusing on one of the two new TWI Kindergarten classrooms in the school and Sra. Soto was the first to be hired. She was already teaching in the school's transitional bilingual program, and when the TWI program was proposed she volunteered for the position.

In fact, I had met Sra. Soto the year before when she was teaching a transitional bilingual 3rd grade class. As described in Chapter 1, transitional bilingual classrooms differ from TWI classrooms in that Spanish language development is not an explicit goal. Nevertheless, Spanish development did seem to feature among Sra. Soto's goals even when she was teaching in the transitional program, while none of the other bilingual classroom teachers I spoke with at that time expressed a concern for their children's Spanish proficiency.

During the year prior to this study, I supervised pre-service teachers who were placed in three of the transitional bilingual classrooms. Sra. Soto's classroom was not actually one of these, and that was because she turned down my request to place pre-service teachers with her. She apologetically explained to me that she was worried that her Spanish-speaking students were not as skilled in Spanish writing as they should be, and that the presence of our monolingual English pre-service teachers would only exacerbate this problem. She did invite me to observe her classroom even though I had no students placed there, and I noted that she spoke in Spanish considerably more than half the time, a striking fact given that this was a transitional bilingual classroom. By contrast, I took some field notes while observing in the other three bilingual teachers' classrooms, noting that all three used Spanish in the classroom only for occasional brief clarification or discipline. These early observations and exchanges highlighted Sra. Soto's strong concern for developing the children's native Spanish literacy, even within a traditional transitional bilingual program where this is not officially part of the curriculum. While she did not have any experience as a TWI teacher before she participated in this study, her wholehearted support for the program's goal of developing Spanish for Spanish speakers was evident even before she started.

Sra. Soto's perspectives on bilingual education and on education in general are essential to this study. My intention was to understand her curriculum design and modification as a function of her own perceptions and evaluations of the classroom, which were necessarily mediated by her personal philosophies of education. In other words, before understanding what Sra. Soto did throughout the year to make her TWI classroom work, it was necessary to understand what she was trying to accomplish and how she herself defined pedagogical strategies as 'working' or 'not working'.

In this chapter, Sra. Soto's understandings are extrapolated from explanations she made to me throughout the study in various contexts, as I took advantage of every opportunity to discuss her justifications of her pedagogical decisions in an attempt to understand her perspective. As described in Chapter 2, my discussions with Sra. Soto took several forms: my interactions with her the year before the TWI program and the study began (which included a tour of Calvary,[1] an established TWI program), four formal interviews during the year, her own summary evaluations of the students at the end of the year, and informal discussions before, during and after the classroom observations, which I recorded in my daily journal. These informal daily discussions proved to be especially powerful in providing insight into Sra. Soto's own perspectives, as they reflected her ideas, concerns and frustrations as they emerged.

Sra. Soto expressed her philosophies of education in terms of reflections and anecdotes rather than in terms of an overarching philosophy. In other words, she never attempted to integrate her actions and beliefs within one consistent philosophy, and her reflections were generally rooted in a specific practice or classroom event. For this reason, I always use the word 'philosophies' in the plural rather than singular form. As described by Simmons *et al.* in their work with beginning science teachers, a philosophy is generally considered to be a collection of relatively consistent beliefs, while people's belief systems are better characterized as a collection of views and assumptions about their roles in the world. Teachers express teaching philosophies by means of statements revealing their views of their own role in the classroom, as well as the nature of teaching and learning, and by studying these statements we can gain some insight into the nature of (and incon-sistencies among) their philosophies (Simmons *et al.*, 1999). Teachers, of course, are not special in this regard, and I would argue that we all possess similar sets of eclectic philosophies that guide our actions, even if we don't always articulate them.

During our Calvary visit, Sra. Soto expressed some of her pedagogical philosophies, particularly those directly relating to the TWI model, through her reflections on the classroom practices of other teachers. When we arrived at the school, we divided into pairs and visited several classrooms. Sra. Soto and I formed a pair, and she kept up a steady commentary on her impressions throughout the visit. When I asked Sra. Soto at that time what she felt to be the most important aspect of the TWI program design, she described a successful TWI approach as one of 'designing instructional activities to promote desired interactions among the children'. In this sense, she explicitly allied herself with the general philosophy behind TWI methodology, which relies on social interaction among learners of both languages (Christian, 1994; Lambert, 1990). This reliance on social interactions among students suggests that effective TWI methodology goes beyond exclusively teacher-directed instruction to the promotion of peer interactions, a fundamental teaching philosophy that may prove difficult to reconcile with implicit philosophies of learning and teaching that historically and culturally underpin our educational system. My observations and discussions with Sra. Soto suggested that she did indeed struggle with reconciling these competing philosophies.

Two-way Immersion: Interactions Among the Children are Fundamental

At Calvary, we observed part of a science class where, as the teacher conducted a lesson on buoyancy in the center of the classroom, some children were standing apart from this activity, alone or in groups of two or three, silently manipulating objects on the table. We did not have a chance to speak to this teacher, as we left before her lesson was finished, so we never found out what exactly these children were doing. Never-theless, Sra. Soto's criticism of this teacher provided an interesting insight into her teaching philosophies.

The majority of the children were gathered around the teacher in the middle of the room as she conducted a science lesson in Spanish about flotation. She began by placing a variety of objects in a tub of water and asking the children to predict which would float and then testing these predictions by allowing them to float (or sink). The children participated verbally in the initial predictions and then stood around the teacher watching as she tested the predictions. Sra. Soto criticized this strategy, commenting to me that the children 'should have been given a more hands-on experience, first experiment on their own (without the teacher), then later coming together in the (teacher-led) group'. Sra. Soto was quite critical of this teacher, both during the visit as recorded in my journal and during an interview at the end of the year, where I asked her to reflect on how her visit to Calvary influenced her pedagogical design. Reflecting on this science teacher, she said, 'Well, I thought her Centers were very teacher-oriented without enough exploration on the part of the kids. She was guiding them and I was disturbed by that'.

This educational terminology concerning teacher- and child-centered learning proves, on careful investigation, to be rather slippery. Definitions vary widely. In one education textbook, child-centered pedagogy, also sometimes characterized as 'constructivism' (Baines & Stankey, 2000), is defined by learners' 'self-regulation':

> The learning process is seen as a self-regulated transformation of old knowledge to new knowledge, a process that requires both action and reflection on the part of the learner. Contrast this idea of learning with the opposite idea, that people learn by absorbing what they are told, or that their minds are like blank pages on which the teachers or others can write. (Howe & Jones, 1998)

One internet resource site for ESL teachers, in its glossary section, defines 'teacher-centered' practice in terms of teacher control and responsibility for determining learning goals:

> Methods, activities, and techniques where the teacher decides what is to be learned, what is to be tested, and how the class is to be run. Often the teacher is in the center of the classroom giving instruction with little input from students. The teacher decides the goals of the class based on some outside criteria. (Gunn *et al.*, 2002)[2]

These definitions highlights what I consider especially problematic in the definitions of child-centered and teacher-centered classroom practices – the notion that, in contrast to a teacher-centered approach, a child-centered approach would allow students to help decide what is to be learned, what is to be tested and how the class is run. Nevertheless, learning within the institution of formal schooling means that learning will be measured and evaluated, goals will be set and methods will be determined by people other than the learner (not just the teachers, but school administration, district requirements, state and national funding bodies, etc.).

Institutionalized schooling in the USA is not only designed and regulated by people other than learners, but has developed a particular culture based on a history of competitive and externally measured achievement that has made certain practices seem common sense and natural (of course we numerically measure progress, of course we provide extrinsic rewards and punishments, etc.). In short, the institution of schooling itself has a culture (Stigler & Hiebert, 1998; Varenne & McDermott, 1998) that is not congruent with the fundamental philosophy of learner autonomy and self-regulation implicit in these definitions of student-centered learning (DePalma *et al.*, 2009; Rogoff *et al.*, 2001). This incongruence may twist attempts to relegate control to learners into absurd situations where students are expected to independently 'discover' the information and skills predetermined by the teacher (in accordance with all the regulating bodies that control teaching).

The practice of embedding supposedly child-centered practice within an authoritarian institutional context is exemplified by an unfortunate teaching experiment in which students studying *Hamlet* were divided into two groups: one group learned through teacher-directed lecture and the other group directed their own learning through group discussions, investigation of web sites and books. Students who followed teacher-directed, lecture-based practices far outscored the 'constructivist' group on the final examination (lecture group on average 82%, constructivist group 67%) (Baines & Stankey, 2000). This study demonstrates that child-centered approaches to learning, when employed with the goal that the children arrive at the teacher's predetermined academic goals, are doomed to fail. This philosophical incompatibility, as I will argue in more detail in Chapter 8, helps account for Sra. Soto's dissatisfaction with her play Centers (Housekeeping and Blocks) as well as the nature of her attempts to intervene in the children's play.

Sra. Soto's criticism of the science teacher's 'teacher-centered' approach seemed inconsistent with her own explicit identification as 'a Madeline Hunter direct instruction teacher'. Madeline Hunter's guidelines for lesson planning clearly require that the teacher strictly control learning goals and outcomes. In the following definition, note the repetition of the word *you* (the teacher) followed by verbs describing the actions initiated by the teacher and directed at *them* (the students):

> You told them what you were going to tell them with **set**, you tell them with **presentation**, you demonstrate what you want them to do with **modeling**, you see if they understand what you've told them with **checking for understanding**, and you tell them what you've told them by tying it all together with **closure**. (Allen, 1998)

I was curious to understand how Sra. Soto reconciled the Madeline Hunter style of teaching with her interpretation of TWI methodology as based on interactions among children. In other words, designing to promote interactions *among* children (as described by Sra. Soto) implies that the teacher is not central to the instructional dynamic (as described by Hunter). She told me that while she had spent many years successfully using Hunter's direct teaching approach in her previous school, she rarely used this approach in her TWI classroom, then she hesitated and said, 'Well, once in a while'. This was the only instance where Sra. Soto explicitly reflected on the application of direct teaching principles in the context of her TWI classroom. The tensions between direct teaching and the apparently more child-centered approach of relying on children's interactions with each other became especially salient in Sra. Soto's own play Centers design, as well as her intervention when she became dissatisfied with the level of Spanish conversation in these Centers. I will explore this in more detail in Chapter 8.

Songs and Chants: Creating a Relaxing and Fun Environment

One of the teachers we observed at Calvary was conducting a lesson dominated by the children's production of formulaic phrases in the form of games and songs. While we observed, Sra. Soto and I both noticed that these students seemed very enthusiastic in their use of Spanish. Aside from the songs and rhyming games we witnessed, we also observed this teacher conduct a lesson on planets, where each student was asked to stand up and name all the planets in Spanish. This constituted a highly repetitive activity, as each student listened to the others recite the planets (more or less) in the same order, and then recited the same list. Afterward, I recorded in my reflection journal that Sra. Soto told me she liked this teacher's methods very much, as these formulaic aspects of language learning give children the confidence to experiment with a new language. She added that games and songs help children build confidence because they are 'fun and relaxing'. She said that this teacher's formulaic approach would be very good, as long as it was balanced with time for 'natural conversation', which she suspected to be the case.

Sra. Soto spoke for a while with this teacher after her lesson, exchanging ideas and resources for songs and word plays that could be used in the bilingual classroom. The data I collected during the year clearly indicate that this faith in the value of formulaic chants and songs is reflected in Sra. Soto's practice, as during the 48 days on which I visited the classroom, I witnessed 17 instances of chants and songs. Most of these instances can better be described as a cluster of activities, usually including a series of dances, chants and songs. These formulaic chants, which were always characterized by enthusiastic and loud participation by the children, will be analyzed in more detail in Chapter 5.

Most interesting at this point was her emphasis on the affective aspects of learning, as she explained the incorporation of formulaic chants into her curriculum design in terms of the children's emotional state: 'fun', 'relaxing' and building 'confidence'. While Sra. Soto made no explicit connection between her concern for the children's affective state and language learning theory, there exists a substantial body of research suggesting that a relaxed affective state can enhance language learning (Arnold, 1999; Krashen, 1985).

Teaching Values in the Classroom

Sra. Soto explained to me that, while the teaching of values was not advocated by many teachers, she firmly advocated values education, 'I'm teaching morals in the classroom, and people will say (that) it's not my job, it's not my job to teach them how to behave. But it is'. School, according to Sra. Soto, is a place where children must be inducted into the norms of society, 'The purpose of school is for us to differentiate ourselves from an animal, domestic or a wild animal, becoming a social animal. Teaching them manners of speaking, teaching them intonation, how to speak without yelling'. At times, she explicitly mentioned incorporating particular values into her curriculum planning. For example, she added dolls to the Housekeeping Center in January and later reflected, 'I added dolls because I felt that I wanted them to understand the purpose of being kind and gentle. Because they were not being kind and gentle with one another. They were throwing things around'.

Throughout the year, this agenda of values education was quite apparent, as she spent a great deal of time encouraging the children to be orderly, neat and quiet. La hora de limpiar (*clean up time*) became a significant activity in the classroom (I recorded 25 instances), and the children were also encouraged to maintain an acceptable degree of order during play time. For example, she criticized the children's disorderly play in the Housekeeping Center, where she had set up a play store (*la tienda*), 'they were throwing stuff around... they were putting things on top of each other, paying for things with 1,000-dollar bills... it was ridiculous'.

Although Sra. Soto characterized her decision to teach values in the classroom as controversial ('people will say it's not my job...'), it is impossible to imagine a valueless classroom. Teaching is implicitly based on a set of cultural values, and we can only choose among ignoring these values, making them explicit or trying to change them (Brint *et al.*, 2001; Gutierrez *et al.*, 1995; Parsons, 2000). Further, many of the moral values that Sra. Soto advocated, such as speaking quietly, cleaning up and playing without fighting, are implicit in the majority of American classrooms.

> It is assumed that the more quiet and orderly the classrooms are, the more likely it is that learning is taking place... students work individually on identical, skill-based assignments to ensure uniformity of learning. Value statements are embedded everywhere in this environment. (Windschitl, 1999: 753)

These implicit classroom values, as well as the strategies Sra. Soto used to explicitly teach moral values, interacted with her language-teaching strategies in interesting ways. For example, her interest in neatness and orderliness manifested (perhaps unconsciously) as a particularly useful language-teaching strategy where the children followed her instructions in Spanish with physical responses (i.e. identifying a misplaced toy and locating its proper place). This process will be described in more detail in Chapter 5. Alternatively, her tendency to minimize conflict among the children, stemming from her interest in preserving a quiet and orderly classroom, at times impeded the realization of her goal of fostering language interactions, since language interactions based on negotiating conflicts were routinely deflated. This process will be described in more detail in Chapter 8.

Contextual vs. Textual Language Learning

The science lesson I observed together with Sra. Soto at Calvary also provided some insight into Sra. Soto's understanding of ideal contexts for language learning (based on her critique of this teacher, whom she felt had not created the appropriate context in her classroom design). While the majority of the children were gathered around this teacher as she conducted a science lesson, some children were scattered around the room in pairs or small groups, working mostly silently and with very little interaction even when there were other children at the same table. Sra. Soto told me later that they were probably engaged in what was intended to be some kind of hands-on 'Centers' activities, but that since children were working alone in a rather disorganized, random fashion, the plan was poorly implemented. She commented to me that Centers worked when well planned, but that, especially in a language learning environment, children need to work in groups. Group work, she explained, encourages conversation, which is essential for language development.

In her final interview, Sra. Soto spoke at length about her concept of language fluency and the importance of a particular kind of language learning context to which conversation is essential. She related fluency to thinking in a target language, 'I, as a second language learner, know that I think in English now. And if I want to talk in Spanish, I think in Spanish. So I knew that if I wanted my kids to speak in Spanish they needed to think in Spanish'. She stressed to me that fluency in a second language can only be achieved in a classroom where the language is practiced in 'natural' conversation, and explained that this is why most people who learn languages in a classroom setting cannot speak that language:

> The difference between acquiring a language and learning a language... is that people learn textually to speak a second language, but they don't know how to apply that second language. Which is why people who have taken Spanish for 5, 7 years don't know how to hold a conversation in Spanish.

She explained how this criticism of what she sees as a typical language classroom led to her own classroom design, 'Acquiring the language meant for them (students) to practice it in contextual sense'.

Sra. Soto uses 'natural' and 'contextual' to describe the kind of setting ideal for language proficiency development, and I believe the key concept in her definition is the use of the verb 'practice'. In other words, in order to become fluent, to think in a second language, to be able to hold a conversation in this language, the learner must practice the language in a natural context. And the traditional language classroom does not provide the kind of natural context afforded by, for example, a period of immersion in a country where the target language is the majority language. In other words, in a language classroom the type of natural context for conversation in the target language provided ideally by natural immersion, i.e. visiting another country, must be substituted by careful design. This theme of designing to approximate 'natural immersion' turned out to be a central feature of her pedagogical practice.

Sra. Soto differentiated between 'learning' and 'acquiring' a language, between 'textual' and 'contextual' language learning (Lafford & Salaberry, 2003). It is clear that she favored the process she referred to as 'acquisition', which requires a 'context', and that for her, 'context' meant an immersion setting where one is forced to use the language in everyday conversation. Sra. Soto criticized typical language classrooms and set out to design a classroom of a different sort, simulating the kind of language acquisition possible in a natural immersion context. This philosophy of language learning was exemplified by her attitudes toward code-switching (shifting from one language to another during an utterance) during instruction. While she sometimes tolerated this from the children, I very rarely witnessed Sra. Soto use any English during what she designated 'official Spanish time'.

Sra. Soto's insistence on avoiding code-switching reflects the principle of language separation fundamental to the TWI program (Lindholm-Leary, 2001), although some have argued that code-switching, particularly inter-sentential shifts, can be usefully employed by bilingual teachers in bilingual classrooms (Aguirre, 1988). It is important to keep in mind that the ability to code-switch provides speakers with an additional richness and flexibility in linguistic expression that schools tend to undervalue (Garcia, 2002; Han Chung, 2006), and which is a particularly important aspect of children's developing biliteracy (Pérez, 2004). Nevertheless, Ebsworth, commenting on Garcia (2002), points out that while it is indeed important to recognize code-switching as a valuable skill, its use in dual language classrooms by teachers is problematic, as it removes the need to attend to the less familiar language (Ebsworth, 2002). Failing to separate the two languages undermines the immersion process, for which attention to the less familiar language is crucial (Lindholm-Leary, 2001).

Refraining from translation or code-switching when teaching in a TWI program reflects a particular understanding of language acquisition rather than a negative attitude toward code-switching in general, 'It is natural for a teacher to be tempted to translate, particularly if there is bewilderment on a child's face. Yet in these programs, the teachers are encouraged to trust the long-term language-learning process' (Torres-Guzmán, 2007: 53). Strategic or even unconscious code-switching by teachers to facilitate understanding also carries connotations of language status. According to a study by Amrein and Peña (2000: 11), a language asymmetry favoring the use of English as the instructional language 'may have combined with social and political preferences to encourage dual language students to become proficient in English, native English speaking students to be apathetic about mastering a second language, and dual language students to believe that English is superior to Spanish'. Switching to English for discipline or key points can imply that English is the language of important things, an implication that Sra. Soto struggled to avoid.

Sra. Soto carefully monitored her own language and also strongly critiqued other teachers who failed to maintain a strict language separation. This included the teacher who substituted for her when she was absent toward the end of the school year and who spoke English during official Spanish time.[3] Sra. Soto told me that although this substitute teacher was a native Spanish speaker (from Peru), she spoke some English to the children during Spanish time. I was able to corroborate her observations in this case, as I observed this substitute teacher switching to English often during Spanish time and translating certain phrases into English, including familiar set phrases such as 'la hora de limpiar' (*clean-up time*), with which all the children were more than familiar in both languages.

The other TWI Kindergarten teacher also received criticism for code-switching. Sra. Soto related to me an event that particularly disturbed her in which this teacher, during Spanish time, made an announcement in English and specifically announced that she was speaking in English so that everyone would understand the important thing she was about to announce. Sra. Soto's stance toward this incident, including her choice to report the incident to me, afforded several important insights into her philosophy. First, Sra. Soto's strong disapproval of this code-switching behavior reflects her politicized stance toward language status, which I describe in more detail below. For her, switching to English because something is 'important' would undermine the value of Spanish and send children the unintended message that English is the language of important things. Second, this kind of code-switching would also undermine the teacher's ability to approximate a natural immersion environment. The power of natural language acquisition lies in the natural environmental constraints: if you could simply switch to English whenever there was something important to say, these important constraints would be weakened.

In Chapter 4, I will examine more closely the ways in which Sra. Soto created a kind of artificial immersion experience in her classroom in order to approximate what she considered an ideal context for language acquisition (that of genuine immersion in a Spanish-speaking country). Nevertheless, despite Sra. Soto's conviction that natural conversation is crucial to language acquisition, my observations suggested that her adherence to certain implicit classroom conventions, such as orderly and teacher-directed speech, turn taking and conflict reduction, sometimes discouraged spontaneous and rich conversation.

Teaching Spanish as a 'Power Language' Within and Beyond Academic Spaces

Although the Centers we saw at Calvary were clearly academic (children were engaged in science learning), Sra. Soto decided to dedicate her own learning Centers as a relatively informal school space where children were encouraged to play, as long as they communicated in the target language. She referred to this strategy as 'play with purpose' (Einon *et al.*, 1986), drawing on a trend in the field of early child education that recognizes play as an integral part of children's learning in academic areas such as math (Ginsburg, 2006), science (Kleinsinger, 1992) and Language Arts (Bellin & Singer, 2006).

Sra. Soto explained that she intentionally tried to extend the use of Spanish beyond academic contexts. She referred to the less structured Centers time as 'non-academic', and her designation of a classroom context as non-academic may be an attempt to import the natural context she valued for language learning into the classroom. When I asked her why speaking in Spanish during Centers time was important, she related this relatively informal classroom space to school-sponsored yet non-academic activities outside the classroom, such as recess and school trips; 'They're realizing that it's not just language learning, academic language, Spanish. That it's play Spanish. That it's going outside Spanish. And going to the city to do something Spanish'.

For Sra. Soto, these non-academic contexts are what give Spanish political significance and status. Sra. Soto told me that speaking in Spanish during these non-academic times is important to developing students' perceptions of Spanish as a valid and valuable language outside the classroom, and she described this as helping the children to understand Spanish as a 'power language'. This conviction became apparent during our Calvary School visit in her discussions with some of the students. She spoke mostly in Spanish to a group of students gathered around a table outside one of the classrooms, and we learned that one of the girls (about 8 or 9 years old) didn't like to speak Spanish, her native language. Sra. Soto knelt next to her and explained in Spanish how important it was for her to be able to speak in two languages, how she herself felt privileged to be bilingual. She commented to me afterward that this girl's attitude was a common phenomenon, one that she had encountered many times and found frustrating. She told me that her younger sister had shared this attitude, refusing to speak Spanish as a child and experiencing a change of heart in later life.

Later, she drew a parallel between her sister's refusal to speak her native Spanish and the preference for English on the part of some of the native Spanish speakers in her own classroom. She told me that Joël and his sister, who also attended Larson, both strongly preferred English, even when talking to each other, despite the fact that their family spoke Spanish at home. She related their attitude to that of her sister, who lost proficiency because she refused to speak Spanish when she moved to the USA as a child. Later in life, when Sra. Soto's sister decided to reclaim her Spanish, she spent some time in Spain. When Sra. Soto reported to me that her sister now has a Castilian (from Spain) accent when she speaks Spanish, she raised her eyebrows pointedly and shook her head, indicating that speaking your native language with a foreign accent was an unfortunate irony. She contrasted herself with her sister, attributing her own fluent adult bilingualism to the fact that, unlike her sister, she did not choose to give up her Spanish as a child.

This story, repeated in parts and alluded to during various discussions throughout the year, comprised an important part of Sra. Soto's auto-biographical narrative that highlighted the dangers of losing fluency in your native tongue. This conviction that adult bilingualism requires continued use of both languages throughout childhood, rooted in Sra. Soto's personal experience and reinforced by her professional experiences (such as her encounter with the Spanish-speaking girl at Calvary), constituted a powerful pedagogical philosophy. Her conviction that the use of a minority language (in this case, Spanish) is a choice made in childhood that is affected by language politics in the broader society shaped her teaching practice, as I will illustrate in more detail in Chapter 4.

Sra. Soto saw language status as strongly related to social class and the assumptions people made based on class (and possibly race), as illustrated by her contrast between attitudes prevalent in the urban and suburban neighborhoods where students in her classroom lived. She described the urban neighborhood of Larson school as a 'very depressed economic area' where Spanish is seen as 'the lower echelon language'.

She contrasted this urban-based, negative attitude with those of suburban White students, as illustrated by twin English-speaking girls in the classroom, who lived in a relatively affluent suburban area and had some Argentinean family background, 'But my twins, who don't come from this area, for them Spanish is the language of their grand-parents. It's a looked-up-at language, they're going to Argentina, their cousins are speaking Spanish; I mean it's (got) more of a romantic flavor to it'.

In this sense, Sra. Soto's conscious use of Spanish in what she considered non-academic school spaces was a political move, an attempt to convince the children that Spanish could be positive and powerful not just within but beyond her classroom walls. The truly extracurricular activities, such as school trips, were outside her power to regulate. Even recess, although it could be counted on as a regular part of the day, was beyond Sra. Soto's regulatory power in that she did not control when and with what frequency she accompanied the children outside. This assignment was based on the school duty roster and the weather, as indoor recess took place in the children's own classroom with their regular teacher. Nevertheless, she reported to me that she saw these extracurricular activities as an opportunity and took full advantage of them to communicate with the children in Spanish, 'Yesterday... we went to the Opera House. I only spoke to them in Spanish. And they were only speaking to me in Spanish. Because it's important to me to make them aware of the fact that Spanish is not just something that you do during, quote, Spanish time'.

However, toward the end of the school year, Sra. Soto began to feel that her academic goals may not be adequately achieved in the short time remaining in the school year. It became apparent that the academic areas of the classroom, which included Language Arts and Tables time in the Spanish-designated morning, began to take precedence over the less academic, informal spaces where conversation, rather than learning a set curriculum, was the goal. Sra. Soto explained to me that as the end of the year approached, she tried increasingly to get the children to work more, moving away from the concept of play that had been such an important aspect of her initial teaching philosophy. She explained that this shift was intended to prepare them for first grade, where play as a form of learning is not as widely tolerated and activities would be more 'academic' and demanding.

In the final interview, when I asked Sra. Soto to evaluate the success of the play Centers, she expressed disappointment, commenting that her need to focus on more academic areas did not leave her enough time to focus her attention on this less academic area of the classroom; 'That's part of having been a first grade teacher, I know where the first grade teacher will want them to be next year, academically'. This division of school learning into academic and non-academic categories, as well as her ambivalence about the relative value of non-academic language learning (through play), reflect a conflict between a philosophy of language learning that requires informal contexts and the values of the institution. She was highly aware of the institutional expectations of herself as a teacher and of her children as students. Assuming the perspective of the first-grade teacher, she anticipated what this teacher would expect from the children in the following year. These institutional expectations pressured her into de-emphasizing the non-academic aspects of her classroom (Centers) and increasingly emphasizing the academic aspects (such as more structured Language Arts and science lessons).

Nevertheless, this ambivalence did not reflect an adversarial stance on her part with respect to the institution, as she did not at any point criticize these institutional values and expectations. Sra. Soto helped design the district's math performance standards for the Kindergarten level, and none of her discussions with me indicated that she was critical of any aspect of these standards, or of the fact that she was expected to use these standards to design her curriculum. In fact, she designed her curriculum explicitly in terms of state standards:

> The state... has given me a book, it's got standards in it, I teach to those standards. And to the best of my ability I've tried to teach to those standards, both in English and in Spanish. So that if (the standards) said to me, "the child will learn about a book, the parts of a book," I make sure they know them both in English and Spanish. They will be able to retell stories, I've taught them in both English and Spanish.

It seems that while Sra. Soto uncritically accepted the institution's expectations, these expectations were not always supportive of her other pedagogical philosophies. This led to a certain ambivalence that became increasingly apparent as the year drew to a close and the academic demands of first grade became more and more imminent. Rather than attribute the relative failure of the play Centers to a certain incompatibility between informal learning contexts and institutional values (as I did), she seemed to find failure in herself, 'I was disappointed in how it developed, and that was truly my fault'.

Connecting the Pieces: Thematic Units

In the car on the way home from our Calvary School visit, Sra. Soto explained to me that she planned to design her curriculum around thematic units, which she said would include poetry, songs and hands-on activities. In her final interview, she expressed a belief that she had achieved this goal of thematic unit organization, 'I think you have gotten that impression from being in my room, that units carried on to units carried on to units, or at least I think you've gotten that impression – that my room had an orderly fashion'. She contrasted her own thematically connected curriculum with what she considers typical teaching, which she criticizes for compartmentalizing learning into distinct subject areas:

> See, sometimes I think that we compartmentalize all subject matter, we say this is math, this is reading... (but) if I'm going to do math, I need reading. If I'm going to do reading, I need to do math.... When I'm doing Calendar with the whole group, I tie in math, science, social studies, everything is tied in together.

She also reflected at the end of the year that this process of thematic design was quite difficult work, 'I have really worked very hard at sitting down and thinking how does this tie with this, tie with that... so planning has been hard'.

As I observed throughout the year, Sra. Soto's curriculum did indeed consist of complicated and interwoven thematic units connecting traditional subject areas such as math and science as well as more personal and more affective elements, such as ethnic pride and self-efficacy. For example, Sra. Soto reflected on one of her units that included several stories from African countries, 'We did Black inventors. We did African tales. I did African numbers... and also tried to build with them language – African animals, the jungle'. This unit included elements of science (inventors), mathematics (numbers in an African language) and Language Arts (names of jungle animals in English and Spanish). Sra. Soto also intentionally implemented this unit during the month of February, Black History Month, to further connect these units to a theme of African pride and history, 'I've been trying to bring pride to my African-American students. Telling them a great number of things that we have, that are fun and good, came from Africa'.

This unit, in turn, was embedded in a larger unit exploring different continents, which involved reading stories from different countries and singing a song about the continents in both Spanish and English. At the same time, the themes were cross-connected; for example, two of the

African stories, *Anansi and the Moss-Covered Rock* and *The Bojabi Tree*, shared a common theme of self-efficacy, which Sra. Soto described as 'stories where somebody little is coming in and helping. It's not a big person it's a little, insignificant person. I'm trying to help them get the idea that they, not the teacher, can help them to learn from each other Spanish'.

This theme of self-efficacy was also reflected in the classroom practice where the children chose a language partner (English-Spanish pairs) to help them throughout the day. To facilitate this practice she posted all the children's photos and names on the board, divided into Spanish and English speakers. She explained that this theme of helping was also connected to a chant, which she implemented in the morning to encourage the children to find a language partner, 'See in the morning I have that new song, you know that new song, right? "Hola Hola como estas? I like you, you like me"? I'm trying in the morning for them to pick already that partner. That English-Spanish partner'.

Sra. Soto described this practice of creating complex thematic connections as a way to facilitate learning:

> I know, as a learner, I need for things to tie in together. If they don't all tie in to knots, I lose it. It's gone. So it's a mesh of tying in knots together so they make a weave. And I do truly believe that people who have a better understanding are people who have a consistent weave in their brain. If you can picture it that way; I can picture weaving and pushing things in together. So the reason I said to you that I think themes work for language development is that I am helping to put that weave together.

More specifically referring to second language learning, she related these thematic weavings to building vocabulary, 'So I knew that if I wanted my kids to speak in Spanish they needed to think in Spanish, which means that they need the vocabulary to do that, and unless that weave was there, it wouldn't be there'. She explained to me that vocabulary is assimilated as we realize that we have learned certain words in another context, and incorporate that word into the present context. To exemplify this process, she explained how one of the English-speaking students, Ian, incorporated the repetitive Spanish phrases he learned during Calendar time to express a novel situation:

> Today (Ian) was trying to say (that) he had three dollars in his pocket because he didn't pay for yesterday. So he tied in the things from our calendar, he said "Tengo (*I have*) three dollars because ayer (*yesterday*)

I did not pay and... tengo uno para mañana (*I have one for tomorrow*)." And I thought, he's tying in the calendar (activity)... and I like that they can move across.

Sra. Soto sometimes referred to her use of themes as scaffolding, 'That's why I'm telling you that I like my themes. That I thought I build a greater scaffold for the kids to learn. That's what I'm doing, I'm scaffolding'. Scaffolds, as defined by Rosenshine (1992), are 'forms of support provided by the teacher (or another student) to help students bridge the gap between their current abilities and the intended goals... the scaffolds are both temporary and adjustable, allowing learners to participate at an ever-increasing level of competence'.[4] In language learning, redundancy itself can be considered a scaffold. Peregoy and Boyle's research in a TWI Kindergarten described the use of linguistic and meta-linguistic redundancy as multiple-embedded scaffolds. These scaffolds, according to Peregoy and Boyle's (1999) analysis, included techniques such as connecting various aspects of the classroom using common vocabulary, for example, by using pretend food items from the play Center in a discussion of healthy dietary practices. In this sense, Sra. Soto's thematic connections may relate, as she explicitly claims, to a concept of scaffolding, in terms of providing target vocabulary practice in different contexts. Sra. Soto described Ian (from the example above) as an example of a child who, within the confines of the available curriculum, has the autonomy to discover his/her own connections, 'The themes help me to give parameters, it's like a scaffold, where you go up, it can go in either direction. Like Ian, he's going up the ladder with me, but he's making these connections to other places'.

Sra. Soto believed that if a teacher does a good job making these connections available to the children through thematic curriculum planning, the children should be able to infer the task required of them when they encounter a new classroom activity from the thematic context, 'And when I just put up a picture and my kids can tell me what it is that I want them to do with it, that to me is amazing – they understood'. She related to me one day with obvious satisfaction that she had noticed Emily, an English-speaking student, spontaneously writing, 'La mamá es una mamífera' (*Mothers are mammals*). She told me that she was very pleased to see that this girl had independently connected two of her classroom themes, family and mammals, in a way that she had planned on making explicit but had not yet done so. She also praised another child who was able to successfully infer some of her thematic connections:

Like today, one of my children, the twins,[5] brought in a book. (She) said, "it's everything we've been talking about" and it was the book I was going to read today. And I thought, see, they even know how thematically things tie in together, and they were now looking at books to bring in that tie in to our theme.

Her satisfaction that this child was able to identify her implicit curricular theme and independently connect an appropriate book suggested that she considered making inferences and connections a desirable achievement. As they follow and connect the teacher's themes, these children are able to access her privileged teacher's understanding in a way that enables them even to predict her thoughts.

Sra. Soto's reflection on her thematic curriculum design reveals two important educational philosophies. First, she believes that language learning best results from language-redundant contexts, as illustrated by Ian's incorporation of 'Calendar time' vocabulary into his personal narrative about money. In other words, there must be multiple contexts where the same vocabulary is required, and language learning is evident when learners begin to transfer vocabulary from one context to another. This concept of learning transfer is consistent with Sra. Soto's overall direct instruction approach, where a particular concern is that the students are able to decontextualize and transfer skills.

Rosenshine (1992: 32) describes decontextualization as the learning stage where 'strategies become free of their original bindings and can now be applied, easily and unconsciously, to various situations'. Transfer is defined as 'the ability to learn in one situation and then to use that learning, possibly in generalized or modified form, in other situations where it is appropriate' (Hunter, 1971). This view is based on the cognitive psychology framework in which skills are seen as independent of the activity, portable, and can be learned in one context and transferred to another. If the skill can be repeated in the new context, this is a demonstration that the skill is decontextualized, that is, that the student possesses the skill in such a way that he/she can recall it in the new context (Anderson *et al.*, 1997). This fundamental cognitive philosophy concerning the nature of learning forms the basis for Sra. Soto's pedagogical design of the Housekeeping and Blocks Centers, where the children's vocabulary knowledge learning in other curricular areas were supposed to transfer to their play. In Chapter 8, I will examine this phenomenon (more specifically, its underrepresentation) in the play Centers.

Second, Sra. Soto's appreciation of the children discovering thematic connections suggests that some degree of autonomy is desirable; children find their own connections, choosing their own direction on the 'scaffold'. Nevertheless, the children's autonomous searching should lead them to certain predesigned discoveries, and Sra. Soto's example of the children guessing their tasks from thematic context illustrates just how much student autonomy is appropriate for the classroom. While Sra. Soto values children who are able to make connections and inferences without direct instruction, these connections should lead to the conclusion she expects. This resonates with the concerns I expressed earlier about child-centered pedagogy within a teacher-directed curriculum (the study where children failed to discover independently what would be on the teacher's Hamlet examination). In this classroom, the potential failure of the children to arrive independently at the teacher's goals seemed to present some problems in the more loosely structured, child-centered aspects of the curriculum (particularly the play Centers, as described in Chapter 8).

Classroom Design: Putting it All into Practice

Sra. Soto explained to me in detail as we toured the Calvary school and in the car on the way home how she planned to design the curriculum of her first TWI classroom. She told me she intended to create 'learning Centers' where children would work together on types of projects that would facilitate conversation. This design coincided with her interest in environments designed for creating natural conversations, creating a 'non-academic' context (consisting of Blocks and House-keeping Centers) within the overall academic environment of the classroom. At the same time, she explained that she saw a need for building vocabulary and confidence in the children by offering some formulaic language use, which would include games and songs. Academic subjects (such as Language Arts and science), play Centers, and repetitive songs and chants would all be organized into thematic units that would allow the children to practice the same vocabulary and concepts in various contexts, allowing them to create strong mental connections.

It was easy to see this theory reflected in the eventual design of her classroom, as Sra. Soto, true to her stated plans, did include both Centers and frequent repetitive and fun exercises like songs and word plays, and she did create thematic units that spread over various classroom activities, including songs, literature and even the relatively unstructured

Centers. In the following chapters, I will describe several aspects of Sra. Soto's pedagogy, analyzing how the various philosophies and goals described here shaped pedagogical practices and how these practices affected learning in this particular TWI Kindergarten classroom.

Notes

1. This school has been assigned a pseudonym.
2. Curiously, this glossary lacks an entry for 'child-centered'.
3. Sra. Soto's family obligations required her to move away shortly before the school year ended, and a substitute teacher took over for the last few days. Sra. Soto reported to me that she took half a sick day to remain in the classroom with the substitute on her first day so the children would have an easier transition.
4. I use Rosenshine's definition because he is a proponent of the direct instruction model of teaching, and so his definition would be most accessible to Sra. Soto (based on her Madeline Hunter training). Other perspectives on scaffolding, which emphasize more joint participation in an activity (problem solving, conversation) are also available (Bruner, 1983; Rogoff, 1990; Wood *et al.*, 1976).
5. This twin is either the same child who observed that mothers must be mammals (Emily) or her twin sister Sandra.

Chapter 4

Making Sure They Don't 'Give it away': Keeping Spanish Alive

As described in Chapter 1, the ideal two-way immersion (TWI) program design is based on a planned symmetrical balance of two languages. In order to qualify for inclusion in the Directory of Two-Way Bilingual Programs in the USA, compiled by the Center for Applied Linguistics, all three of the following criteria must be met:

> **Integration:** Language-minority and language-majority students are integrated for at least 50% of instructional time at all grade levels
> **Instruction:** Content and literacy instruction in English and the partner language is provided to all students, and *all students receive instruction in the partner language at least 50% of the instructional day*
> **Population:** Within the program, there is a balance of language-minority and language-majority students, with each group making up between one-third and two-thirds of the total student population (Center for Applied Linguistics, 2008, italics in original)

This definition relies strongly on the assumption that children will be fully proficient in the language to which they are officially assigned as dominant, and that they will be eager to communicate in this language. Nevertheless, the unequal sociopolitical status of the majority and minority languages can affect children's language preferences and even abilities. The hegemony of English in US society skews the actual implementation of this ideal.

The Hegemony of English as a Majority Language in the USA

Hegemony is a social process that attributes value to certain practices over others. Based on the social construction of 'the natural order of things' or 'common sense', hegemony is domination by means of intellectual social control rather than through coercion (Gramsci *et al.*, 1972). Asymmetrical power relations are maintained by reinforcing the ideologies of the dominant group and converting their practices into cultural capital, that is, knowledge, behaviors and habits that become associated with status and success (Bourdieu, 1986). A language or dialect that is used by a powerful group becomes cultural capital, and so it becomes common sense that this language or dialect is highly valuable, and perhaps even inherently superior (Pennycook, 1998).[1] Common sense in this context does not imply wisdom; rather it implies a socially and politically constructed, value-laden assumption that comes to be taken for granted.

English is a hegemonic language in the USA: it seems natural that English is the 'common' language (despite a history of linguistic diversity), it seems to be common sense that English is virtually the only language of opportunity (in terms of education and employment) and it seems obvious that learning English will bring everyone, regardless of skin color or other ethnicity markers, opportunities for success. While bilingualism is, in fact, nothing new to the USA, there is a strong tendency to consider assimilation to 'mainstream' language and cultural practices at the expense of home language and culture the only path to success (García, 2005). Spanish-speaking children may tacitly adopt these assumptions even when their parents, and even they, value learning Spanish. In Sra. Soto's words, children from Spanish-speaking families can feel pressured to 'give away' their home language in favor of a language that they perceive as more powerful.

While TWI programs are sometimes touted as enrichment programs, particularly as a marketing strategy for attracting English speakers who value foreign language education (Lindholm-Leary, 2001; Valdés, 1997), this notion can have problematic connotations. Pérez (2004: 178) describes how teachers, parents and school administrators came to redefine one TWI program in terms of 'linguistic rights, reclaiming language and cultural heritage' rather than enrichment, thus situating the program firmly in terms of basic rights for language-minority children rather than as a luxury that might easily fall victim to funding cuts.

Several studies have pointed out that Spanish, as a minority language in the USA, risks significant underrepresentation in TWI classrooms. In a study of TWI programs in California, Collins (1998: 39) identified several of these programs as weak models, or ones that 'may have poor integration, balance, and/or dual language use'. Collins' (1993) ethnographic study of a third-grade TWI class revealed that English-speaking students did not use Spanish as much as their Spanish-speaking classmates used English, and that teachers spoke English two-thirds of the classroom time and used Spanish almost exclusively for disciplinary purposes.

Riojas-Cortez (2001) described a TWI Kindergarten where, despite the fact that all the children were of Mexican heritage, 11 out of 12 children were more fluent in English than in Spanish. Alanís' (2000) study of a fifth-grade TWI classroom found that while participants developed high levels of English proficiency, English speakers never achieved high levels of Spanish proficiency, and Spanish speakers did not develop their native language much beyond the initial years of the program. She attributes this asymmetrical language development to the children's overall preference for speaking English (Alanís, 2000). While native English speakers in US TWI programs do not tend to achieve very high levels of Spanish proficiency, Spanish native speakers in a Mexican bilingual school that used a 50-50 English-Spanish approach were found to achieve high English proficiency, suggesting that the broader sociolinguistic context is an important factor (Graham & Brown, 1996).

Potowski's (2004) ethnographic study of Spanish use in a fifth-grade TWI classroom revealed that children used Spanish only about half the time during official Spanish time. Potowski's analysis suggested that language choice reflects not a resistance to the official Spanish curriculum, but rather the sociolinguistic complexity of social hierarchies and identity management. Her observations also point out that peer group work, a collaborative learning technique that has been recommended for TWI classrooms (E.R. Howard *et al.*, 2007), can nevertheless result in high levels of majority language use among peers (Potowski, 2004).

Wiese (2004) described a second-grade classroom where the perceived English language deficits of some native English speakers, predominantly minority students who spoke a non-standard dialect of English at home, resulted in shifting emphasis for these particular students from Spanish to English literacy. Weise's study also serves to remind us that there is internal hegemony even within the dominant language, so that even certain dialects of English come to be understood as inferior (Labov, 1974).

The challenge of maintaining equity in a program that attempts to integrate children from majority and minority language groups is demonstrated in Amrein and Peña's (2000) study of a newly implemented TWI program in Phoenix, Arizona. While the school officially attempted to foster an atmosphere of language and cultural equity, the authors describe instructional asymmetry (e.g. the tendency to speak more English than Spanish), resource asymmetry (e.g. the increased availability of English written material) and student asymmetry (e.g. the tendency for Spanish speakers to speak relatively good English, while English speakers remained predominantly monolingual) (Amrein &

Peña, 2000). Schools where children are expected to achieve a high level of Spanish literacy have difficulty finding advanced literacy materials, since publishers adjust their production to a market consisting mainly of transitional bilingual programs, where only moderate levels of Spanish literacy can be expected (Smith & Arnot-Hopffer, 1998). Other potential risks to the balance of Spanish in a TWI program include lack of administrative support for teachers (Riojas-Clark, 1995), being housed as a specialty program within an English-speaking school (Hayes, 2004) and the higher status of English in the broader American society (Shannon, 1995; Valdés, 1997).

Studies like these that examine the ways in which both minority and majority languages are actually used in TWI classrooms are invaluable in understanding the classroom-based reality behind the ideal TWI model. In this chapter, I explore the effects of English hegemony on this Kindergarten classroom, as well as Sra. Soto's strategies to encourage Spanish as well as English speakers to see Spanish as a valuable and powerful resource in its own right. I will first provide an overview of the linguistic competencies and preferences of the children in this Kindergarten classroom and then describe the strategies employed by the teacher to support the use of Spanish during official Spanish time. It is my hope that systematically analyzing one teacher's classroom practice will provide guidance for other teachers working in environments of language hegemony.

The Children: Language Proficiencies and Preferences

There were 21 children in the classroom, 11 of whom had been identified as Spanish natives and 10 identified as English natives.[2] According to Sra. Soto, all the assigned English speakers spoke English at home, and none had had any significant experience with Spanish before the school year began (see Table 4.1).

While some of these English speakers had relatives who were able to speak Spanish, Sra. Soto's questioning of the parents revealed that none of these relatives spoke Spanish with the children. For example, Sandra and Emily, who were twin sisters, lived with a Spanish-speaking father, but their mother, who also lived with them, spoke no Spanish. Kathleen had a Spanish-speaking grandmother with whom she did not live. James' parents both had Latino backgrounds, but only James' mother spoke any Spanish, and she did not live with him. Ian's father was Latino, but Sra. Soto was not sure if he was able to speak Spanish, and he did not live with Ian. The remaining four English-speaking children had no known

Table 4.1 English speakers' experience with Spanish

Name	Gender	Spanish experience
Emily/ Sandra	Girl	One parent bilingual, other parent English monolingual
Kathleen	Girl	One Spanish-speaking relative, does not live with child
James	Boy	
Ian	Boy	
Mark	Boy	No known contact with Spanish speakers
Jamaica	Girl	
Dorinda	Girl	
Rashid	Boy	
Khamil	Boy	

relatives or friends who spoke Spanish outside the school. Four of these children were African-American and lived in a predominantly African-American neighborhood near the school. Overall, according to Sra. Soto's assessment of the families, which she based on her communications with the parents, the English speakers did not have much opportunity to use Spanish outside the classroom.

The Spanish natives, by contrast, had had significant exposure to English before beginning the TWI program. According to Sra. Soto's records, most of the children had attended the district's English language public preschool. Sra. Soto's conversations with parents further revealed that some of these children habitually used English in the home. She also told me that she noticed that several of them preferred to speak English with their siblings in the school (see Table 4.2).

Of the 11 children who had been officially designated as Spanish speakers, Sra. Soto only identified three as, in her terms, good 'Spanish role models'. Berto left early in the school year, and so Sra. Soto did not provide information on his language background. Sra. Soto identified two children, Emilio and Norma, who spoke mostly English in the home. Norma's parents were from Puerto Rico, and spoke in Spanish to each other in the home but, according to Sra. Soto, they always addressed Norma in English. Emilio lived with a father who spoke Spanish and a monolingual English-speaking mother. Sra. Soto criticized the district

Table 4.2 Spanish speakers' experience with English

Name	Gender	English preschool	Other English experience
Emilio	Boy	Yes	Spoke predominately English at home
Norma	Girl		
Lucía	Girl		Preferred to speak English with siblings
Joël	Boy		
Wilma	Girl		
Oscar	Boy		
Amalia	Girl		Rarely spoke English
Alberta	Girl	No	Rarely spoke English
Alicia	Girl		Rarely spoke English
John	Boy		Very little, arrived from Mexico middle of year
Berto	Boy	No	Unknown – left school early in the year

screening process for mis-assigning children's language proficiency: 'How was the screening done? By surname. Only by surname. Not by ability. And not by the parent saying, yeah, my child does speak Spanish at home. Not true. I mean, that just wasn't the case. But this is an imperfect world'.

Of the remaining children who did speak mostly Spanish at home, Sra. Soto reported that four of them (Lucía, Joël, Wilma and Oscar) preferred to speak English, at least when she saw them in the school talking with friends and siblings. Joël and his sister, she told me, can always be seen talking together in English. She also mentioned that Joël, at the beginning of the year, had directly told her that he would not speak Spanish in the classroom. This problem of language preference seemed to persist throughout the year, as Sra. Soto reported to me in May that she noticed and reprimanded Oscar and Norma for talking together in English. She reported that Oscar and Wilma also preferred to speak to their siblings in English, although their families spoke Spanish at home. In Oscar's case, Sra. Soto clearly separated the influence of family and society, as she reported that Oscar's mother was 'distressed to see that he preferred to speak only in English'. While there has been research into the direct (Tannenbaum & Howie, 2002) or mediating (Luo & Wiseman, 2000) influence of family dynamics on language loss and maintenance, it is important to keep in mind that these children's parents all registered their children for the TWI Kindergarten, suggesting at least some commitment to promoting Spanish language and cultural enrichment on the part of Spanish-speaking parents and those families with Latino heritage. Sra. Soto found that the children's preference for English had a detrimental effect on their Spanish language development. For example, she commented on Lucía, who preferred to speak with her siblings in English; 'Lucía's verbal Spanish was very poor in the beginning of the year'.

Sra. Soto's reflections on the effects of English hegemony in her classroom

Although Sra. Soto's comments described here indicate that she was particularly worried that Spanish speakers preferred to speak English due to social pressure, she told me in our final interview that she sometimes had problems encouraging some Spanish speakers to speak English during English time in the afternoons. I was not able to corroborate that statement, since my data collection focused on Spanish time, but it is important to take into consideration that language learning is difficult in any case, and that the effects of language hegemony only serve to exacerbate this difficulty in the case of minority languages.

Sra. Soto never used the term 'hegemony' in her formal interviews and informal discussions with me, but this is the concept that seems to me to best describe her sociopolitical understandings of language. In our final interview, she reflected on the low status of Spanish in the urban area of the school; 'You have to remember environmentally where they are living... We are in a very depressed economic area, our school is. And they see Spanish as the lower echelon language. The language of people they do not like'. She reflected on several Spanish-speaking children who preferred English in the classroom, 'Wilma switches to English, every single time. And that's because she gave away her Spanish in nursery school last year... She decided last year in nursery school that her not speaking any English was not good for her'. It's clear from this statement that Sra. Soto sees a conscious choice, whether to keep or give away a language, at the root of bilingualism.

Sra. Soto expressed with conviction that the school environment in this case encouraged this decision to reject Spanish, and specifically implicated Crestfield, the district's public preschool program, which does not have a bilingual component, 'It's interesting that they all went to the same (pre) school, and they all gave up their Spanish, and you know why, it's Crestfield. And it's the city kid that's in there... and they said, "We're not going to get banged"'. Sra. Soto characterized the atmosphere at Crestfield as strictly monolingual. Despite the fact that many of the children attending the program live in the Latino neighborhood of the city, the language of Crestfield's classrooms is officially English. Further, she characterizes the overall environment of Crestfield as threatening, as evidenced by her reference to the children's fear of getting 'banged', a term for 'attacked' often associated with gang rivalry.

Sra. Soto implicated personality traits of the child in this decision, and explained why three girls (Amalia, Norma and Wilma) who went to the same preschool differed in the extent of their decision to 'give up' Spanish, 'The three of them went together. Amalia's a very timid child. She didn't pick up any English there. Wilma, very competitive. Norma, almost as competitive. They realized that the language of command was English, and by God they were going to learn it'. Interestingly, in Sra. Soto's view, the danger of language loss seems to be greater for the competitive, aggressive child than for the timid child, as the more competitive child recognizes opportunity in the hegemony of English and consciously decides to ally with the stronger language, rejecting the weaker.

Sra. Soto's comments cast the social environment as a powerful factor in the children's decision to become or not to become bilingual adults, an assumption that implies a certain faith that modifying this early social environment can affect the learner's eventual success in achieving bilingualism. Further, these comments reveal that Sra. Soto viewed the children's Spanish proficiency as constantly threatened by environmental forces and requiring compensatory strategies. These strategies, as she described during our discussions, were social strategies designed to counter the social signals children were receiving from both teachers and peers that English was, as she described, 'the language of command'. In the following sections, I analyze strategies for strictly enforcing a Spanish-only policy during official Spanish time, thus effectively creating a tiny, local zone of Spanish hegemony within what Sra. Soto's descriptions characterized as a broader English hegemonic society.

Redressing Structural Asymmetry: A Strand Within a School

As mentioned in Chapter 2, the school day was divided into official Spanish time in the morning and official English time in the afternoon, and the transition took place at lunch (11:30 am). It's important to keep in mind that this classroom was one of two TWI Kindergarten classes in an otherwise English-dominant school. All the other classrooms were either English-only or traditional transitional bilingual, where Spanish use is minimized as much as possible. Even the neighborhood surrounding the school was not largely Spanish speaking, although it was near a predominantly Latino neighborhood. While Sra. Soto reported to me in her interviews that she tried to use Spanish a little during recess and other informal school spaces, the children spent the time from 11:30 am to 12:15 pm eating lunch and playing in this mainly English-speaking whole school environment. If this default-English time were not counted, the division of languages in Sra. Soto's classroom would have approached the even division implied by the 50:50 model. Official Spanish time lasted from 8:40 am to 11:30 am, a total of 2 hours and 50 minutes. The official English time began after lunch and recess, at 12:15 pm, and lasted until dismissal at 3:10 pm, a total of 2 hours and 55 minutes.

Nevertheless, lunch and recess did occur in the school cafeteria and playground, where the dominant school language was English, and this 45-minute period effectively extended the English time to 3 hours and 40 minutes. This situation was exacerbated later in the year, when administrative complications required the children to go to lunch a half hour earlier at 11:00 am, effectively reducing the official Spanish time by another 30 minutes. Sra. Soto restructured her schedule in response to this, adding a half hour of Spanish to the afternoon. Of course, this did mean that Spanish time was interrupted by the *de facto* English period of lunch and recess, so it was hardly an ideal situation. Even so, Sra. Soto reported that she was criticized by the school principal for 'over-emphasizing Spanish'. The other Kindergarten teacher did not adjust her schedule to compensate for the lost half-hour of Spanish time.

Sra. Soto also reported that Spanish time was truncated by interruptions, Specials and occasional auditorium events, all of which were, of course, in English. These interruptions certainly must have taken place during the afternoon English time as well, but they would have been congruent with the official language. In fact, Specials (library, gym, music and art), for which the children left Sra. Soto's classroom and learned in a completely English context, took place in the afternoon. Yet this did not entirely prevent the broader English school environment from seeping into Spanish time. My classroom observations during morning Spanish time supported Sra. Soto's perception of this phenomenon. Auditorium events, loudspeaker interruptions and occasional visits from other school employees generally took place in English out of necessity, because most of the members of the broader school community, teachers, administrators and children alike, were monolingual English speakers.

Sra. Soto attempted to compensate for this inequality as best she could. Aside from her rather controversial decision to increase official Spanish time by a half hour each day, she sometimes modified or reversed her language schedule for the day, telling me that she was attempting to compensate for sudden changes in the school schedule. For example, one morning I entered at 9:00 am during official Spanish time and saw that the children were engaged in English Language Arts. Sra. Soto explained that the children were to participate in a school-wide activity in the auditorium this morning, which would necessarily take place in English, and so she had decided to reverse the languages, moving Spanish time to the afternoon just for this day.

As far as English-language interruptions were concerned, there was little Sra. Soto could do to avoid them. Furthermore, when a response was needed, she had to break her own very strictly self-imposed sanction against code-switching (as described in Chapter 3), since the speaker from the main school office was always a monolingual English speaker. I recorded three intercom English interruptions during Spanish time. My observations of these suggested that Sra. Soto employed a sort of damage-control policy, where she attempted to minimize the inevitable effect of English interruptions on her carefully constructed Spanish immersion zone.

The following example of an intercom interruption during official Spanish time is perhaps particularly inopportune, since Sra. Soto has just finished scolding Rashid, an English speaker, for continuing to speak in English:

Sra. Soto: [In a sharp voice] Mira, Rashid. ¿Por qué sigues tú hablando de eso en inglés? Si tú vas a hablar conmigo en inglés...
(*Look, Rashid. Why do you keep talking about that in English? If you are going to talk with me in English...*)
Unknown woman: [Voice cuts in over the intercom] Mrs. Soto?
Sra. Soto: Yes?
Unknown woman: The number you gave for Kathleen, is it a new number?

Sra. Soto: No, it's her old number.
Girl: [to Sra. Soto] What do I have to do?
Sra. Soto: Tu alfabeto. (*Your alphabet*) [Saying the letters in Spanish]
A, B, C, D, E, F...

In this case, not only is Sra. Soto's sharp insistence that Rashid speak to her in Spanish undermined by the English interruption, but also the interruption itself seems to be a rather unnecessary request for information that is not particularly urgent. Furthermore, Sra. Soto is required to respond in English, since the speaker from the office is not bilingual, thus breaking the very rule that she has been trying to convince Rashid to follow. In fact, the child who speaks immediately after Sra. Soto's English response does follow this code-switch and speaks in English as well. Nevertheless, Sra. Soto minimizes the effect of the interruption by responding to the child in Spanish as if nothing has happened.

Overall, Sra. Soto's responses to intercom interruptions can be described as damage control strategies that follow three basic guidelines:

(1)   She does not respond unless she has to.
(2)   She responds as briefly as possible when she does.
(3)   She immediately returns to Spanish and requires that the children do the same.

Sra. Soto's Compensatory Strategies: Creating Artificial Spanish Immersion

Since the broader language of this school, like that of mainstream English society, was English, occasional interruptions and incursions of the majority language into official Spanish time were beyond Sra. Soto's control. Nevertheless, within her own classroom, official Spanish time was a carefully constructed and maintained microcosm of artificial Spanish immersion, and seemed to reflect the faith she had in natural language immersion experiences as described in Chapter 3. This term 'artificial' is not meant to be derogatory, but to reflect the conscious construction of a micro-environment that is not reflected in the broader school or societal environment. In other words, while she was perfectly capable of understanding and speaking English, and most of the children, including many of the designated Spanish speakers, were perfectly capable of speaking English, she employed various strategies to maintain a Spanish-only atmosphere during Spanish time.

Sra. Soto's Spanish immersion strategy can be divided into five main approaches:

- Strictly enforce 'Spanish-only' policy during Spanish time.
- Explicitly assign Spanish speakers the responsibility of being Spanish resources.
- Adopt the assumption that speaking Spanish is a choice, not an ability.
- Cultivate a game-like atmosphere based on pretend Spanish constraints.
- Involve children in maintaining and enforcing the game rules.

Strict enforcement of Spanish-only policy (punishment and praise)

This enforcement of a Spanish-only policy during official Spanish time included both explicit praise for speaking Spanish and explicit punishment for failing to do so. For example, Sra. Soto praises Emily (English), for asking her a question in Spanish:

> **Sra. Soto:** Emily, bien hecho, que me lo preguntaste en español. ¡Muy lindo! (*Emily, well-done that you asked me that in Spanish. Very nice!*)

Interestingly, despite the extremely limited experience the English speakers had with Spanish, Sra. Soto identified five English speakers as positive Spanish role models: Sandra, Emily, Dorinda, Ian and Kathleen. Sra. Soto's praise for the English speakers who served as Spanish role models was based largely on their efforts. Sra. Soto reported to me that Ian had been trying to speak in Spanish to his Latino father, who did not live with him and that Sandra and Emily, the twin sisters whose bilingual father did not speak Spanish at home, had tried to speak 'a few words' with their father. She mentioned that Dorinda was an especially enthusiastic participant in Spanish chants and songs, and identified Kathleen as a very enthusiastic language learner, whose strong social motivation contributed to her success as a Spanish language learner.

This relatively easy praise for English speakers based on their efforts reflects Valdés' criticism (1997) that in TWI programs an inequality emerges as English speakers are praised for minor advances in Spanish acquisition, while Spanish speakers must perform at a higher level in English to earn similar appreciation. Since these English speakers had far less exposure to Spanish than their Spanish-speaking peers had to English, failure to lower expectations for their progress might have resulted in frustration and resistance. Simply having the same expectations for

English and Spanish speakers was not feasible, and while Sra. Soto did praise her English speakers for their efforts, she also chided them readily for lack of effort. Nevertheless, my observations did support Valdés' critique.

Speaking English during Spanish time was clearly a punishable offense, and this rule applied to both English and Spanish speakers alike. One day, while the children were working together at their tables, Sra. Soto chided Joël (Spanish) for speaking English during Spanish time. Emily (English) immediately pointed out to Sra. Soto that Joël *can* speak Spanish:

> **Emily** (English): [addressing Sra. Soto] Joël español. (*Joël Spanish*)
> **Sra. Soto:** Sí. Joël sabe español. Así que no tiene ninguna razón para estar hablando en inglés. (*Yes. Joël knows Spanish. Therefore he has no reason to be speaking in English*)

While this exchange emerges because of Sra. Soto's insistence that Spanish speakers speak only Spanish during Spanish time, it seems in this context that she was inadvertently penalizing Joël for knowing Spanish, as his bilingualism was conceptualized as a reason for castigation. It was because he knew Spanish that he had no reason to speak English.

Spanish speakers as Spanish resources

Sra. Soto not only expected the English speakers to speak Spanish, and chided them when they seemed to be making insufficient effort, but she also explicitly assigned the Spanish speakers the responsibility to help her in her role of supporting Spanish use. For example, one day when Sra. Soto was trying to encourage the children to retell a rather complicated Spanish story in which a little girl tries to change her hair in various ways, she chided Alicia (Spanish) for not participating. This story was a bit confusing and Sra. Soto had been receiving incorrect answers to her questions:

> **Sra. Soto:** ¿La niña quería tener pelo, ¿qué? (*The girl wanted to have hair, what kind?*)
> **A couple of children:** [calling out] ¡Lacio! (*Straight!*)
> **Sra. Soto:** No, rizado. (*No, curly*) [turns to Alicia, who had not responded] Alicia. ¿Por qué es que tú, que te necesito, para que me contestes a mí las preguntas, estás mirando al aire? (*Why is it that you, who I need to answer my questions, are looking into space?*)

In this case, she makes it clear that she is expecting Alicia to participate in her lesson as a way to help her teach Spanish.

She also seemed to expect the Spanish speakers to maintain a general Spanish-only atmosphere, despite the fact, as mentioned above, that some of them were more comfortable, and even more proficient, in English. To this end, I frequently noticed her chiding the Spanish speakers for speaking to each other in English during Spanish time. One day, for example, she caught Wilma asking Norma about her project in English, despite the fact that both girls were Spanish speakers:

> **Wilma** (Spanish): [to Norma] Were you tracing it?
> **Sra. Soto:** No le digas esto en inglés, a ella, por favor. (*Don't say that to her in English, please*)
> **Norma** (Spanish): [repeats Wilma's phrase in Spanish]
> **Sra. Soto:** Gracias, Norma. (*Thank you, Norma*)
> **Sra. Soto:** [this time addressing Wilma] Wilma, si no puedo contar contigo, hablando en español, ¿con quién cuento? (*Wilma, if I can't count on you, speaking in Spanish, who can I count on?*)

Speaking Spanish is a matter of choice, not ability

Sra. Soto's comments to me suggested that she tended to characterize English speakers who tended to speak English during Spanish time, even those who particularly seemed to struggle with the new language, as unwilling rather than unable to speak Spanish. For example, she told me that '(Jamaica's) stubbornness was what impeded her progress at acquiring Spanish skills'; James 'had a high interest in learning Spanish' until his Spanish-speaking mother left the family during the year, after which he 'dropped' the effort; and Mark's immaturity 'impeded his language acquisition'. In addition, toward the end of the year, she expressed to me her approval for Oscar and Joël, two Spanish speakers, for increasing their use of Spanish in the classroom, and she described this as a choice rather than an improvement of ability. Joël, she told me, 'opted to speak more and more his mother's tongue... and a power language in our classroom'. While she occasionally allowed children, at least the English natives, to speak to her in English, she frequently insisted that they speak to her in Spanish. The following comment she made to Rashid (English), for example, indicates that she believed, or at least was pretending to believe, that he could speak Spanish:

> **Sra. Soto:** Rashid, ¿por qué es que tú insistes hoy en hablar en inglés? (*Rashid, why is it that today you insist on speaking English?*)

This quote suggests that Rashid was speaking English (on that particular day) as a personal caprice rather than a logical result of his inability to speak Spanish. In other words, Rashid should be speaking what little Spanish he knows rather than drawing on his extensive English skills, a sort of behavior that Rashid might have resorted to if he had been in a genuine monolingual Spanish environment. In effect, Sra. Soto compensated for the fact that her classroom was not actually a monolingual Spanish environment during the official morning Spanish time by trying to convince the children to participate in her fantasy that it was. Given her professional and personal experience with bilingualism, Sra. Soto's characterization of Spanish use as a question of choice rather than ability seemed to reflect a teaching strategy rather than a naïve view of the complexities of language learning.

Playing the Spanish game

Aside from her direct orders to speak Spanish or to not speak English, Sra. Soto also employed some more imaginative strategies for maintaining her artificial Spanish environment. Having stocked the Housekeeping play Center with attractive dolls to encourage the children to play house, she declared that the dolls could not speak English:

> **Sra. Soto:** Las muñecas entienden no más que español (*The dolls don't understand anything except Spanish*)

These same dolls, of course, only understood English during official English time.

Later in the year, she brought more toys into the Housekeeping Center to simulate a grocery store: a couple of cash registers, a scale, some baskets and a toy scanner. She declared that it was a Mexican *tienda* (store). At one point, I heard her chiding Ian for speaking English in the *tienda*, telling him that the *tienda* was in Mexico and therefore nobody spoke or understood English.

In addition to the monolingual dolls and the Mexicans in the *tienda*, Sra. Soto herself played the role of monolingual Spanish speaker, but only in the morning. For example, one day when the children were playing in the Housekeeping Center, she entered and insisted that she didn't understand them:

> **Sra. Soto:** Yo estoy escuchando a ciertas personitas hablando en un idioma que yo no entiendo. (*I am listening to certain little people speaking in a language that I don't understand*)

Since she also rather mysteriously spoke English (and only English) in the afternoons, her true bilingualism was revealed during the course of each school day. This strategy demanded complicity from the children, who were expected to play along with her monolingual game despite her obvious grasp of both languages. However, occasionally, the children did not play along. For example, in the following segment, Berto has just spoken to Sra. Soto in English and Sra. Soto has just informed him, in Spanish, that she does not understand English. Berto resists her ruse, while Sandra attempts to get him to play along:

> **Berto** (Spanish): [to Sra. Soto] Yes you do speak English.
> **Sandra** (English): [to Berto] Only in the afternoon, but she doesn't understand in the morning.

Berto seemed suspicious of Sra. Soto's refusal to speak English in the morning, while Sandra seemed willing to participate in Sra. Soto's fantasy as a game whose rules she is willing to accept. In this sense, the rules of the game were constantly under negotiation. The exchange between me and Rashid (English) that introduced Chapter 1 is another example of this. Both Rashid and I knowingly and rather guiltily spoke English during Spanish time. When I glanced over at Sra. Soto, Rashid seemed to sense betrayal and retreated, retracting his subversive claim that he did not speak Spanish. These incidents where the children (and the researcher!) momentarily disrupted the artifice and then attempted to re-establish it only served to highlight the fact that we all (usually) played along.

Children collaborate in maintaining the game

As the year progressed, the children began to collaborate actively with Sra. Soto in preserving her Spanish-only artifice. Although the Spanish speakers and English speakers alike continued to speak English at times when Sra. Soto's rules clearly required Spanish, they began to turn each other in for transgressing the rules. The classroom began to resemble a game whose rules could be invoked by anyone, and sometimes strategically for personal reasons.

It became clear to the children as the year progressed that Spanish had become, during official Spanish time, the 'power language' (to use Sra. Soto's own term) in this classroom. Speaking Spanish, as well as turning in another child for not speaking Spanish, allowed the children the chance to gain the moral high ground. In many cases, Sra. Soto chastised the children for speaking English by asking them, rhetorically, what language they were speaking. Other children were often quite eager to answer this incriminating question for them. For example, in the following segment, Sra. Soto enters the Housekeeping Center and begins to chide Ian for speaking to his dolls in English. Wilma eagerly turns him in:

> **Sra. Soto:** [to Ian] Sabes que...¿Qué te pasa? No te entiendo. ¿Qué idioma estás hablando con ellas? (*You know... What's going on with you? I don't understand you. What language are you speaking with them?*)
> **Wilma** (Spanish): ¡En inglés! (*In English!*)

This example shows a Spanish speaker turning in an English speaker for speaking English, suggesting that at least in this classroom where Sra. Soto has consciously converted Spanish into the 'language of power', the Spanish speakers possess some degree of cultural capital (to apply Bourdieu's term). Nevertheless, English speakers invoked the rule as well. For example, one day when Sra. Soto entered Housekeeping to chide Alicia (Spanish) for speaking English, Sandra (English) identified her transgression:

> **Sra. Soto:** [to Alicia, who is speaking English] ¿Tú sabes lo que alguien me dijo? Piensa. (*Do you know what somebody told me? Think*)
> **Sandra** (English): Que estaba hablando en inglés. (*That [Alicia] was speaking in English*)
> **Sra. Soto:** [smiles, adopts an exaggerated and comical expression of shock] ¿Mi Alicia? ¡No! (*My Alicia? No!*)

At one point, Sandra introduced her own brand of fantasy play into the enforcement of the Spanish-only policy by turning in fellow English speaker, Dorinda. Sandra reported Dorinda's transgression not to the teacher, but to Dorinda's own (imaginary) mother, whom Sandra pretended to call on the toy telephone in Housekeeping. Sandra spoke into the toy phone in a curious mix of English and Spanish:

> **Sandra** (English): [picks up the toy phone and pretends to dial, then speaks into the mouthpiece] Hola, Dorinda's mother? Dorinda's mamá? Dorinda is hablando inglés en la casa. (*Hello, Dorinda's mother? Dorinda's mother? Dorinda is speaking English in the house*)

The children collaborated in maintaining Sra. Soto's Spanish-only rule not only by turning each other in, but also by helping each other. For example, one day when Sra. Soto chided Khamil for speaking English while playing with the dolls in the Housekeeping Center, Sandra took over when Sra. Soto's attention shifted to other children:

Khamil (English): [addressing the dolls he has placed in the crib] It's time to go to sleep.

Sra. Soto: [calling over from outside Housekeeping] ¿Por qué todos ustedes muchachos están hablando en inglés? (*Why are all you guys talking in English?*)

Khamil (English): [a few seconds later] It's time to go to sleep.

Sandra (English): Khamil, en español, es 'hora de dormir'. Es esto en español, es 'hora de dormir'. (*Khamil, in Spanish it's 'time to go to sleep'. It's this in Spanish, it's 'time to go to sleep'*)

These examples demonstrate ways in which Sra. Soto actively created an atmosphere where language use was constrained, that is, where speakers were discouraged from speaking the unofficial language (English) and encouraged to speak the official language (Spanish). It is also clear that the children participated in maintaining this artificial immersion by both helping each other follow the rules and turning each other in when they didn't.

As far as my interviews and discussions with Sra. Soto indicate, she never explicitly categorized her strategies for maintaining Spanish immersion in the way I have presented them here. These strategies seem to be based on earlier (both personal and professional) experience and reflective classroom practice, as described in Chapter 3. I have extrapolated her strategies from her actions and words and organized them here in a way that I hope will make them available for others to study and evaluate in light of their own practice contexts.

Focus on Berto: Successful Spanish Speaker, Unsuccessful Spanish Role Model

Berto was a bit of an enigma in this classroom, since he left early in the school year and we did not get a chance to get to know him very well, or to see how his abilities and behaviors changed over time. He was the only child that Sra. Soto did not include in the summary evaluations that she wrote for me, although I do have some of her comments about him recorded in our early interviews. We didn't know much about his family either, except that they enrolled Berto in the TWI program. This decision suggests that they had some interest in the development of his Spanish abilities, although we can't be sure how long they intended to remain in the USA.

According to Sra. Soto, Berto had recently arrived from Mexico shortly before the beginning of the school year, and his family left the country suddenly a few months later. His English was marked by a Spanish accent and occasional hesitancies and lapses in vocabulary. However, we did know him as one of the most resistant Spanish speakers, despite the fact that he was officially designated as a Spanish speaker and came from a nearly exclusively Spanish-speaking background.

Berto made an interesting contrast with John, who arrived from Mexico shortly after Berto left and was actually identified by Sra. Soto as a strong Spanish model because of his relative lack of English fluency. While the two boys shared similar language backgrounds, their attitudes toward the languages contrasted sharply: John was happy to speak Spanish, a more familiar language. Berto preferred to speak English, even though it was not his stronger language. This had some serious implications for Berto's position in the classroom: since he was not willing to take up the (Spanish) expert role that he was qualified for, his only possibility was to take on the role of incompetent speaker (of English) and resister of classroom norms. Recall that it was Berto who openly challenged Sra. Soto's pretense of being a monolingual Spanish speaker in the morning.

Berto tended to speak English even when the other children spoke Spanish to him, and he spoke almost exclusively English with Sra. Soto as well. This example of Berto working with Wilma, another Spanish speaker, and Mark, an English speaker, illustrates Berto's dogged insistence on speaking English:

> **Wilma** (Spanish): [to Mark] Mira, primero tú tienes que pintar esto. (*Look. First you have to paint this*)
> **Berto** (Spanish): Oh, no!
> **Wilma** (Spanish): Oh, ¡sí! (*Oh yes!*)
> **Berto** (Spanish): Oh, no!
> **Wilma** (Spanish): ¡Oh, sí! Porque, mira, antes dijo la Sra. Soto… (*Oh, yes. Because look, before Sra. Soto said…*)
> **Berto** (Spanish): [cuts Wilma off] You don't gotta color it.
> **Wilma** (Spanish): Sí, porque antes dijo la Sra. Soto… ¡mira… mira! (*Yes, because before Sra. Soto said… look!… look!*)
> **Berto** (Spanish): OK. I'm looking. But you don't have to talk… I should know what… everything what I'm doing, girl.

Later, when Sra. Soto was watching them work on the same project, Berto addressed her in English as well, despite the fact that she had been speaking to the children exclusively in Spanish (this vignette is described in more detail in Chapter 7).

As the vignettes in this chapter suggest, Berto tended to reject Sra. Soto's efforts to promote Spanish use in Spanish time, resulting in the ironic fact that he was one of the poorest Spanish role models despite being one of the few truly Spanish-dominant children in the classroom. For Berto, failure was waiting for him when he arrived in this classroom, although he did not stay around long enough for us to know whether or not it would have eventually claimed him. This specter of failure was a sad irony, given that what little we knew of his immigrant family's unstable situation suggested that he was the kind of child that bilingual programs were designed to support. He was also the kind of child that Sra. Soto passionately advocated for: in her ideal world and the world imagined by the TWI model, Berto would embrace both English and Spanish. We don't know why Berto was so reluctant to speak Spanish and so eager to 'become' an English speaker, but he seemed to embody the hegemonic processes described at the beginning of this chapter: for Berto, English was simply and obviously better.

Focus on Emily and Sandra: Can Success be too Easy for English Speakers?

Emily and Sandra were White twin sisters and were officially designated as English speakers. They lived with their monolingual English-speaking mother and bilingual Argentinean father in a suburban area outside the city where the school was located. According to Sra. Soto, who knew the family personally, the father did not speak Spanish in the home. Early in the year, the father and his parents said that the girls would not respond whenever they tried to speak a little Spanish with them, yet toward the end of the year, the family reported that they were able to speak some Spanish with the twins. Sra. Soto did not believe that the girls had any appreciable Spanish ability when they entered this TWI classroom in September, but they were very highly motivated to speak Spanish, perhaps due to the family situation, and they progressed rapidly. The twins seemed to exemplify the case of a monolingual English-speaking child who is particularly motivated to learn Spanish by a supportive, if not bilingual, family environment.

Based on my own observations of Emily and Sandra, they also seemed to exemplify mainstream middle-class White children who, perhaps because of a cultural congruence between school and home (Heath, 1983) and an ingrained confidence in the institution of schooling as a means to personal success and growth (Foley, 2004; Willis, 1981), consistently strive to please the teacher and tend to be good at it. They possessed, in Bourdieu's terms, tremendous cultural capital. In Sra. Soto's terms, as she wrote in her summary evaluations of Emily and Sandra, 'Their solid skills base in their native tongue I felt facilitated their language acquisition'. I would add that the twins' willingness to play by the rules, their pleasant and respectful demeanor and their ability to improvise within the acceptable parameters of school discourse comprised additional cultural capital that resulted in their recognition as both academically strong and good 'Spanish role models'.

In sharp contrast to Berto, Emily and Sandra not only knew how to play the school game, but also were more than willing to do so. It was Sandra who took up the teacher's role in reminding Khamil (above) how to tell his dolls to go to sleep in Spanish. Recall from Chapter 3 that it was Emily who delighted Sra. Soto by spontaneously writing that mothers are mammals. Furthermore, Emily wrote this in Spanish, following the rules as she effectively surpassed the teacher at her own game, identifying and further connecting her implicit classroom themes. Later, in Chapter 5, we will see that Emily further delighted Sra. Soto by interrupting a lesson to point out her own observation that many of the Spanish days of the week end in *-es*. Because she was able to demonstrate the kind of independent yet academically appropriate thinking that Sra. Soto advocated, Emily was praised, rather than chided, for the interruption.

Emily and Sandra actively supported Sra. Soto's pedagogy in various ways. When they took the initiative, as in these examples, they did so within the appropriate limits: somehow, they knew what kind of independent initiative would be rewarded and what would not, when they could get away with calling out and when they might be chastised (Kathleen, by contrast, tended to lack this judgment, as we will see later). Both twins obediently tried hard to speak Spanish and sometimes joined the teacher in making sure that others did, too. In short, they understood and played the game of school well. In one of her interviews, Sra. Soto described the kind of acceptable initiative that contributed to their designation as good Spanish role models, despite the fact that English was their dominant language, 'My two twins are a good role model, in that Emily asked today, "Can I sit at Norma's table?" And Sandra said, "can I sit at Wilma's table?"... They wanted their Spanish partner to sit at their table with them. So they're starting to get the gist of what I said'. The twins actively took up Sra. Soto's suggestion that the children try to work with a 'language partner', someone strong in the language in which they were weakest. Not only did they learn quickly, but they also collaborated actively and eagerly with Sra. Soto in her pedagogical design. In return, they received a great deal of praise and encouragement for effort, if not for the level of Spanish proficiency that a Spanish native might have achieved in English in the same short time span.

Analysis: Cutting Our (Language) Losses in the Face of English Hegemony

On visiting the bilingual program in a 'blue-ribbon school' in Texas, Robert Bahruth (2000: 203) describes an encounter with a boy who had entered the program as a monolingual Spanish speaker only to develop the attitude that there was no need to develop his native language; 'can we call a program bilingual if the final interpretation of success affirms monolingualism?'. Sra. Soto's personal experiences with bilingualism (in terms of her own efforts to remain bilingual and her sister's failure) as well as her encounters with bilingual children with attitudes similar to the boy in Baruth's narrative (as I witnessed during our trip to Calvary) led her to develop a stance toward bilingualism as a basic yet fragile human right that did not come without a great deal of effort and support. This conviction, not a methodology or even a learning theory *per se*, strongly shaped her classroom practice.

Sra. Soto's notion of Spanish speakers 'giving away' their home language under social pressure in the USA echoes throughout the literature on immigrant bilingualism, and has been associated with pressure from Spanish-speaking peers (Hakuta & Garcia, 1989), the broader society's negative associations of foreign languages and accented English as 'improper or unintelligent' (Chen-Hayes *et al.*, 2001), teachers' negative attitudes toward Spanish in schools (Godina, 2004; Nieto, 1999) and parents' insistence that English be spoken at home (Gurza, 1999). Rather than think about children's language learning and use in terms of motivation or personality factors, it is more useful to consider their investment in the language; how their relationship with the language has been socially and historically constructed (Norton, 2000). The desire to speak perfect 'unaccented' English, and even the desire to speak as little Spanish as possible suggests that even bilingual children from similar Latino backgrounds position each other in terms of language as cultural capital (Nuñez-Janes, 2002b; Orellana *et al.*, 1999), a dynamic that reflects minority adults' attempts to blend into what they perceive to be a color-blind, monocultural and monolingual society (Nuñez-Janes, 2002a). This ambivalence toward the home language, the sense that one must choose a high-status language over one's own low-status native language, is described more poetically in journalist Richard Rodriguez's melancholy autobiography. Rodriguez's (1983) now famous quote, 'The loss implies the gain', poignantly expresses the feeling that one must lose Spanish to gain entry into mainstream American society.

In order to create an experience of language immersion, effective TWI teaching 'necessitates establishing and enforcing a strong language policy in the classroom that encourages students to use the instructional language and discourages students from speaking the non-instructional language' (Lindholm-Leary, 2005: 17). This is especially important for the minority language, since there are many sociocultural and logistical forces that act against it. The sociolinguistic situation in this school was far from unusual; even schools that do use both Spanish and English tend to distribute their use in ways that reinforce Spanish as the lower-status language, for example, by only using Spanish when it seems necessary, or switching to Spanish for disciplinary purposes (Escamilla, 1994).

Sra. Soto compensated for what she perceived as the tendency of English to invade the official Spanish time by consciously creating and enforcing an artificial Spanish immersion. As with any constraints, these restrictions of freedom can be perceived as threats to individual freedom and esteem. Nevertheless, I argue that artificial constraints are necessary to replace the absent natural language constraints that one might find in a true Spanish immersion situation (such as a classroom in Mexico). The uncomfortable effects of these artificial constraints can be mitigated by creating an atmosphere of familiarity, warmth and humor in the classroom (Takahashi-Breines, 2002).

My observations of Sra. Soto showed that she frequently hugged the children, joked with them and called them pet names. Her creation and invocation of shared fantasy elements (e.g. that she and the dolls switch language proficiencies at midday) seemed to create a community with special shared practices. While the children's willingness to smilingly turn each other in for language infractions might seem disturbing to some outside observers, the children's concurrent tendency to help each other produce the target language and the general air of camaraderie in the classroom suggested that Sra. Soto was successful in cushioning her constraints with the creation of a warm and supportive classroom community.

However, the cases of Berto, Emily and Sandra exemplify Valdés' (1997) concern that Spanish speakers might inadvertently suffer from the language dynamics of a dual language classroom. Berto's Spanish proficiency was undermined by his at times dogged reluctance to use the language, while enthusiastic English speakers like Emily and Sandra received relatively easy praise for effort. In encouraging the understandably slower and less experienced English speakers, are we unconsciously sending the Spanish speakers the message that their accomplishments aren't as valuable? I believe that Sra. Soto attempted to compensate for this by explicitly praising Spanish speakers for acting as resources and allies and by encouraging them to help her police Spanish use, but Valdés' concern continues to trouble me. My time spent in this classroom has left me with a lingering question: given the inherent asymmetry of language proficiencies and preferences demonstrated in my own and other studies, how can we avoid implicitly penalizing Spanish speakers for faster and higher (English) language achievement?

Notes

1. For a clear overview of how Bourdieu's concept of cultural capital can be applied to language, see (Pennycook, 2001: 123–127).
2. One Spanish-speaking child, Berto, left in the middle of the year. Another Spanish-speaking child, John, arrived in the middle of the year. The rest were present throughout the entire school year.

Chapter 5

Daily Rituals and Routines: Safety in the Familiar

This chapter and the following three chapters are each dedicated to a different kind of classroom activity structure. Activity structures are recurring classroom situations whose communication patterns remain relatively stable over time; they tend to be organized by content (such as vocabulary or art) as well as by the kind of work involved (such as seatwork or small group discussion) (Doyle, 1981). In schools, teachers design and control activity structures, which come to be characterized by different implied values, norms for participation and opportunities for learning. Different classroom activities involve different patterns of 'interactional rights and obligations of various members of the interacting group' (Erickson, 1982: 154).

When I refer to an activity structure in general, and a classroom activity structure in particular, I mean to consider the nature of the activity as a whole: what kinds of participation are accepted as legitimate and encouraged, what is forbidden (or marginally/occasionally tolerated), what kinds of interactions among the participants tend to emerge during the activity and what kind of relationships might form during or as a result of this activity?

For example, in the activity structure I describe as Calendar time, legitimate participation consisted of responding to a set of fixed routine questions, although some deviation from this pattern was acceptable under certain circumstances. The children were expected to speak one at a time, and the teacher maintained a strict hierarchy (children must listen to the designated speaker, who must in turn listen to the teacher). By contrast, in the Housekeeping and Blocks Centers (described in more detail in Chapter 8), the children were expected to initiate their own interactions with each other independently, and in Tables time (described in Chapter 7) the children were expected to focus on a specific task and interact verbally with each other in ways that were guided not directly by the teacher nor independently by the children, but by the common goal of accomplishing the task at hand. Analyzing these activity structures separately will allow us to contrast them. What kinds of language learning might chants and songs afford or constrain that Centers play might not, and vice versa? How did children's behaviors and social positioning shift across these different activity structures? Erickson (1986: 129) points out that classroom activity structures establish local micro-cultures that contribute to the social construction of learners, 'Within a given moment in the enactment of an event and during the overall course of shared life together, particular sets of individuals come to hold distinctive local meanings-in-action'.

This chapter specifically focuses on the repetitive routines and rituals of this classroom, highly structured activities that were designed to foster confidence and relaxation. As described in Chapter 3, Sra. Soto believed that a good two-way immersion (TWI) classroom would incorporate both formulaic and predictable activities and opportunities for natural conversation. In this chapter, we will examine those predictable routines and rituals that usually centered around daily classroom management: lining up, sitting down, moving to another part of the classroom, cleaning up and receiving instructions to prepare the children for smooth transitions among curricular activities. Chants and songs usually accompanied these transitional activities, and the children often engaged in brief teacher-directed exchanges that incorporated target vocabulary. I have also included here the Calendar time activity, which was actually officially a part of Language Arts, because of its highly ritualized and repetitive nature.

Picking up on the Routines

Early on in the school year, it became clear that Sra. Soto relied heavily on the establishment of routine, and she made an effort to ensure that her classroom was as organized and predictable as possible. This does not mean that it was boring, but that the children could easily and quickly recognize what was happening in the classroom and what was expected of them at any given time without relying heavily on linguistic explanation. So, for example, as the children moved from one activity to another, the cry 'clean-up time' in English and 'la hora de limpiar' in Spanish quickly became familiar and meaningful, and the children generally engaged immediately in what they knew to be the expected tidying behaviors.

One persistent classroom routine that the children quickly became used to was writing their names on assignments before turning them in. Throughout the year, this routine was established by verbal repetition. Sra. Soto regularly repeated some version of the command 'Pon tu nombre'

(*Put your name*) or the question, '¿Tiene tu nombre?' (*Does it have your name?*), as the children approached her with their finished work, as the following excerpt exemplifies:

> **Sandra** (English): Emilio asks to go and play.
> **Sra. Soto:** ¿Apuntó su nombre? (*Did he put down his name?*)
> **Sandra** (English): ¿Cómo se dice? (*how do you say it?*)
> **Sra. Soto:** [turns to Emilio] ¿Pusiste tu nombre? (*Did you put your name?*)
> **Emilio** (Spanish): [looks down silently at his paper]
> **Sra. Soto:** [to Emilio] Ponga el nombre. (*Put your name*) [turns to Sandra] Dile que apunte su nombre y puede jugar (*Tell him to put his name and he can play*)
> **Sandra** (English): [to Emilio] Ponga el nombre, Emilio. (*Put your name, Emilio*)

In the following segment, we see that Dorinda has become so used to this routine that she protests when she feels the routine has been disrupted. The children have been working on a paper project during Tables time when Sra. Soto announces that it is time to stop the activity and prepare to go downstairs for lunch. She has just told the children to leave their papers neatly on the table to finish when they return from lunch, and she has not included her characteristic instructions to write names on papers:

> **Sra. Soto:** Ay, ¡qué lindo que veo a todo el mundo limpiando su área! (*Oh, how nice that I see everybody cleaning their area!*)
> **Dorinda** (English): [runs up to Sra. Soto holding out the paper she has been working on] ¡No pone no name (sic)! (*No put no name!*)
> **Sra. Soto:** Déjalo por ahora. No te preocupes. ¿Y cómo se dice esto en español? (*Leave it for now. Don't worry. And how do you say that in Spanish?*)
> **Mark** (English): [calls over from another table] ¡No nomble (sic)! (*No name!*)
> **Sra. Soto:** No hay nombre. Gracias, Mark. Dorinda, ¿qué dices? (*There's no name. Thanks, Mark. Dorinda, what do you say?*)
> **Dorinda** (English): [smiling] No nombre. (*No name*)
> **Sra. Soto:** No tiene nombre. (*It doesn't have a name*)
> **Mark** (English): No tiene nomble (sic). (*It doesn't have a name*)
> **Dorinda** (English): No tiene nombre. (*It doesn't have a name*)

In this example, while Sra. Soto insists that Dorinda (and Mark) keep trying to produce the correct phrase in Spanish, it is Dorinda who initiates the exchange, inspired by her expectation of the classroom routine. The routine of the children constantly being reminded to write their name on their work has provided Dorinda with frequent repetitions of (variations of) the appropriate phrasing as well as the implicit understanding of this routine. When the routine is broken, Dorinda is able to approximate the command in Spanish, eliciting a response from Sra. Soto and initiating a didactic language exchange between herself, Mark and Sra. Soto.

Similarly, another routine that became conventional was Sra. Soto's admonition not to run ('no corras' in the singular; 'no corran' in the plural) as the children line up by the classroom door, for example:

> **Sra. Soto:** Hormigas, no corran, hormiguitas, en una fila. (*Ants, don't run, little ants, in a line*)

Later in the year, Rashid appropriates this customary command not to run and, like Dorinda in the previous example, elicits correction from Sra. Soto:

> **Sra. Soto:** [to the children who are lining up to leave the room] Busquen sus sacos y se ponen en la línea sin hablar. (*Find your jackets and get in line without talking*)
> **Rashid** (English): [to another child, who was running] ¡No corre! (sic). (*Doesn't run!*)
> **Sra. Soto:** [correcting him] ¡No corras! (*Don't run!*)

As the children were guided verbally to comply with certain classroom routines, they heard the same commands in slightly different versions, again and again. As they gained confidence, the children began to initiate verbal participation using the basic language structures that had become familiar through repetition, as illustrated by Dorinda's and Rashid's statements above. These kinds of repetitive physical instructions were scattered throughout the school day, but were particularly characteristic of the activity structure referred to in this classroom as Clean-up time.

Clean-up Time: Children Respond Physically to Directions in Spanish

Clean-up time was a transitional activity that usually occurred between lessons. When Sra. Soto announced that it was 'la hora de limpiar', the children were expected to put materials away and prepare for the next activity. Clean up was carefully guided; Sra. Soto often gave detailed instructions to the children, who responded by physically carrying out these instructions. This type of activity closely corresponds to the second-language teaching methodology referred to as total physical response (TPR) in which the teacher gives commands and models the physical responses and the children respond by performing corresponding physical actions (Asher, 1984).

Sra. Soto never explicitly discussed TPR methodology with me or named it as such, and so I have no evidence to suggest that she was consciously employing this methodology as a teaching strategy. However, Clean-up time did reflect Sra. Soto's expressed belief that children needed to learn to maintain an orderly and neat classroom. As discussed in Chapter 3, Sra. Soto advocated the teaching of values, which she characterized as 'becoming a social animal'. Whether or not she meant to employ TPR strategy, her concern for imparting to the children a sense of responsibility for maintaining a neat classroom area gave rise to an activity characterized by the children's physical responses to her instructions, as illustrated by the following vignette. Oscar, Norma, Lucía (Spanish) and Emily (English) have been seated around the table in the Housekeeping Center and Sandra (English) has been serving them 'food' using small plastic pieces representing food items, plates, cups, etc.

Sra. Soto calls over from the Tables area, telling the children to clean up and reminding them to speak in Spanish. Then she begins to give more specific instructions to Emily and Lucía concerning what they are to do with the plastic cups that are colored either white to represent glasses of milk or yellow to represent glasses of orange juice:

> **Sra. Soto:** Emily, agarra los vasos de leche y tú los guardas. (*Emily, gather those milk glasses and you'll put them away*)
> **Emily** (English): Sí. (*Yes*) [begins to gather up the glasses of milk]
> **Lucía** (Spanish): [walks over and picks up a white 'milk' glass and a yellow 'orange juice' glass]
> **Sra. Soto:** [to Lucía] Le dije, Lucía, le dije a ella que guarde los vasos de leche. (*I told her, Lucía, I told her to put away the glasses of milk*)
> **Lucía** (Spanish): [silently hands out a white glass]
> **Emily** (English): [silently reaches out and takes the milk glass Lucía hands her]
> **Lucía** (Spanish): [takes the one glass of juice to the cabinet and places it inside]
> **Emily** (English): [places all the milk glasses in a basket on the table, takes this basket to the cabinet, places the basket inside next to the juice glass]

Neither Emily nor Lucía has trouble following Sra. Soto's orders. They may not need any contextual cues at all, but if needed, cues are inherent in the limited range of activities possible during Clean-up time. For Emily, the glasses of milk are right next to her on the table, so even if she could only understand the phrase 'vaso de leche' (*glass of milk*), the context of Clean-up time would tell her what to do with these glasses of milk, as putting things away is the only acceptable activity during Clean-up time. The context provided through routine is further evident in the fact that both Lucía and Emily successfully placed the glasses in the wooden cabinet, even though Sra. Soto did not specify where to put them, demonstrating that the activity of 'putting away' has become a familiar routine.

Further, when Sra. Soto tells Lucía that it is Emily's task to put away the milk glasses, she is expecting that Lucía will offer Emily the milk glass and that Emily will accept the milk glass. If either Sandra or Lucía is uncertain of the action expected, they can receive guidance through observing the reaction of the other. In this case, all these contextual cues are available to the girls, and their actions flow so smoothly that it is impossible to know whether the children need to rely on contextual cues as they perform the physical responses required by Sra. Soto.

As the segment continues, Sra. Soto shifts her focus to Sandra, telling her where to place the plastic building shapes and cucumber she has in her hands:

> **Sra. Soto:** Sandra, me gustaría que todas las verduras... que las pongas en el canasto. (*Sandra, I would like that all the vegetables... that you put them in the basket*)
> **Sandra** (English): [walks over and drops the cucumber into a basket in the corner, which is filled with plastic vegetables, and then walks over to the cabinet and puts the building shapes in a bin inside]

Sandra accurately interprets that the cucumber, not the plastic shapes she is also carrying, belongs in the basket. As the basket is already filled with vegetables, this provides a contextual cue to support Sra. Soto's statement that vegetables should go in this basket. Then Sra. Soto engages Sandra in some more directed clean up, this time using gestures to assist her comprehension:

> **Sra. Soto:** [pointing to a basket on the floor] ¿Saben qué? Este canasto, que está en el piso, por el espejo, ¿lo guardan también? (*You know what? This basket, that is on the floor, in front of the mirror, will you put it away, too?*)

Sandra (English): [walks over to the basket and picks it up]

Sra. Soto: Sandra, ponlos arriba del gabinete. (*Sandra, put them on top of the cabinet*)

Sandra (English): [places the basket she just picked up, along with the basket she already had in her hand, on top of the cabinet]

Sra. Soto: Mira, y esa silla que está allí. (*Look, and that chair that's over there*) [points to the plastic chair next to the table, which is normally in the corner]

Sandra (English): [looks up at Sra. Soto and then over at the chair, then walks over and drags it into the corner]

Sra. Soto: Agarra las verduras que están en el piso en el canasto, y ponlo allí, arriba del baúl (*Put the vegetables that are on the floor into the basket, and put it on top of the chest*)

Lucía (Spanish): [standing near the vegetable basket, picks up the vegetables from the floor, puts them in the basket, and then picks up the basket and carries it over to the toy chest, placing it on top]

Again, the children carry out the actions smoothly, and they *seem* to understand perfectly Sra. Soto's Spanish orders. Yet this appearance of perfect language comprehension might be supported to some extent by the available contextual cues and gestures. As Sra. Soto directs Sandra to first pick up a basket from the floor, and then move a chair, she gestures toward them. Therefore, if Sandra has any doubt about the meaning of 'canasto' or 'silla', she can use these gestures, along with the experiential context (the classroom routine that this plastic chair is kept in the corner, not next to the wooden table, and that the plastic vegetables are always kept together in the same basket) to aid her in performing the correct actions with the correct objects.

These vignettes illustrate how children can draw on these extra-linguistic cues to perform *as if* fully competent in the language. While this apparent competence is probably a reality in the case of Lucía, a native Spanish speaker, these cues allow Sandra and Emily, the English-speaking twins, to perform as flawlessly as their Spanish-speaking classmate *even before* they have achieved the necessary level of language competence.

While Clean-up time was consistently characterized by these kinds of teacher-directed physical activities, Sra. Soto's concern for orderliness was not limited to this designated cleaning time. Opportunities for this TPR-type pedagogical engagement occurred throughout the day. It is also significant that the orderly nature of Sra. Soto's classroom itself provides an informative context: everything had its place. The children quickly learned that plastic glasses and silverware go in their respective baskets in the cabinet, while vegetables go in a separate basket on top of the toy chest. This order created a contextual limitation of possibilities and allowed the children to follow clean-up instructions with an accuracy that, in some cases, allowed them to seem more competent in the language of instruction than they really were. This not only helped them seem and feel more competent, but the congruence between the words spoken (*verduras, canasto, silla*) and objects seen supported the important task of vocabulary learning.

Chants: Confidence can Precede Ability

Recall from Chapter 3 that Sra. Soto expressed an enthusiasm for chants during our visit to the Calvary School, arguing that the repetitive structure gives children confidence to use their new language. Sra. Soto's practice strongly reflected this stated philosophy, as chants were a regular part of the classroom, and the children, judging from their loud and often boisterous participation, did in fact learn the repetitive chants quickly and participate enthusiastically. For the purpose of this study, I include as 'chants' any repetitive language activity following a set script that was meant to be repeated over time and gradually memorized by all the children. In this classroom, chants were a significant part of the curriculum, including atonal chants as well as songs, some accompanied by stylized physical movements. During the data collection period, I recorded 15 chanting activities in Spanish and 2 in English, each of which included one or several chants in a row.

Two of the chants were associated with books, *Chana y su Rana* (Avalos & Caminos, 1992) and *Bojabe Tree* (Rickert, 1958), and the children repeated them during the course of the Story time phase of Language Arts, and at times before and after the story as well. The rest of the chants took place during transitional periods, while the children were waiting in their seats or on the floor for the next activity to take place. Sometimes they were integrated into the process of organizing the children for the next activity. For example, *El Canto Vegetal* (The Vegetable Chant) was used as a lining up activity. The text of the chant is as follows:

> Brócoli, tomate, ñame y habichuelas. Calabazas, papas, zanahorias y el maíz. Nabo, berza, pepinos, y la cebolla. Ahora ya tú sabes, el canto vegetal. El canto vegetal. El canto vegetal. Ahora ya tú sabes, el canto vegetal.

The English translation is as follows:

Broccoli, tomato, yam and beans. Squash, potatoes, carrots, and corn. Turnip, cabbage, cucumbers, and the onion. Now you know the vegetable song. The vegetable song. The vegetable song. Now you know the vegetable song.

As the following segment indicates, the children participated enthusiastically, but not always accurately. In this segment, the children are standing behind their chairs, and Sra. Soto has just told the children that they will line up using the vegetable chant. She has placed placards representing the vegetables on the floor in the front of the room. Sra. Soto explains to the children that they are supposed to volunteer to identify the vegetable and, if successful, they may get in line:

Sra. Soto: Voy a poner las cosas en el piso. Cuando yo llamo a la persona, la persona tiene que venir y ponerse en línea. (*I'm going to put the things on the floor. When I call the person, the person has to come and get in line*)

Sra. Soto initiates the activity by reciting the whole chant once and the children, obviously familiar with the chant, join her loudly and enthusiastically. Then she begins again, stopping at the first vegetable (broccoli) and selecting a child to identify the appropriate placard and line up, then repeating the song each time and stopping at the next vegetable, repeating the process. The children hold their hands up, impatiently vying to be selected. Sra. Soto calls on Dorinda (English) to identify the tomato, but Dorinda selects the wrong vegetable and has to return to her seat. Then Sra. Soto calls on Alberta (Spanish), who correctly selects the tomato and lines up.

When the children have finally lined up with their vegetable placards, there are a few children left in their seats. Sra. Soto directs them to line up, asking each child in line to name their vegetable and place it in the plastic yellow bin she offers them one by one. When they have trouble naming the vegetable, she corrects them. For example, Mark (English), who is standing in line holding a placard labeled 'maíz' (*corn*), seems to have forgotten the name of his vegetable:

Sra. Soto: Mark, ¿qué es lo que tienes? (*Mark, what do you have?*)
Mark (Spanish) [no response]
Another child: [calling out from the line] ¡Maíz! (*Corn!*)
Sra. Soto: [to Mark] Maíz.
Mark: Maíz.

Sra. Soto: [still looking directly at Mark] El maíz. (*The corn*)
Mark: El maíz.
Sra. Soto [takes Mark's corn placard and puts it in the yellow bucket]

Only when Sra. Soto is satisfied that Mark has successfully learned to say his vegetable in Spanish does she accept his offered corn placard and move on to the next child in line.

In keeping with Sra. Soto's idea that chants provide children with confidence, it is evident from this segment that the children eagerly participated in the chant even when they did not actually know the correct Spanish words. These chants seemed to reduce the children's performance anxiety to the point where they didn't mind revealing the gaps and flaws in their understanding. Although Mark accurately selected the photo of corn to represent 'maíz', he was unable to repeat the Spanish word when asked. Dorinda volunteered (enthusiastically, with much arm waving and jumping up and down) to identify the tomato even though it turned out that she was unable to accurately associate the Spanish word *tomate* with the photo of a tomato. In this sense, the chants provided a forum where the children could join in and they seemed to enjoy this participation even before they were competent enough to do so accurately.

Calendar Time: Support through Repetitive Language

Calendar time was actually part of the daily Language Arts activity. In Sra. Soto's classroom, Language Arts took place twice every day, every morning in Spanish and every afternoon in English. Therefore, Calendar time, which consisted of a series of formulaic activities related to the day, date and weather, took place every day in both languages as well. Each day, children were selected to perform a series of routine physical tasks, such as changing the squares on the classroom calendar to indicate the correct time and day and transferring straws from one container to another to indicate the number of days that have elapsed in the school year. The day's weather was also established using placards with weather words and illustrations. The other children participated by answering questions individually or as a group, helping the leading child if she/he had a problem and joining in on chants.

The following segment illustrates the overall repetitive and routine nature of Calendar time, and also the potential for brief child-initiated inquiry to emerge within this highly teacher-structured activity. During the course of the usual recitation of the days of the week, Sandra and Rashid (both English speakers) notice a pattern in the spelling of the days of the week in Spanish. The children are sitting on the rug and Sra. Soto is sitting on the chair in front of them, in typical Calendar time formation. Rashid has been selected to physically manipulate the calendar, which consists of rearranging the calendar squares to indicate today's date. As the designated child, Rashid stands near Sra. Soto's chair. Sra. Soto leads all the children in a chant about the days of the week:

> Los días se van, los días vienen. Los días que se van, ahí vienen. Domingo, lunes, martes, miércoles, jueves, viernes, sábado. (*The days come and the days go. The days that go, come back. Sunday, Monday, Tuesday, Wednesday, Thursday, Friday, Saturday*).

> **Rashid** (English): [selects the placard with the day of the week, 'jueves' (*Thursday*), and places it in the correct position]
> **Sra. Soto:** Rashid sabe justo... (*Rashid knows just...*)
> **Sandra** (English): [interrupting] March is almost done. [starting to translate her own English utterance into Spanish] Marzo... es... (*March... is...*)]
> **Sra. Soto:** [finishes the sentence for Sandra] Marzo se está terminando. (*March is ending*)

Having guided Sandra through her attempt to translate her own English statement into Spanish, Sra. Soto returns to the daily Calendar time script and asks the children to spell the word 'jueves' using Spanish letters. She and the children spell the word together, and then everyone repeats the word together.

On this day, Calendar time proceeded much as it did every day, with Rashid performing the usual tasks, and the children answering questions, and chanting and spelling as requested. Nevertheless, when Sandra called out her comment in English, interrupting Sra. Soto's sentence, Sra. Soto did not chide her for interrupting, but helped her finish her sentence. Clearly, this is an acceptable interruption, perhaps because Sandra's comment is directly relevant to the Calendar time theme of orientation in time (March is, in fact, almost over) and possibly because she makes an effort to translate her initial transgressive English outburst into Spanish. As this segment continues, Sandra continues her successful attempt to deviate from the Calendar time routine script:

> **Sandra** (English): Sra. Soto, en español, los días, muchos de los días tienen... (*Sra. Soto, in Spanish, the days, much of the days have...*) [stands up and points to the last two letters of each day of the week, repeating, 'e-s, e-s, e-s...' naming the letters in Spanish]
> **Rashid** (English): Domingo, no. (*Sunday, no*)

Sra. Soto: Domingo, no. Y sábado, tampoco. (*Sunday, no. And not Saturday, either*)

Sra. Soto: [points out that the days that end in 'es' are days when they have 'escuela' (*school*), repeating this phrase for each day of the week in turn, stressing the first syllable of 'escuela' each time] Lunes estamos en la *es*cuela, martes estamos en la *es*cuela... (*Monday we are in school, Tuesday we are in school*...) [leans over, smiling and congratulates Sandra, patting her on the leg, and then sighs, smiling broadly] Ay, qué cosas que descubrimos. (*Oh, the things we discover*)

Despite the strongly teacher-led and scripted nature of Calendar time, Sra. Soto takes Sandra's lead and supports her independent observation that many Spanish days of the week end in 'es', even spontaneously making up a little chant to illustrate that school days end in 'es', the same letters that begin the Spanish word for 'school' (*escuela*). Sra. Soto's words as well as her expressions and gestures indicate that she is quite pleased with Sandra's behavior, explicitly referring to Sandra's observation as a 'discovery'.

The rest of this Calendar time activity proceeds more regularly. Rashid is still standing in front of the classroom, and this time he is expected to repeat three standard phrases, the current date, yesterday's date and tomorrow's date:

Sra. Soto: [to Rashid] Bien duro, bien alto. ¿Qué palabra estás buscando primero? (*Nice and strong, nice and loud. What word are you looking for first?*)

Jamaica (English): [calls out] ¡Hoy! (*Today!*)

Sra. Soto: [acknowledges Jamaica, although a couple of other children also called out the correct answer] Jamaica te está ayudando. ¡Muy bien, Jamaica! (*Jamaica is helping you, very good, Jamaica!*) [turns to Rashid] ¡Di! (*Say it!*)

Rashid (English): [haltingly and softly] Hoy es jueves... (*Today is Thursday*...)

Child: [interrupts him] ¡Bien duro! (*nice and strong!*)

Rashid (English): [continues in a louder voice] El día 25 de Marzo... (*The 25 of March...*)

When Rashid finally finishes reciting the current date, Sra. Soto and the rest of the children repeat the sentence together, and then he continues the script, following the same pattern for yesterday and tomorrow.

For Rashid, producing these scripted sentences took some time, and he relied heavily on the guidance, support and encouragement he received from the teacher and his peers. The repetition and support seemed to help Rashid, a native English speaker who was generally reluctant to speak Spanish. He began his oration speaking very slowly and haltingly, but he seemed to be a bit more confident and fluent by the time he got to the third sentence. It is also interesting that when a group of children offered Rashid the advice to begin as usual with the word 'hoy' (*today*), Sra. Soto singled out Jamaica as the helper and praised her for her contribution. This reflected Sra. Soto's overall strategy of strongly encouraging the more timid speakers, like Jamaica, when they do speak up.

Later in this segment, Mark is called on to spell the current month in Spanish. Mark reaches up and points to every letter in the word 'marzo' (*March*) as he says it in Spanish. Sra. Soto and the other children repeat each letter as he says it, and then everybody repeats the spelling of the entire word after Mark is finished. Rashid, no longer the lead child in the activity, attempts to take the lead as Sandra did earlier and points out a pattern in the spelling of the Spanish month 'marzo' and the English equivalent (*March*):

> **Rashid** (English): [pointing to the two words 'March' and 'marzo' that are right next to each other on the board] Sra. Soto, m- a- r-, m- a- r- [pointing to each letter as he says it in Spanish]
> **Sra. Soto:** Tienes razón. M- a- r-, m- a- r- (*You're right. M- a- r-, m- a- r-*)

Here Rashid attempts to make a 'discovery' similar to Sandra's above. While he is acknowledged, he is not quite as successful as Sandra in initiating a new discussion about his discovery, and his praise is not quite as effusive. While it might have been just as productive to pursue Rashid's observation, since there are several other months that begin with the same letters in both Spanish and English, Sra. Soto did not linger over Rashid's discovery as she did with Sandra's similar one, moving quickly on to the next series of formulaic activities. Rashid's bid to take the lead might have fallen flat simply because Sra. Soto noticed that there was little time left before moving on to the next activity, or because she was simply not as interested in Rashid's pattern as she was in Sandra's weekday spelling pattern. Nevertheless, this discrepancy also suggests that the children's positionings in the classroom, specifically Sandra's developing reputation as a good role model and Rashid's reputation as a bright but somewhat unruly child, might have played a part in Sra. Soto's rapid decision making.

Using the Familiar as Scaffolding: Making (the Right) Independent Connections

In Chapter 3, Sra. Soto elaborated on the importance of scaffolding, which she described as a temporary support or 'weave' of new and old information that allows learners to make their own connections. These connections, however, should not necessarily be too creative, but should fall within the parameters of the planned curriculum. In a sense, children move independently on the scaffold provided, but they are ultimately guided to make certain kinds of connections. Even independent discoveries that receive positive recognition, like Sandra's day-of-the-week discovery, fall within certain parameters (a focus on spelling patterns, a relevance to the school calendar).

One kind of activity structure that was common in this classroom consisted of strongly guided exchanges between the children and Sra. Soto that usually took place during, before or after Clean-up time. These exchanges seemed at first glance to be casual conversations about what would happen next, but on closer inspection it became apparent that Sra. Soto was consciously guiding the children to connect the vocabulary they learned in the repetitive and routine learning contexts described in this chapter to their everyday lives in terms of weather, food, clothing, etc.

During these exchanges, the children generally attended to Sra. Soto, who gave instructions and embedded in these instructions known-answer questions involving relevant vocabulary, such as the menu for lunch or the weather outside. For example, in the following segment, the children have just finished cleaning up and are waiting at their assigned tables to line up and go downstairs to the lunch room. Sra. Soto is standing in the middle of the classroom addressing the children, who are seated at or standing by their tables:

> **Sra. Soto:** Nosotros tenemos que ir abajo para comer. ¿Vamos a ir afuera hoy? (*We have to go down to eat. Are we going outside today?*)
> **A child:** Sí (*Yes*)
> **Sra. Soto:** Sí. ¿Por qué? (*Yes. Why?*)
> **Ian** (English): [shoots up his hand]
> **Sandra** (English): [calls out] Porque no hac (sic) frío. (*Because it's not cold*)
> **Sra. Soto:** Porqué no hace frío... y además no está... ¿qué? (*Because it's not cold, and also because it's not... what?*)
> **Several children:** [calling out in unison] ¡Sol! (*Sun!*)
> **Ian** (English): [shaking his head] Sol. No sol. (*Sun. No sun*)

Wilma (Spanish): [finally completing Sra. Soto's sentence] Lloviendo. (*Raining*)
Sra. Soto: No está lloviendo. ¿Hay sol afuera? (*It's not raining. Is the sun out?*)
Several children: ¡No!
Sra. Soto: No, está nublado. Pero de todas maneras, ¿podemos ir a jugar afuera? (*No, it's cloudy. But anyway, can we play outside?*)
Several children: ¡Sí! (*Yes!*)

In this excerpt, Sra. Soto, who certainly knew better than anybody whether they were going to go outside and why, attempted to lead the children to the correct conclusions, which she already knew: they would be able to go outside to play because it was not too cold and, most importantly, it was not raining. When the children offered other responses to her questions, in this case the true but irrelevant piece of information that the sun was not shining, she restated the comment using different vocabulary (no sun = cloudy, 'nublado') and connected it to her own theme (even though it was cloudy, it was not raining, so they could go outside).

Because Sra. Soto constrained the discussion by asking specific closed-ended questions, she was able to practice a very specific set of vocabulary, the vocabulary concerning weather that they had been using habitually as a part of Calendar time, which was reinforced by visual context, as the children could see through the window that it was cloudy but not raining.

Taken together, these activities that I have categorized as daily rituals and routines shared some important characteristics: choices were restricted, which left little room for improvisation, but allowed the children to relax and focused them on certain core vocabulary and expressions. These choices were restricted through the establishment of scripts (chants, formulaic phrases), classroom routines (rules and schedules) and teacher guidance (closed-ended questions and specific instructions). In these activities, the teacher was central to initiating and guiding interactions, even where these interactions seemed to be everyday conversations about food and weather. The strongly teacher-centered nature of these activities ensured that the children became familiar with certain key aspects of Spanish and applied the language they learned under certain very controlled circumstances (following instructions, discussing the weather, etc.). As we will see in Chapter 8, the children were not as likely to draw on curricular vocabulary and well-practiced phrasings or to self-monitor their use of the official language when they guided their own activity in the play Centers.

Focus on Amalia and Jamaica: Supporting Reluctant Speakers

These highly structured activities provided particular support for timid speakers, whatever the reason for their reticence to speak. As described in Chapter 4, most of the English speakers had considerable difficulty with Spanish, since they had had little or no exposure to the language before beginning the school year. This did not make them all timid, necessarily, but lack of proficiency certainly contributed to their reticence. Of course, not all Spanish speakers were confident and enthusiastic contributors during Spanish time, either. Jamaica, an English speaker, and Amalia, a Spanish speaker, were perhaps two of the most reticent speakers during Spanish time.

Sra. Soto described Amalia as 'a very timid child'. She was also one of only two Spanish-speaking children who 'had no English' when they entered the program in September. Recall that it was Amalia whom Sra. Soto contrasted with the more aggressive girls who had given away their Spanish in pre-school when they realized that English was the more powerful language, implying that Amalia's very timidity might have protected her from English hegemony. As a strongly Spanish-dominant child, Amalia might have been quite a valuable asset to this TWI classroom if it were not for timidity and reluctance to speak in either language. Sra. Soto identified Amalia as a child who not only spoke very little, but also had some speech problems that required some special services that were not available in the district. When she did speak, which was rare, it was usually difficult to hear her, as she was extremely quiet. Amalia was physically small and delicate as well, and she often worked or played by herself so quietly and created so little disturbance that she went practically unnoticed.

In the following excerpt, for example, it is Sandra, an English speaker, who initiates a conversation in (mostly) Spanish with Amalia, who barely participates. Sandra asks Amalia whether another teacher in the school, Sra. Jones, will be on the playground that day:

> **Sandra** (English): Amalia. ¿Está Sra. Jones abajo? (*Is Sra. Jones downstairs?*)
> **Amalia** (Spanish): [does not respond]
> **Sandra** (English): [perhaps asking which grade this teacher teaches] Is it second grade or primero? (. . . *first?*)

Amalia (Spanish): [does not respond]
Sandra (English): Primero (sic) grado o segundo grado? (*First grade or second grade?*)
Amalia (Spanish): [does not respond]
Sandra (English): First grade or second grade, ¿está abajo? (... *is downstairs?*)
Amalia (Spanish): [shrugs]
Sandra (English): ¿No sé? (sic) (*I don't know?*)

It is easy to see from this exchange why Sra. Soto might consider certain English speakers like Sandra to be better Spanish 'role models' than Amalia, despite the fact that Amalia was a much stronger Spanish speaker. Sra. Soto considered that Amalia 'did improve in English as the year progressed thanks to her friendship with the twins (Sandra and Emily)', but she seemed to believe that Amalia, rather than acting as a Spanish-language resource in the classroom, needed a lot of support in speaking both languages.

In the following segment of Calendar time, for example, Sra. Soto explicitly asks the rest of the children to be quiet and pay attention to Amalia because she is not very strong. She selects Amalia to come forward and transfer straw counters from one container to another to indicate how many school days have passed since the beginning of the year:

Sra. Soto: Amalia necesita que todo el mundo la preste apunte. Ella no es tan dura. (*Amalia needs everyone to pay attention. She's not so strong*)
Amalia (Spanish): [counts the straws out loud in Spanish, but barely audibly, first a group of 100, then 2 groups of 10, then five ones, placing the straws in the container as she counts them]

Since the other children are quietly counting along with her, Amalia is asked to perform in a relatively low-stress situation: the children are paying attention to her, as Sra. Soto requested, but in a sense supporting her by speaking along with her. It may seem odd that Amalia, a native Spanish speaker, would need this level of support, but, as demonstrated by her exchange with Sandra above, she often seemed reluctant to respond verbally even when it was well within her ability to do so. In this sense, Amalia's need to build confidence in public (Spanish) speaking may have been as strong as that of the less proficient Spanish speakers.

As this segment continues, Sra. Soto calls on another timid speaker, Jamaica, an English speaker who was extremely reticent to speak

Spanish. Sra. Soto described Jamaica as 'a very obstinate child... her stubbornness was what impeded her progress at acquiring Spanish language skills'. Unlike Rashid or Dorinda, who were highly social and interacted frequently and happily with the other children (although mostly in English), Jamaica tended to be quiet and withdrawn and had what Sra. Soto described as 'temper tantrums' involving sullen silences and refusals.

When Amalia has finished her straw count, indicating that they have so far spent 125 days in school, Sra. Soto calls on Sandra to walk to the board and write the number 125 on the notepad there. Then, Sra. Soto leads the children in counting by tens to 125 (they add 5 at the end). Finally, she calls on Jamaica to come to the front of the room and lead the group in repeating the count by tens:

> **Sra. Soto:** Jamaica, A ver si me ayudas. Estamos contando en grupos de diez. (*Jamaica, let's see if you can help me. We are counting in groups of 10*)
> **Jamaica** (English): [walks over and stands next to the teacher as everybody counts together] diez, veinte, treinta... (etc.)... noventa. (*ten, twenty, thirty... (etc.)... ninety*)
> **Sra. Soto:** [when they have reached a hundred, pauses and turns to Jamaica] El número que a ti te gusta (*The number that you like*)
> **Jamaica, Sra. Soto and the children:** [continue to count until 125]
> **Sra. Soto:** A Jamaica le gusta escribir el número cien. Lo escribe en todas partes. Sobre todo. Le gusta el cien. Ándate, muy bien. (*Jamaica likes to write the number one hundred. She writes it everywhere. All over. She likes one hundred. Go on, very good*)
> **Jamaica** (English): [smiling, walks back to her seat on the floor]

Sra. Soto invited Jamaica to lead the counting, inviting her to take up a relatively prestigious position: she was standing next to the teacher in front of the other children, who were sitting on the floor. She was leading, the rest were following. Yet this relative prestige demanded little of Jamaica. First of all, they had already counted straws, written the number 125 on the board, and then counted by tens once again. Jamaica was asked merely to repeat what had already been recited several times. In addition, the children were counting aloud along with her, as they had done for Amalia above. Therefore, this was a performance that was strongly supported by repetition and by the other children's social participation and, at the same time, symbolically placed Jamaica in a temporary position of honor. In addition, Sra. Soto connected her personally to the counting, pointing out that she had a special affection for the number one hundred, a connection that obviously pleased Jamaica, judging from her smile.

Like Amalia, Jamaica was able to enjoy being the center of attention without the performance anxiety that might have accompanied such a position. Although Jamaica was in many ways unlike the quiet but affable Amalia, the two shared a need for social support that was easiest to meet during these highly structured activities. Furthermore, while it might be tempting to assume that only the English speakers would need this level of support during official Spanish time, it is important to keep in mind that other factors, such as particularities of native language development, temperament and social positioning, influenced the degree of social support the children required to speak in public.

Focus on Dorinda: Reluctant to Speak Spanish, but Happy to Chant

Sra. Soto singled Dorinda out early in the year, suggesting that I watch her carefully as an example of a native English speaker who was especially motivated to learn Spanish, specifically noting that Dorinda seemed to 'always sing and chant the loudest in Spanish'. I noticed that Dorinda tended to participate enthusiastically in the more highly scripted activities such as chants and Calendar time. Sra. Soto noted that Dorinda quickly learned the formulaic chants and participated eagerly, as exemplified in the following segment. When Sra. Soto signals the shift from official English time to official Spanish time,[1] Dorinda begins a chant automatically, reciting the words alone:

> **Sra. Soto:** ¿Están listos? Es la hora de español. (*Are you ready? It's Spanish time*)
> **Dorinda** (English): [chanting alone, and making the accompanying movements with her arms] Arriba, abajo, al lado, detrás... (Up, down, next to, behind...)

Dorinda is in the back of the classroom and Sra. Soto is in the front, so it's possible that Sra. Soto does not notice Dorinda's chanting. She ignores Dorinda's chant and instead continues to prepare the children for the 'pajaritos' chant in the customary manner:

> **Sra. Soto:** Necesito pajaritos. Espera. Alas para arriba. Tengo varios pajaritos que no están listos. Mira, niños. Alas para arriba, alas para abajo... (*I need little birds. Wait. Wings up. I have several little birds that are not ready. Look, children. Wings up, wings down...*)
> **Dorinda** (English): [stops her own chant and joins in with the rest]

In this segment, Dorinda enthusiastically begins to chant on her own and just as enthusiastically switches to another when Sra. Soto guides her to do so. My observations of Dorinda during chants and other similarly scripted activities supported Sra. Soto's impression: she genuinely seemed to have fun, usually chanting loudly and making any accompanying body movements strongly but not in an exaggerated fashion. She did not seem to see chants as a chance to act silly or attract attention (as occasionally happened with some children), but followed the script of speech and movement with a curious combination of joyful abandon and precision. She learned them quickly and accurately.

By contrast, Dorinda seemed reluctant to use Spanish in the less structured play-like activity of the Centers. Sra. Soto commented, 'Dorinda is great in the classroom, academics, speaking Spanish, but does not when they're playing'. Recall from Chapter 3 that Sra. Soto divided classroom activities into academic and non-academic activities, suggesting that what Sra. Soto meant by non-academic activities include both scheduled classroom 'play' time (the play Centers, which will be described in more detail in Chapter 8) and informal school times (such as lunch and recess). Dorinda participated well in teacher-directed activities such as the ones described in this chapter (and Language Arts and Tables time, which will be discussed in more detail in the following two chapters), but she did not voluntarily incorporate her new Spanish vocabulary into activities over which she had more control. Some of the other English-speaking children, like Kathleen and the twins Sandra and Emily, did make some attempt to speak Spanish in these informal classroom spaces, with some encouragement from Sra. Soto. Others, like Jamaica and Khamil, were reluctant to speak Spanish in structured as well as less structured activities. Of all the English-speaking children, Dorinda showed the most striking contrast in behavior between the more and less teacher-structured aspects of the classroom. Sra. Soto, who had hoped that the children would incorporate aspects of the learned curriculum into their play time, found this contrast frustrating.

Toward the end of the year, she explicitly forbade Dorinda to play in the Centers with her friend Rashid, another native English speaker. According to Sra. Soto, Rashid and Dorinda spent too much time speaking in English when they were together, and she told them that they couldn't play in the Centers together or share a table as they completed their projects during Tables time. Dorinda's case illustrates how the nature of the activity structure not only shaped children's participation but also helped to construct learner identities: the same child that was identified by Sra. Soto as an enthusiastic participant during highly formulaic activities was characterized as reluctant and even rebellious during the less structured activities.

Analysis: Supporting Learners through Structure and Repetition

The activities in this chapter might be characterized as the most highly teacher-centered of all the classroom activity structures, and these were the most congruent with the Madeline Hunter direct teaching approach (Allen, 1998), which Sra. Soto identified as the model guiding much of her formal training and experience. While she also embraced the TWI principle of promoting children's interactions with each other in the classroom (Christian, 1994; Lambert, 1990), she seemed to excel in and to be most confident during these strongly teacher-directed activities.

Indeed, her skill at direct teaching and her concern for maintaining an orderly and tidy classroom combined to construct a highly successful activity structure that resembled TPR methodology (Asher, 1982, 1984), although she never identified it formally as such. Furthermore, while TPR commands can seem a bit arbitrary ('stand up', 'put your hands in the air', etc.), the TPR-like commands during Clean-up time were embedded in the everyday familiar routines of the classroom, making it even easier for children to smoothly follow more complicated and language-rich commands. Owing to its high degree of visual contextualization, TPR activities are particularly well-suited to the early years of TWI instruction (Quintanar-Sarellana, 2004), and Sra. Soto seems to have, apparently unconsciously, improved on the model by incorporating these activities into the everyday collective maintenance of the classroom community.

In addition to the non-verbal responses characterizing the TPR-like activity, Sra. Soto also planned for repetitious chants and songs that permitted the children to produce formulaic phrases in a relaxed, familiar and fun context, as she also described in Chapter 3. This recognition of the importance of affect in language learning (Arnold, 1999) echoes Krashen's (1985) notion of lowering the 'affective filter' of learners, inhibitory attitudes and emotions that prevent second language learners from understanding a new language. Not only does anxiety impede comprehension, but it also inhibits learners from seeking and attending to language input (Krashen, 1985). In the vegetable chant vignette described in this chapter, for example, Mark's ability to participate only faltered when Sra. Soto stopped the game and directed a question to him, requiring him to perform independently and resulting in a brief awkward silence when he could not produce the correct word. These chants and songs also served to enhance automaticity, an important aspect of fluency that involves 'the development, through extended and consistent practice, of rapid, smooth, comfortable speaking skills that do not consume the attentional resources necessary for other aspects of performance' (Gatbonton & Segalowitz, 1988: 474). Unlike less structured speech contexts, these chants and songs removed the responsibility for thinking and planning inherent in independent communication and engaged the children in a relatively low-risk form of language performance.

This chapter illustrates how simple and repetitive language activities as well as strong teacher support can build confidence for reluctant or timid speakers like Amalia and Jamaica, while permitting some room for child-initiated improvisation, as illustrated by Rashid and Sandra's attempts to point out language patterns they discovered during the Calendar time activity. Pérez and Torres-Guzmán (1996: 68) point out that routine classroom tasks, such as calendar activities, attendance and weather reports, can provide opportunities for literacy development in the bilingual Kindergarten; 'Teachers can establish daily routines not only in ways that encourage children to interact with and experience print, but also in ways to assume the role of the leader'.

At the same time, Sra. Soto's different responses to Rashid's and Sandra's similar improvisation attempts suggest that teachers' willingness to follow children's leads might be affected by their perceptions and expectations of children as learners, which are in turn constructed through the activity structures designed by teachers. Recall from Chapter 4 that Sra. Soto praised both Sandra and her twin sister Emily for being good 'role models.' It may be that Sra. Soto's characterizations of Sandra as a bright child whose curricular insights are generally productive helped influence her decision to follow Sandra's lead, while her characterization of Rashid did not inspire the same kind of engagement. It is impossible to know for sure exactly how these factors influenced Sra. Soto's decisions about which interruptions to accept and follow during her strongly teacher-directed activities such as Calendar time. Nevertheless, it is important for all teachers to consider how our understandings of children might impact the hundreds of split-second decisions like this one that teachers make every day, which contribute to the social construction of children as learners.

Finally, Dorinda's case illustrates the difficulty of designing a TWI classroom to approximate the experience of actual immersion, or what Sra. Soto referred to as 'natural' or 'contextual' experiences (Lafford &

Salaberry, 2003), such as spending time in a Spanish-speaking country. As we saw in Chapter 4, she tried to re-create a foreign language immersion experience as much as possible, replacing natural constraints with artificial language constraints. However, when the teacher was not there to provide these artificial constraints, Dorinda and her friend Rashid took advantage of the possibility, clearly attractive to both, of speaking together in English whenever possible. In a sense, the inherently rule-governed nature of chants and songs released the teacher from some of the responsibility of enforcing language rules and constraints. This implies that the introduction of other less highly structured but still internally rule-governed activities such as play productions, dramatic readings, role plays, etc., might have provided an intermediary space for structured improvisation. These kinds of dramatic productions might have helped bridge the gap that seemed to prevent Dorinda's enthusiasm and competence from spreading into the less formal spaces of the classroom, a problem that we will explore in more detail in Chapter 8.

Note

1. Although Spanish time normally preceded English time, there were occasional days when this order was reversed, as described in Chapter 4.

Chapter 6

(Spanish) Language Arts: Participating in the Narrative

There were two official Language Arts periods every day, one during official Spanish time and one during official English time. The Language Arts period varied somewhat in content and time allotment but, generally speaking, centered on story reading. Stories were often repeated again and again and the children were expected to participate actively in retelling the stories. The children generally participated eagerly in Language Arts activities, and Sra. Soto seemed to have little trouble maintaining their attention and finding volunteers to contribute to the group activity.

Every Language Arts period consisted of two, and sometimes three, separate activities. There was always Story time, the central story-reading activity, as well as the Calendar time activity described in Chapter 5, where the children performed various predictable and formulaic activities concentrating on the current day, date, month and season. Some Language Arts periods also included Vocabulary, an explicit lesson in which Sra. Soto sat in front of the class and asked guiding questions about vocabulary using visual props, books, illustrations or charts. All three Language Arts activity phases were highly teacher-centered in that the children were expected to pay careful attention to Sra. Soto at all times and participate as requested; talking with each other and engaging in other activities during the Language Arts activity were strongly discouraged.

This chapter focuses mainly on Story time, and it is interesting to contrast the different ways in which the children's engagement was maintained in Calendar time and Story time. Calendar time was more closely structured and repetitive, which provided a great deal of support for individual children to speak. Only in Calendar time were the children asked to stand in front of the room and recite as part of the routine, and the very narrow range of variation in this activity provided maximum support for this potentially stressful performance activity. In Story time, by contrast, children were expected to participate, but were rarely called on to provide more than a very brief public response. More typically, the children remained seated with the group and vied to be selected to provide the requested answers, or they simply called out answers.

I will illustrate various aspects of storytelling using different stories told on different days. While Story time was much less formally scripted than the formulaic memorized chants and the Calendar time routine, the activity was still strongly teacher-directed. The children were expected to participate in the teacher-led narrative, contributing their own knowledge, interpretations, opinions and even personal experiences, but without deviating much from Sra. Soto's (implicit) intended path. Story time was characterized by the children's attempts to contribute to the classroom narrative and Sra. Soto's strategies for encouraging and guiding this participation.

The Bojabi Tree (1): Weaving a New Story into the Curriculum

Stories were read over and over in Sra. Soto's class, and the children never seemed to tire of them. This might be because of Sra. Soto's highly creative and participatory way of 'reading' the stories, which had very little to do with actually reading the text aloud from the printed page. I observed one Language Arts activity where a new story was introduced for the first time, and this happened to be during English time. While the overall focus of this book is on patterns of Spanish use during official Spanish time, I think a brief excursion into English time is useful at this point, since Sra. Soto's first reading of *The Bojabi Tree* (Gerardo, 1994) illustrates some of her characteristic techniques for introducing new material into the classroom. We will first look at the ways in which Sra. Soto introduced *The Bojabi Tree* for the first time and then look at how the patterns of interaction changed when the same story was read just one week later, when the children were more familiar with it.

The Bojabi Tree is about a magic tree that, during a time of famine, is able to give fruit but only if addressed by name, and the problem of the story is that nobody can seem to remember the tree's name. Every time one of the animal characters goes to ask the snake for the tree's name, the animal forgets the tree's name. Eventually the little turtle, the story's hero, is able to remember the tree's name, using a chant as a mnemonic device.

The story was introduced in February, when classroom routines and many curriculum themes were already well established. As usual for the Language Arts story reading activity, Sra. Soto sat in front of the class, and the children sat on the rug in front of her. This example takes place during English time, on one of the rare occasions when Spanish and

English times were reversed to accommodate a change to the school-wide schedule (as described in Chapter 4).

In the following segment, Sra. Soto introduces the story they are about to read for the first time, *The Bojabi Tree*, situating it both in the context of their recent geography unit on the continents and a science unit on plants. She reminds the children about the chant they did on the continents during an earlier Spanish Language Arts period, and places the colored map of the world on the easel behind her, flipping it over so that the continents are now labeled in English:

> **Sra. Soto:** I've got an African tale I'd like to tell you. [gesturing to the map behind her] You know how to do our song in Spanish... [launches immediately into the Continent Chant in English]
>
> **Children:** [chant the names of the continents in English as Sra. Soto points to each continent on the map behind her]
>
> **Sra. Soto:** [holds up the book that she has on her lap] This book is from Gabon, called *The Bojabi Tree.* [attends briefly to a intercom interruption, and then returns to the children] What kind of animal is that? [pointing to the turtle on the cover of the book]
>
> **Children:** [calling out several versions of the answer at once] Turtle, it's a turtle!
>
> **Sra. Soto:** It's a turtle
>
> **Children:** [several calling out in Spanish] ¡Tortuga! (*Turtle!*)
>
> **Sra. Soto:** Tortuga.
>
> **Children:** [calling out various things at once] My brother used to have a turtle... My name begins with a 't...'

In this initial reading, the children participate, even though they are still unfamiliar with the story, because Sra. Soto connects the story with familiar aspects of the curriculum (the continent song) and also with everyday experience (such as turtles/*tortugas*). The children call out more personal connections: one boy relates the story to his own name while another relates it to his brother, who has a turtle. Sra. Soto waits patiently while the children call out their personal connections; she doesn't respond, but neither does she discourage these unsolicited observations.

When Sra. Soto did finally begin to tell the story, she started out by making an explicit connection to the famine-struck land in which the story takes place and the broader scientific concept of plant growth. She made a specific reference to the tree that they planted recently as part of a science unit on plants. As the above vignette illustrates, she also specifically situated the story in the African country of Gabon, and began the story with a chant about the continents. In this way, Sra. Soto connected this story to two already familiar themes she had established elsewhere in the curriculum, specifically in science and geography.

As described in Chapter 3, Sra. Soto's thematic weaving encompassed but extended beyond curriculum content areas (such as plants, animals, counting and weather) to include values and personal development lessons. This story was introduced during Black History Month (February) as part of an African tales unit celebrating African-American achievements and contributions, and it was also linked to an overall theme of self-efficacy: small people (like the clever *Bojabi Tree* turtle) could be resourceful and help others. The small people in her class were expected to emulate the turtle's resourcefulness and helpful nature and to draw on each for support as part of her English-Spanish language partner policy, connections she made explicit through her comments to the children. From the very first reading of *The Bojabi Tree*, she began to establish these connections, carefully incorporating the new story into the complex thematic weave of the classroom.

This segment also illustrates that even the first time through the story reading was hardly a smooth monologue. In this first reading, Sra. Soto did read from the pages of the book, but she never read two pages consecutively, and even frequently stopped in the middle of the page to make comments. In this segment, aside from the frequent interruptions (intercom announcements, parent visitors, discipline), Sra. Soto inter-sperses her reading with curricular connections (geography-Africa, science-tree nutrition), vocabulary explanations (definition of the word 'famine') and closed-ended questions ('What kind of animal is that?' 'Without rain, what doesn't happen?'). As the children became familiar with the story, their role in the retelling became more active and also more complex, as Sra. Soto made decisions about which contributions to include and exclude from the narrative they co-constructed.

The Bojabi Tree (2): Reconstructing Together a Familiar Story

After the children had heard the story several times, they were expected to participate in the retelling of the story. The following excerpt illustrates the children's very different experience of *The Bojabi Tree* just one week later. *The Bojabi Tree* has a chant as part of the story, and this time the children are asked to chant the Bojabi Tree chant even before the story begins:

Sra. Soto: [picks up *The Bojabi Tree* and puts it on her lap] What is this story?

Children: [calling out together] Bojabi Tree!

Sra. Soto: [begins to chant the Bojabi Tree chant from the story]

Children: [join in, enthusiastically and loudly] Bojabi Tree. Strong and tall. Soon Bojabi fruit will fall. [they raise their hands above their head and lower them as they sing, indicating the fruit above falling down]

Sra. Soto: I want your help in retelling this tale. [holds up the book] Let's see. Let's start with Mark. Mark, what's the problem in this story?

In this reading, the children are expected to participate more directly. Instead of reading the title herself, as she did on the first reading a week earlier, Sra. Soto now expects the children to tell her what the title is when they see the book on her lap. They are expected to know the chant, and they join in automatically as she begins, even without being explicitly invited.

Just one week after the first reading, Sra. Soto does not read the text; she does not even open the book. Her role is more that of a director than a story-teller, orchestrating the children's retelling of the story through questions. She weaves the children's contributions into a retelling of the story by elaborating on them and sometimes asking for clarifications and definitions:

Sra. Soto: Who did they go ask for the name of the tree?

Children: [calling out together] The snake!

Sra. Soto: The snake goes and tells the antelope, 'Oh, I know the name of the tree'.

A couple of children: [together] Bojabi!

Sra. Soto: Bojabi. Remember it well. But what happens? Dorinda?

Dorinda (English): He forgot the name.

Sra. Soto: Why did he forget the name?

Dorinda (English): Cause a splash came.

Sra. Soto: What do we call that?

Rashid (English): A wave.

Sra. Soto: A wave came...

Children: [interrupt her by calling out so many different things at once it is impossible to hear anything]

Sra. Soto: [continues her statement, raising her voice over the children's shouts] ...and he forgot.

This segment illustrates the children's enthusiastic and chaotic participation, but also Sra. Soto's careful guidance of this apparent chaos. Notice that she is unsatisfied with Dorinda's description of the wave that washes over the animals and makes them forget the tree's name as a 'splash', and she encourages Rashid's correction. At times she addresses her questions to a specific child (such as Mark or Dorinda, above), and sometimes she addresses the questions to everyone. Sometimes she acknowledges one child's contribution (in this case, by repeating Rashid's comment and incorporating it into her own statement), and sometimes she pauses to allow everyone to call out their own contributions at once.

The story continues as various animals attempt, unsuccessfully, to go to the snake and ask for the tree's name, and then forget when a large wave sweeps over them. The events are repetitive, only the animal changes. When the little turtle, the hero, enters, there is some dialogue, but it is entirely reconstructed by Sra. Soto, who continues, still without opening the book, to invite the children's help in reconstructing both events and dialogue:

> **Sra. Soto:** The little tortoise said 'Let me try'. And what did all the other animals do?
> **Children:** [laugh loudly, to imitate the laughter of the animals]
> **Emilio** (Spanish): [laughs particularly loudly]
> **Sra. Soto:** [waits a few seconds as the children laugh] They all laughed. That's right, Emilio, a big hearty laugh. They said, 'You are so little. How are you going to remember?'
> **A few children:** [calling out together suggestions for the turtle's dialogue] I can try!... I'm going to try!... I'll try!...
> **Sra. Soto:** He did. He said, 'I am going to try. It doesn't matter if you're big. It doesn't matter if you're little. It's whether or not you...' [allows her voice to trail off, indicating that the children should complete the invented dialogue]
> **Children:** [loudly, together] Try!
> **Sra. Soto:** Try.

As the story continues, the little turtle's mother advises him to remember by singing a song, and he sings the Bojabi Tree chant that the children chanted before beginning the story. The children repeat the chant with great enthusiasm, especially Dorinda, whose voice is particularly loud. The magic chant works: the turtle remembers the tree's name and the tree releases fruit for the hungry animals waiting below.

When they have finished retelling the story, Sra. Soto asks the children what was the moral of the story, and it is clear that she is hoping to connect it to her classroom theme of little people being resourceful and effective:

Sra. Soto: This story was trying to teach us something. What was it trying to teach us? Rashid?
Rashid (English): How to remember.
Sra. Soto: How to remember? [in a hesitant voice] Yes, it teaches us how to remember. What else is it trying to teach us?
Sandra (English): I know!
Sra. Soto: What, Sandra?
Sandra (English): It doesn't matter if you're small.
Sra. Soto: It doesn't matter if you're big or small. All you've got to do is... what?
Children: [call out together] Try!

Sra. Soto clearly has a correct answer in mind, and while Rashid's answer is perfectly reasonable, it is not the expected answer. Sra. Soto hesitates, apparently unwilling to deny the validity of Rashid's response, but continuing to seek the desired answer. After all, Rashid's answer is correct, as indeed mnemonic devices are a good way to remember things. Other interpretations of the book's message might be possible as well, for example, not to rely on snakes, not to laugh at other people, to listen to your mother's advice. Nevertheless, Sra. Soto wanted to link this story to her own theme, as she described to me later, 'The little turtle who came and helped all the other animals, even though she was really little... that's the whole concept'.

Better Move On, Frog: Negotiating Terms of Participation

Throughout the two English time readings of *The Bojabi Tree* we see the children negotiating their participation in Sra. Soto's narrative, while the norms for participation shifted from strictly teacher-centered (children must raise hands and quietly wait until called on) to child-centered (children call out comments and answers, at times in unison). This inconsistency is further illustrated with the reading of *Better Move on, Frog* (Maris, 1982) during Spanish time and, as we will see, may have had some strategic advantages as well as some confusing effects.

The book was written in English, but Sra. Soto translated it into Spanish during Spanish time. This was not an uncommon practice in Sra. Soto's classroom, and served as a strategy to compensate for the somewhat less diverse availability of Spanish language materials in the USA (Gonzalez-Jensen, 1997). The story, very simple and repetitive, consists of a frog encountering various animal homes and looking inside to find pairs of eyes peering out from the darkness. For each new animal home the frog encounters, the first page displays a different animal home with mysterious eyes shining out of the darkness and the following page displays an inside view of the dwelling, revealing the nature of its inhabitants.

In the following segment, Sra. Soto has been asking the children to retell the story, which mainly consists of counting the pairs of eyes and then predicting what kind of animals will be revealed on the following page. The frog has just encountered several pairs of eyes in a dark hole in the ground, which, when Sra. Soto turns the page, is revealed to belong to a family of rodents:

> **Sra. Soto:** [turns the page slowly] ¿Qué están dentro? (*What are inside?*)
>
> **Children:** [call out answers as she turns the page]
>
> **A child:** ¡Tejones! (*Rodents!*)
>
> **Sra. Soto:** Tejones. (*Rodents*) [claps her hands] Mejor es que te muevas, rana, esta casa está llena de tejones. (*Better move on, frog, this house is full of rodents*) [points to a large rodent on the page] ¿Quién es este tejón? (*Who is this rodent?*)
>
> **Children:** [call out] ¡Mamá! (*Mom*)
>
> **Sra. Soto:** [points to a smaller rodent] Y ¿quién es este? (*And who is this one?*)
>
> **Children:** [call out] ¡Bebé! (*Baby*)
>
> **Sra. Soto:** El bebito (*The little baby*)

Having accepted called-out answers to these three questions, Sra. Soto suddenly shifts her strategy. She explicitly reprimands Kathleen for calling out an unsolicited answer and selects Amalia to provide the same answer, then she continues to focus exclusively on Amalia and then Dorinda, ignoring the contributions of the others:

> **Sra. Soto:** [turns to a new page, which consists entirely of white pairs of eyes shining out of a dark background]
>
> **Kathleen** (English): [calls out] ¡Ojos! (*Eyes!*)
>
> **Sra. Soto:** Si me quieren contestar, levanten la mano. (*If you want to answer me, raise your hands*) [looks directly at Amalia] ¿Qué ves? (*What do you see?*)
>
> **Amalia** (Spanish): Ojos. (*Eyes*)

Sra. Soto: [still looking directly at Amalia] Cuéntalos. (*Count them*)
Amalia: [begins to count quietly]
Children: [while Amalia is counting, yell out numbers]
Rashid (English): [with hand raised, calls out] ¡Sra. Soto! ¡Sra. Soto!
Sra. Soto: [ignores Rashid, turns the page and selects Dorinda to identify the animal]
Rashid (English): [calls out quickly, before Dorinda can respond] ¡Conejo! (*Rabbit!*)
Sra. Soto: ¡Yo no te estoy hablando! (*I am not talking to you!*) [addressing the whole group] Ayúdame (*Help me*) [claps her hands and launches into the refrain] ¡Mejor es que te muevas, rana, esta casa está llena de conejos! (*Better move on frog, this house is full of rabbits!*)
Children: [join in the chant, loudly]

In this segment, we see Sra. Soto shift her strategy, first encouraging the children to call out responses, then suddenly directing her questions to Amalia and then Dorinda, explicitly excluding Kathleen and Rashid's correct but unsolicited answers. She then shifted back by inviting all the children to engage in the refrain. This may well have been a conscious strategy to make sure that the quieter and less confident children participated. As we have seen in earlier chapters, English-speaker Dorinda was quite confident with Spanish chants but hesitant about using Spanish in other classroom contexts. Spanish-speaker Amalia was shy about speaking out, even in her native language. By contrast, Sra. Soto characterized Rashid and Kathleen, both English speakers, as particularly aggressive children who tended to take the spotlight if you let them. She may have been trying to give the center stage to Dorinda and Amalia.

Whether conscious or not, this inconsistency provided an uncertainty that encouraged participation and attention. As calling out was often accepted, the children called out answers frequently during Story time, apparently understanding this to be potentially acceptable and at times even praiseworthy behavior. At the same time, the possibility existed that, even if the children didn't participate voluntarily, they might be called on at any time (as in the case of Dorinda and Amalia above).

Chana y su rana: Embedded Literacy and Numeracy Activities

Another Story time activity pattern consisted of a closer focus on the printed text, which included embedding explicit school-type literacy lessons in the reading. These lessons focused on specific print literacy conventions: spaces are left between words, names begin with a capital letter, letters indicate particular sounds, etc. The reading of *Chana y su rana* (Avalos & Caminos, 1992) illustrates this close reading variation of Story time.

For most of the *Chana y su rana* (Chana and her frog) Story time segment illustrated here, Sra. Soto takes a more traditional story reading approach, reading the text directly from the page and asking the children to repeat her reading (in the form, as she describes, of an echo). Nevertheless, she does not read smoothly, but interrupts herself repeatedly to pay a great deal of attention to the analysis of print conventions as they are encountered in the story. She also takes advantage of the fact that there are countable items in the illustrations (specifically apple cores) to ask the children to count during the story. This segment also illustrates Sra. Soto's insistence that the children sit in an orderly fashion and pay attention to her although, as with the previous Story time segments, her rules for participation shift frequently.

As Story time begins, the children are still cleaning up from an earlier activity and arranging themselves around the teacher on the rug. Sra. Soto sits in her chair with the closed book on the easel next to her and, while the children are still cleaning up and finding seats on the rug around her, she places the book on the easel and begins the chant from the story:

> **Sra. Soto:** Sana, sana, culito de rana. Si no sanas hoy, sanarás mañana. *(Get better, get better, little frog bottom. If you don't feel better today, you'll feel better tomorrow)* [calls out instructions to the children] Ven acá, por favor, Rashid... No, Mark... Khamil, no te puedes sentar en la silla... Alicia, Joël, y John, ahora mismo... muévete un poquito para atrás, por favor... *(Come here, please, Rashid...No, Mark... Khamil, don't sit in the chair... Alicia, Joël, y John, right now... move back a little please...)*

The beginning of this story reading is interspersed with Sra. Soto's attempts to call the children to order. As Sra. Soto tries to impose order while the children prepare for the story reading, her priorities are apparent. The children should quickly find a seat on the rug in front of her and sit down (with bottoms on the floor and legs crossed), and they should be paying attention to her.

Nevertheless, throughout this activity, Emilio, a Spanish speaker, has been counting out loud, in Spanish, the frogs on the cover of the book. He has been sitting at the front of the rug, leaning forward and pointing as he counts, and now he gets up and stands in front of the easel, touching the frogs as he counts. As the segment continues, Sra. Soto's interactions with Emilio are quite different from her interactions with the other children, despite the fact that he is not following her commands, either:

> **Sra. Soto:** [turns her head and watches Emilio as he finishes counting] ¡Muy bien! Siete manzanas comió. (*Very good. He ate seven apples*) [looks back at the other children and resumes her instructions] Ven, Amalia... Rashid, Rashid, ¿tú sabes que estoy esperando? ¡Ven acá! ¿Quién no me está mirando? (*Come here, Amalia . . . Rashid, Rashid, do you know that I am waiting? Come here, who is not looking at me?*) [gets up and walks to the back of the rug area, addressing children individually as she goes] Es la hora de nuestra lectura en español, y varios de ustedes no están acá conmigo... Déjalo, muchacho. Ven acá, por favor, Sandra, estoy esperando. Tú, culo para abajo, piernas cruzadas. Sandra, ahora. Joël, ahora. Ian, ahora. Déjala en paz, Wilma, ella está prestando más apunte que tú. (*It's time for our reading in Spanish, and several of you are not with me. Leave it alone, boy. Come here, Sandra, I'm waiting. You, bottom on the floor, legs crossed. Sandra, now. Joël, now. Ian, now. Leave her alone, Wilma, she is paying more attention than you*)

While Sra. Soto directs the children to sit down and pay attention to her, Emilio is not doing either of these things. He gets up from his seat, walks to the book and begins to count apples out loud. Nevertheless, Sra. Soto praises him, suggesting that Emilio's inappropriate behavior is excused by the nature of his actions. In fact, he has chosen to engage in behavior that, as we can see from the rest of the segment, is clearly encouraged by Sra. Soto: close attention to the book, finding things to count in the illustrations and use of the appropriate language, Spanish. Before Sra. Soto begins the story, she asks the children to analyze the print features of the text, which also involves counting:

> **Sra. Soto:** [pointing to the title of the book] ¿Quién me puede decir cómo llamamos esto? (*Who can tell me what we call this?*)
> **Norma** (Spanish): [raises her hand]
> **Sra. Soto** [gestures to select her]
> **Norma** (Spanish): Libro. (*Book*)
> **Sra. Soto:** Lo llamamos un libro. ¿Cómo llamamos este libro? (*We call it a book. What do we call this book?*)
> **Emily** (English): Chana y su rana. (*Chana and her frog*)
> **Sra. Soto and a few other children:** [join in as Emily says the title] ... y su rana. (*and her frog*)

Sra. Soto: ¿Cuántas palabras hay en este título? (*How many words are in this title?*)

Norma (Spanish): Cuatro. (*Four*)

Sra. Soto: Contamos ya, uno... dos... tres... cuatro. (*Let's count now, one... two... three... four*) [pointing to each word in the title as she counts]

A few children: [join in the counting]

Sra. Soto: Muy bien, Norma. ¿Cómo sabemos que hay cuatro? (*Very good, Norma. How do we know that there are four?*)

Again we see a question that received a reasonable answer, but not the one Sra. Soto was expecting. Norma's response of 'book' rather than the title suggests that she misinterpreted what Sra. Soto was referring to by the word 'this', effectively an accurate answer to the wrong (perceived) question. Sra. Soto accepts Norma's answer but without praise, and modifies her question to get the desired answer, which Emily then provides. Recall that Emily has a history of success in interpreting Sra. Soto's wishes, and she may have been drawing on both the subtle rejection of Norma's answer and Sra. Soto's general practice of reading out the title of the book at the beginning of every Story time activity to once again come up with the desired response. Later, when Norma offers exactly the desired answer (there are four words in the title), Sra. Soto praises her, since this time she not only knows the right answer, but she has also correctly interpreted Sra. Soto's question.

As the segment continues, we can see that Sra. Soto has a specific curriculum she wants the children to 'discover' by answering her questions: she wants them to notice that words are separated by spaces and to identify the sound-letter correspondences for the words in the title:

Sra. Soto: ¿Cómo sabemos que hay cuatro? ¿Qué dejo entre mis palabras? (*How do we know that there are four? What do I leave between my words?*)

A few children: [call out] ¡Espacio! (*Space!*)

Sra. Soto: [covers most of the title with her hand, leaving only the first two letters visible] Acá de vuelta tengo este sonido de esta mañana. ¿Qué dice esto allí? (*Here I have again this sound from this morning. What does this here say?*) [begins to make the sound corresponding to the letters she indicates] Ch... ch... ch... che. Ch... ch... chibo... chile... Chana. Digan conmigo. Chana y su rana. (*Say it with me. Chana and her frog*) [points at each word in the title as she says it]

Children: [join in] ...y su rana. (*... and her frog*)

In this pre-reading phase, Sra. Soto focuses on analysis of the short title, including phonetics (the sound made by the Spanish letter 'ch') and print conventions (spaces are left between words). Again we see that Sra. Soto asks questions with specific answers in mind. When Norma tells her that what she is pointing to is a book, she acknowledges this reasonable response, but continues to seek the desired answer (the title of the book). All Sra. Soto's questions have unambiguous answers (there are four words in the title, we know there are four words because they are separated by spaces) and, even when a reasonable alternative is offered, as in Norma's case, Sra. Soto continues to guide the children to the answer she was expecting. The dynamic of this story time activity is largely comprised of the children vying to demonstrate that they know the correct (expected) answer.

After this period of intense focus on the text, Sra. Soto switches the focus to the illustration on this page, now asking the children to count the number of apples. She directly addresses Emilio, who has already counted the number of apples on the cover as they were preparing to read the story:

> **Sra. Soto:** Emilio, dime cuántas manzanas comió en esta página. (*Emilio, tell me how many apples he ate on this page*)

Despite the highly structured nature of this activity and Sra. Soto's obvious apparent narrow focus on textual characteristics, the incorporation of Emilio's activity into a teacher question effectively legitimizes his earlier independent practice by now integrating it into her official narrative.

Focus on Mark: How to be the Center of (Positive) Attention

Sra. Soto described Mark as a boy whose family spoke only English at home, and whose Spanish language acquisition and academic development were delayed by immaturity and behavior problems. Furthermore, she felt that Mark had a tendency to emulate in the classroom the home behaviors of his father, whom she described as authoritative and 'a bit abusive with him'.

In the following excerpt, we see one of the rare examples of Mark gaining public recognition as a successful learner. Interestingly, as in the case with Emilio's spontaneous apple counting, Mark is praised not because he carefully follows explicit classroom protocol, but because he skillfully violates it. During Story time, Sra. Soto is seated next to a large easel holding the book *Chana y su rana*, and she is reading it aloud with the children, who are seated on the rug in front of the easel. The pattern here is highly repetitive and predictable: Sra. Soto reads a small section of text out loud while the children watch and listen, then the children repeat what she has just read as she points to the words on the page. Suddenly she stops and asks Sandra (English) a question about punctuation:

> **Sra. Soto:** Mira, Sandra (*Look, Sandra*) [holds the book so that one page is showing, and continues] Tengo de vuelta esos (*I have these again*) [points to two places in the text with exclamation points, which always appear in pairs in Spanish] ¿Qué son? (*What are they?*)
> **Mark** (English): [calling out immediately] ¡Puntos! (*Points*)
> **Sra. Soto:** [accepts this answer, repeating and correcting it] Puntos de exclamación. (*Exclamation points*)
> **Mark** (English): [stands up and begins to walk to easel]
> **Sra. Soto:** [continues, pointing to the exclamation marks] Aquí en una línea, porque está hablando. Porque está hablando. (*Here in a line, because she is talking. Because she is talking*) [looks at Mark as he approaches] ¿Sí? (*Yes?*)

Although Sra. Soto has specifically called on Sandra and Mark interrupts by calling out an answer before Sandra can respond, Sra. Soto accepts Mark's answer. Furthermore, as the conversation continues and it becomes apparent that Mark was actually referring to other 'puntos', Sra. Soto allows his unsolicited observation to change the focus of her lesson:

> **Mark** (English): [now standing by the open book, points to the colon before the quote] Puntos. (*Dots*)
> **Sra. Soto:** [emphasizing the first word] Dos puntos. Viste, sí, porque está hablando, Mark. Mark, está muy bueno que notaste eso. Los dos puntos me dice que alguien va a hablar. Se acuerdan ustedes, cuando yo le dije que a veces podemos... (*Colon.[1] You saw, yes, because she's talking, Mark. Mark, it's very good that you noticed that. The colon tells me that someone is going to speak. Remember, when I told you that sometimes we can...*) [her voice trails off as she gets up and begins to walk over to the desk by the wall to get a marker, and then she adds] Muy bien, Mark. (*Very good, Mark*)

Sra. Soto allows Mark to lead the topic of the lesson away from her intended topic, even though he violates classroom rules (his comment is unrelated to the teacher's question, and he calls it out when someone else had specifically been elected to provide the answer). Nevertheless, he is successful in diverting Sra. Soto's attention to the topic of his choice, and he receives extensive praise. Quite possibly this is because Mark chooses to ask about a punctuation mark related to the one she is planning to discuss.

Completely forgetting Sandra and the exclamation points, Sra. Soto continues with a detailed explanation of the use of the colon that Mark has discovered, using examples and drawings to illustrate that a colon can be used to introduce reported speech in the same way as a speech bubble (which the children have already learned about). Finally, she finishes the elaborate explanation and sits down again, directing her final comments to Mark:

> **Sra. Soto:** [sits down and opens the book again] Esos dos puntos, Mark, es en vez de hacer este globo. En vez de usar un globo, diciendo que alguien está hablando, usan dos puntos y esta raya. (*Those two points, Mark, is instead of using this balloon. Instead of using a balloon, saying that someone is talking, they use two points and this dash*)

As she finishes the explanation, she calls Mark by name, addressing the final point to him directly, with the result that this entire explanation, which has been delivered to the class in general, seems to have been devoted to Mark.

Sra. Soto often seemed to grab opportunities to involve the children she was particularly concerned about, such as extremely shy Amalia and frequently disengaged Kathleen, in her ongoing narrative. Her characterization of Mark as a generally problematic learner might also, then, have influenced her decision to divert from her planned curriculum and follow his lead. As illustrated earlier, Sra. Soto's turn-taking policy was highly inconsistent, in that sometimes she required the children to raise their hands, sometimes she selected in advance a specific child to answer a question, and sometimes she acknowledged the children who called out comments and questions without raising their hands. Her desire to involve children like Mark, whom she viewed as less competent and engaged learners, may have partially accounted for her frequently changing rules for legitimate participation, although the pattern was not nearly regular enough to draw any strict conclusions. Most likely, the decisions that Sra. Soto made about whose participation to honor and whose to reject were the result of split second calculations based on a variety of factors, including explicit and implicit goals and assumptions.

Focus on Kathleen: The Social Construction of a Behavior Problem

A White, English-speaking child, Kathleen, lived with her mother in a low income, mainly Latino neighborhood of the city. Sra. Soto saw Kathleen's home life as problematic: she was a frequent witness to the trading of 'stuff' (drugs) and her basic needs (food, clothing, glasses) were not met. She told me that she made several home visits but 'never did get too far'. Her written development was 'far below level' and, at the end of the year, Sra. Soto felt that she was not academically or emotionally ready for first grade.

Although toward the end of the year, Sra. Soto did say she wished she could have had Kathleen tested for a learning disability, she tended to characterize Kathleen's problems as social and resulting from environmental, rather than organic, deficits. She tended to describe Kathleen's problems in terms of an unfortunate mismatch between the social expectations and practices at home and at school, a mismatch that would only increase as Kathleen progressed through the school system. She told me that she was concerned about what would happen to Kathleen in the following years, because as each year progresses, the teachers would 'have to be stricter'. She contrasted what she expected would be increasingly teacher-directed and restrictive activity structures in school with what she imagined Kathleen's home activity structures to be, 'You can see that she is allowed to do whatever she wants at home, you can see that, can't you?'

As Sra. Soto indicated, she often stretched the rules of her own classroom activity systems to permit the flexibility that Kathleen seemed to need. She sometimes accepted Kathleen's participation on her own terms even when that violated classroom protocol. On one occasion, for example, when Kathleen was becoming increasingly upset as she was working on a Tables project, Sra. Soto allowed her to go and play in the Blocks Center, which, normally, children were permitted to do only after their Tables project was completed (these two activity structures are described in more detail in Chapters 7 and 8). She explained that teachers in higher grades would not allow Kathleen to wander around the room and do whatever she wanted, because they would have to worry more and more about ensuring that she learned particular content.

Nevertheless, Kathleen's reputation as a behavior problem was firmly established during some of the more restrictive activity structures in this Kindergarten classroom. The ways in which Sra. Soto, Kathleen and her classmates contributed to Kathleen's social construction as a sort of frustrating but beloved class clown were particularly evident one October morning during Story time. They were reading a story called *The Rain Puddle* (Holl & Duvoisin, 1968), in which several animals see their own reflection in a rain puddle and believe that an animal who looks just like themselves has fallen in. True to her usual style, Sra. Soto made various curricular connections before and during the reading of the story: a focus on the letter 'R', the scientific nature of reflection, symmetry and evaporation, and the naming of the animals.

The following segment takes place during English Language Arts. Sra. Soto is seated in front of the classroom with the children on the rug around her, and Kathleen is seated in front. Kathleen is identified as disruptive almost as soon as the lesson begins, and engages in what seems like a progressive battle for control with Sra. Soto, until Sra. Soto eventually physically picks her up and puts her in a chair in the back of the room.

> **Kathleen:** [sitting quietly, watching Sra. Soto and holding a book on her lap]
>
> **Sra. Soto:** [to Kathleen] You shouldn't have brought your book with you. [To the class in general] I need everyone's eyes and ears on me. [holding a cardboard cutout of the letter 'R', begins a discussion about whose name begins with this letter. Removes the cardboard to reveal a mirror behind it]
>
> **Kathleen** (English): [begins to move out of her seat to try to position herself directly in front of the mirror to see her reflection]
>
> **Sra. Soto:** When you see yourself in the mirror we call that a...? [Interrupts herself and addresses Kathleen] Do nothing that will keep the teacher from teaching and the other students from learning.

As Sra. Soto begins to read the story, she frequently stops to make the usual sorts of curricular connections, but she also stops frequently to chide Kathleen for behaviors that consist of either looking at her own book instead of up at the teacher, sitting with her head resting down on her knees, or lying on the floor. Sra. Soto begins by silently taking Kathleen's book without interrupting her own reading. Then she attempts to attract and hold Kathleen's attention by involving her in another discussion of the letter R. Later, when Kathleen has put her head down, Sra. Soto stops reading, and finally addresses Kathleen directly again:

> **Sra. Soto:** Kathleen, that's it. You must sit up, because I can't teach.

After some attempts to verbally encourage Kathleen to sit up, Sra. Soto apparently gives up and returns to reading. After a few more minutes, she stops reading again and physically picks Kathleen up and moves her to a chair at the back of the circle of children. Finally, as the story comes to an end, Kathleen is permitted to go to the bathroom. As she wraps up the summary of the story, Sra. Soto contrasts Kathleen with the wise owl, who is the hero of this story:

> **Kathleen** (English): [walks slowly toward the bathroom]
> **Sra. Soto:** We usually say you need to be a wise owl and not a SILLY GOOSE (saying these last words more loudly and looking toward Kathleen's retreating form) But Kathleen's a silly goose.
> **Rashid** (English): Kathleen is being a silly goose.
> **Sra. Soto:** But she's gone now.
> **Khamil** (English): No she's not, she's in the bathroom.

Sra. Soto conducts a brief lesson about reflection and fingers to illustrate that we have symmetrical fingers on our left and right hands. She then calls the children to line up one by one after each has correctly answered a question about today's lesson. After calling on two other children, she calls on Kathleen:

> **Sra. Soto:** Kathleen, what do you see when you look in a mirror?
> **Kathleen** (English): My face.
> **Sra. Soto:** That's right and a beautiful face that is when you're on your best behavior. Kathleen, go get in line.

This segment reveals some of the processes underlying Kathleen's social construction as a problem learner in this classroom. First, Kathleen began the Story time segment by quietly sitting in the front of the circle with her eyes on the teacher. This was completely acceptable behavior, except that she had a book in her lap. Even though at the beginning Kathleen was not reading the book, Sra. Soto interpreted this as a disruptive act and immediately chided her ('You shouldn't have your book with you'). Kathleen obviously resisted this rule, albeit passively, as she continued to clutch her book throughout the segment. In fact, none of Kathleen's acts could technically be interpreted as disruptive, as her resistance to classroom norms was completely silent. Her disruption seemed to stem from failing to focus attention on the teacher. Whatever Kathleen's original intentions, bringing a book to a Story time reading was interpreted as an act of defiance. Later, Kathleen's silent acts of putting her head down and then curling up on the floor were so distracting to Sra. Soto that she stopped reading the story and physically removed her to the back of the room. An outsider might not have interpreted these behaviors to be disruptive, but the strongly teacher-centered nature of this activity constructed these behaviors as highly transgressive. Sra. Soto seemed to be distracted by Kathleen's transgression of the activity structure norms for participation rather than any noise or movement that might literally have distracted her from teaching.

Second, one of Kathleen's disruptive behaviors seemed to result from an *excessive engagement* with one of the main aspects of this lesson, the mirror. Her eagerness to see her reflection in the mirror that Sra. Soto had brought for exactly that purpose temporarily distracted her from other aspects of the lesson that were occurring simultaneously (the story itself and the focus on the letter 'R'). Furthermore, her fascination with the mirror caused her to move slightly from her seat (she was seated almost in front of the mirror), thus attracting further attention to her transgressions and invoking an immediate accusation of disrupting the class ('Do nothing that will stop the teacher from teaching...'). This seemed to upset Kathleen, as it was at this point that she began to exhibit obvious disengaged behaviors, such as opening and reading from her book, putting her head down and eventually curling up on the floor.

Finally, Kathleen was explicitly assigned an identity during this episode. She was determined to be a 'silly goose' during her absence. As this segment demonstrates, Rashid immediately accepted this construction, echoing Sra. Soto's comment that Kathleen was a silly goose. Just a few days later, echoing the 'silly goose' comment, Kathleen was explicitly compared to a lost duck, a character in another story the class was reading. Interestingly, Kathleen seemed to enjoy this running joke.

During this later Spanish Language Arts Story time segment, Sra. Soto was reading *Has Visto a Mi Patito?* (Tafuri, 1991) in which a mother duck searches for her lost adventurous duckling. At the beginning of this Story time, Kathleen was at the back of the group, playing with another child's nametag and not paying very much attention to the story. When Sra. Soto compared the lost duckling in the story with Kathleen, however, she looked up, moved to the front of the room and began to watch the book closely as Sra. Soto read. Throughout the story, Sra. Soto and the other children made several more references to Kathleen as the lost duckling, which seemed to engage Kathleen's attention.

Several months later, in March, it was clear that this had become a running joke in the classroom. When they are about to read another book involving ducks, Sra. Soto reminds the children of the earlier story as well as Kathleen's role as the 'lost duckling':

Sra. Soto: [directly to Kathleen] ¿Recuerdas? ¿El cuento que contamos sobre ti? (*Remember? The story we told about you?*)

Kathleen: [smiles and ducks her head]
Children: [laugh]

The children, and even Kathleen, seem to participate eagerly in the construction of Kathleen as the lost duckling of the class, a process that seems to have begun with the earlier construction of her as a 'silly goose'. This was hardly a process of social exclusion, as Kathleen was actually an extremely popular child with her peers. In fact, one February morning, after she had been absent for only one day, Kathleen was mobbed by an enthusiastic group of children who hugged her and asked her why she had been absent. Sra. Soto commented to me, 'It's not that she's not well liked, she's too well liked'. Nevertheless, Kathleen's reputation as a problem learner was firmly established relatively early in her first year of school.

Analysis: Negotiating Participation, Defining Learners

Overall, Story time was a strongly teacher-centered activity structure, although the rules for participation were inconsistent and had to be negotiated by the children. Sra. Soto sat in the front of the room and led the lesson while the children sat on the floor at her feet and, ideally, paid close attention to her and participated according to her directions, whether this meant retelling a story or answering a question. While teacher-centered activities are sometimes associated with little participation or response from the children (Gunn *et al.*, 2002), in Story time the children were invited to participate in the teacher's ongoing narrative in carefully structured and guided ways.

Story time provided relatively rich language modeling on Sra. Soto's part, as she maintained a constant narrative entirely in the target language that was more or less rooted in the children's book they were reading. In this manner, the children's close attention to the teacher, enforced directly (by command) or indirectly (by the ever-imminent possibility of being called on to answer a question), provided them with considerable quality linguistic input (Krashen, 1985), whose comprehensibility was enhanced by repetition, narrative context and visual cues. Reading aloud, particularly the dramatic, participatory strategies used by Sra. Soto, can help familiarize children not only with the technical aspects of the target language (in terms of vocabulary, grammar and punctuation), but also with the cadence and intonation of the spoken language, aspects of writing style and genres, and practices of inference and prediction; furthermore, reading together can simply be a fun class activity, as 'laughing or emoting together about the character's escapades makes for cohesive group dynamics' (Pérez & Torres-Guzmán, 1996: 76).

It's important to keep in mind that Sra. Soto did not enjoy the support of a cohort of teachers who participated in the design and implementation of a coherent Spanish-language arts program (Smith & Arnot-Hopffer, 1998), nor did she have much access to Spanish materials in a school where acquisition of Spanish language materials was not a high priority (given that, at the time, there were only two two-way immersion (TWI) classrooms, both at the Kindergarten level). She had to improvise, in terms of both materials and strategies, since her training had been in English as a second language (ESL) rather than foreign language teaching or bilingual education.

This improvisation can be seen here not only in terms of her use of English materials during Spanish Story time, but also in the ways in which she expanded a simple story reading event into a more complex discursive event that included not only connections to other curricular activities, but also to the children's own lives and interests. Sra. Soto's narratives were broad and complex. Brief and redundant questions and answers were embedded in richer narratives involving animals, plants and weather that linked their own lives with far-away places and general scientific phenomena. It was Sra. Soto who wove these complicated narratives, and the children negotiated their participation in them according to her terms. In designing her classroom literacy events and controlling the terms of participation, Sra. Soto sent important messages to the children about what does and doesn't count as legitimate practice and participation, 'Teachers lead children to particular kinds and levels of reading practice... through this the students learn what "counts" as writing and reading, what "counts" as response and interpretation, and what "counts" as a legitimate function and use of literacy' (Pérez & Torres-Guzmán, 1996: 55).

Characteristic of Story time was the rather narrowly prescribed zone of acceptable participation. Generally, children provided answers to questions that had specific and unambiguous answers, whether their response was elicited or volunteered. The repetition of the same story and redundancy of the vocabulary, as Sra. Soto connected the story to other curricular activities, provided support as the children searched for the correct (expected by the teacher) response. Answers to questions were usually expected to be found in the text or by remembering previous related lessons. For example, before and after reading *Better Move on, Frog*, the children's answers to Sra. Soto's questions included that animals have babies in the springtime, that bees have queens and that rats are mammals, all information recalled from previous science lessons. Participation initiated by the children was accepted, as in the case of Emilio's spontaneous apple counting and Mark's observations on punctuation, if it related to Sra. Soto's overall curricular goals. Recall from Chapter 3 that Sra. Soto referred to this dense cross-curricular weave as scaffolding, a practice that has been identified as an effective TWI Kindergarten practice (Peregoy, 1991; Peregoy & Boyle, 1999).

This focus on her own curricular themes served Sra. Soto's stated purposes of teaching certain values and reinforcing learning through repetition and embedding in multiple contexts, but it also meant that sometimes the task of the children was to guess correctly Sra. Soto's understandings, rather than producing their own. This tended to undermine creativity and individual expression, and it also tended to favor children, like Emily, who were particularly good at making (the right) thematic connections.

The classroom also benefitted children who were able to correctly intuit how to conform to classroom norms that were not consistent, even within the same activity. The rules for legitimate participation seemed to shift continually: one moment Sra. Soto waited patiently while children called out various comments at the same time, and the next moment she admonished children to raise their hands and wait until they were called on. While at times she accepted a range of contributions (including personal connections), she sometimes rejected even reasonable inter-pretations for the one she was looking for. The children who were consistently quiet and obedient might avoid reprimand, but the real rewards of attention and praise were won by those who knew when and under what circumstances to speak out of turn.

Mark's success in capturing the attention of the teacher is a good example of this kind of rule-bending strategy. Quite possibly his success was partially because, as in the case of Emilio counting the apples, Mark chose to focus on a topic that met Sra. Soto's criteria as an appropriate curricular activity. The fact that Mark spoke his one word query in Spanish ('puntos') may have also had an effect on her responses since, as described in Chapter 4, she tended to reward English speakers for their attempts to speak in Spanish. However, she also seemed to bend her own rules at times to accommodate children like Mark and Amalia, who needed extra support to participate in group activities. In this sense, her inconsistent rule patterns seemed, at least in part, to be a strategy to selectively support less confident learners. This inconsistency also seemed to help maintain children's attention: you never knew, really, when you might be allowed to call out an answer, or when you might just be singled out to provide an answer.

Yet over time, the characteristic ways in which the children negotiated the norms for participation in these different activity structures contributed to their construction as learners in this classroom, and perhaps beyond (as the teacher's evaluations were passed on to parents and future teachers). Over time, the children came to be described by Sra. Soto, and even acknowledged by their peers, as particularly capable in particular areas or as particularly problematic learners. Emily and Sandra were able to skillfully intuit the teacher's wishes and become role models for a language in which they are not proficient, while Kathleen failed to embrace the classroom norms and began to develop what might become enduring behavior problems. Interestingly, Sra. Soto described Kathleen as particularly socially adept, and considered this to be an important part of her problem.

According to Sra. Soto, Kathleen was 'really attuned to listening to what everybody else is saying', which made her an unsuccessful 'content learner'. She was more likely to focus on the social interactions around her than on content that the teacher was trying to transmit (whether that was a story, a lesson on letters or a demonstration of scientific principles). This conceptual division between social interaction and classroom content implies that there is a teaching and learning process going on in the classroom that is divorced from the social context, a division that my own analysis of classroom activity systems does not support. It is not that there is a content separate from social interactions, but that some kinds of social interactions (listening to the teacher and vying to answer the teacher's questions) are privileged over others (independent reading, certain postures and lack of eye contact) in particular classroom activity structures (Erickson, 1982).

In many ways, Kathleen operated in exactly the opposite way from Mark in these Story time segments, and this seemed to be more a matter of understanding and adhering to the implicit social rules rather than a reflection of social engagement or content relevance. While Mark was able to violate protocol and incorporate his own relevant interests into the strongly teacher-directed lesson, Kathleen's interests (reading a book, examining her reflection in a mirror) were excluded and she was strongly chastised, despite the fact that these interests were also relevant to the teacher's Story time agenda.

In fact, many of the behaviors for which Kathleen was chastised during the 'silly goose' segment were not social at all with respect to her peers, but violated particular kinds of required social engagement with the teacher (e.g. she read her own book instead of listening to the teacher read; she lowered her head instead of watching the teacher). Mark, by contrast, explicitly interrupted the teacher and demanded her attention and, by walking to the front of the group and taking center stage next to the easel, demanded social engagement from his peers as well. In this sense, Kathleen's problems seem to consist not so much of an excess of social engagement, but in an insensitivity to or lack of interest in the ways in which social interactions must be negotiated with the teacher in this particular activity structure.

Recall that Sra. Soto contrasted Kathleen's impoverished and (in her opinion) poorly structured home life with what she predicted would be an increasingly structured school life as Kathleen advanced through the grades. While this was largely cast as a mismatch between school and home culture, Sra. Soto's implicit acceptance of school culture and rejection of what she characterized as Kathleen's more permissive and even neglectful home culture suggested an implicit deficit theory, which might have been tied to assumptions about Kathleen's social class and urban environment (Sautter, 1994). Since the causes of Kathleen's problems were identified as enduring and external to the classroom, the effect of the activity structure itself remained invisible and unanalyzed.

While the long-term consequences of her construction as a problem learner may very well prove to be damaging (Varenne & McDermott, 1998), the short-term consequences were that she received rather a lot of attention: the teacher stopped the lesson frequently to speak to her, carried her from one place to another and developed a running classroom joke about her being a lost duckling. Kathleen very rarely capitulated and, as the 'silly goose' segment illustrates, she was more likely to persist or even escalate the behavior that bothered the teacher than to stop. Kathleen's responses suggested that, as a highly socially motivated person, she may have preferred attracting what the teacher saw as negative, disciplinary attention to participating in these activity structures where everyone's attention was (supposed to be) focused on the teacher.

Interestingly, Sra. Soto told me that this same 'excessive' social motivation was what made Kathleen a particularly successful language learner. Sra. Soto attributed this to her tendency to be an auditory rather than visual learner. My interpretation of Kathleen's strangely divergent 'content' and 'language' learner identities was different: Kathleen was highly successful in the less teacher-directed, more loosely structured aspects of the classroom, where her interest in and ability to foster social interactions was an asset rather than a deficit. In my opinion, it was the vastly different nature of the activity structure that enabled Kathleen to shine, particularly in the Housekeeping and Blocks Centers, where the children were expected to initiate and maintain extended verbally mediated social exchanges. In Chapter 8, Kathleen will be featured again, this time focusing on her social construction as a successful language learner.

Note

1. The colon in Spanish is called 'dos puntos', literally translated in English as 'two dots'. The period is translated as 'punto', or literally 'dot'. Therefore, Mark's naming of the colon as 'punto' was quite close to the correct term.

Chapter 7

Tables Time: Language in Activity

Tables time was meant to facilitate group interaction as the children worked together in small groups to accomplish assigned tasks. In fact, Sra. Soto originally conceptualized this type of activity as a learning Centers activity. Recall from Chapter 3 that after our visit to the Calvary two-way immersion (TWI) school, she told me that she wanted children to work together on projects in learning Centers. Her original idea was that this collaboration would facilitate conversation, but over time it became apparent that the children tended to work separately on the same task. As the year progressed, this project-based activity came to be known simply as 'Tables' and the term 'Centers' was reserved for the Housekeeping and Blocks play Centers.

Nevertheless, the children were expected to engage in conversation during Tables time, and they were carefully arranged at the tables in mixed-language groups in the hope that they would speak in Spanish during Spanish time. Unlike in Language Arts, where the children were expected to focus their attention on the teacher, the children were expected to work relatively independently during Tables time. However, this activity was carefully and strictly teacher-designed. The children were expected to focus on a specific task and interact verbally with each other in ways that were guided not directly by the teacher nor independently by the children, but by the common goal of accomplishing the task at hand.

The children were assigned to one of five tables. Either all tables worked on the same project simultaneously or each table was assigned one out of a set of projects that rotated the following day, so that within several days every table had worked on all projects in the set. Tables time actually consisted of two distinct phases, characterized by very different activity structures. In the task-completion phase, the children sat at their assigned tables to complete their projects while Sra. Soto moved among them, helping children who needed assistance. This task-completion phase was usually preceded by an explanation phase, a whole-class activity where Sra. Soto introduced the assignment of the day and explained it. The explanation phase was strongly teacher-centered: the children watched the teacher as she used various verbal, textual and graphic cues to make sure they understood the task they were meant to accomplish. As mentioned earlier, when the children finished their Tables time project for the day, they were permitted to go to either the Housekeeping or Blocks Center, which required that they approach Sra. Soto, demonstrate that they had finished the project to her satisfaction, and ask permission in the appropriate official language. Usually, Tables time took place in mid-morning, after Spanish Language Arts and before lunch.

Tables time tasks generally consisted of physical projects that required some degree of construction, including activities such as coloring, painting, folding and pasting paper, and occasionally the use of yarn or other materials. These activities generally related to a broader theme in the curriculum, reflecting the enthusiasm Sra. Soto expressed for a thematic curriculum (see Chapter 3). For example, each of the four seasons consisted of an overall seasonal unit that was referred to frequently in the context of various activities throughout the day. During Tables time, the children painted and folded paper to make butterflies in the spring, and they engaged in projects involving mittens and snow-flakes in the winter. These activities usually involved some kind of embedded academic skill. The butterflies, for example, exemplified symmetry, as the children painted colored circles on one-half of the paper and then folded it to spread the color onto the other half. Often projects required that the children match and or divide objects. For example, one science-related Tables project required the children to cut out pictures of animals and paste them together according to their habitat. On another occasion, when they had been talking about growing babies and plants during the spring, the children had to cut out and divide items depending on whether they grow or shrink over time and then paste them in the appropriate category.

While the activities were conceptually embedded in broader cross-curricular themes and the children were physically grouped together at tables, the goal of each particular Tables time activity was to complete the project independently. The children followed instructions and completed the project in accordance with an unambiguous goal set by the teacher (i.e. group all animals living in water together, construct your own names from letter blocks). While the children physically worked together and shared materials with others at the same table, these activities did not share any characteristics of group activities, and therefore did not particularly afford linguistic interaction. The exchanges that occasionally arose among the children at the same table while the activities were progressing smoothly were characteristically brief. The children sometimes checked each other's progress, called attention to their own activity, or asked for materials. The children often simply ignored each other's brief comments, for example:

> **Dorinda** (English): [addresses Oscar, who is sitting next to her] What are you doing?
> **Oscar** (Spanish): [no response]

Sometimes there was just a brief response, or even a simple repetition:

> **Ian** (English): [folding his paper mitten over his hand] Alright! Look at my glove!
> **Oscar** (Spanish): [in a mocking voice] Alright, look at my glove!

Often the children's comments and questions elicited non-verbal responses. The children often asked each other for shared supplies, for example:

> **Ian** (English): Where's the blue?
> **Oscar** (Spanish): [silently hands Ian the crayon bag]

These examples typify the nature of interactions as the children followed the routine, non-problematic Tables time activity. It is also no coincidence that all these brief examples are in English, despite the fact that they were all recorded during official Spanish time. As demonstrated in Chapter 4, the children tended to speak in English unless Sra. Soto was there to enforce the Spanish-only rule. While Sra. Soto apparently imagined that the children would happily converse as they completed their Tables time tasks together, it seemed to me that the real opportunities for language learning in this activity structure arose in different ways. In the following section, I will illustrate the ways in which Sra. Soto's explanations provided opportunities for comprehension, and then I will illustrate how conversation was afforded when problems arose in the completion of the task.

Explanation: Listening Assisted by Rich Visual Context

In the initial explanation phase of Tables time, the children gathered around Sra. Soto as she explained their task for the day, usually assisted by audio-visual aids (photographs or diagrams mounted on her easel). She often demonstrated the activity as she talked. These explanations were characterized by gestures and highly contextual language, and Sra. Soto demanded that all the children attend carefully to her throughout her explanation. To ensure this, she frequently called on children to answer closed-ended, known-answer questions to advance her narrative, rather than simply speaking continuously.

In the following excerpt, Sra. Soto is sitting next to a large easel with five sheets of paper pinned to it. She explains the papers one by one, as each table is to complete a different project. After completing instructions for Tables 1–4, she finishes with instructions for Table 5, which involve some complicated steps:

> **Sra. Soto:** [holding up a large cardboard mitten] Un mitón grande. (*A big mitten*) [places a stack of different-colored construction paper on her lap and holds up one piece at a time] ¿Qué color es esto? (*What color is this?*)
>
> **Children:** [calling out in unison, more or less, the name of the color in Spanish each time she holds up a sheet of paper and asks this question] Rojo... morado... azul... verde... anaranjado... morado (*Red, purple, blue, green, orange, purple*)
>
> **Sra. Soto:** [repeats each color after the children] Ustedes pueden elegir el color que quieran. (*You can choose the color you want*)
>
> **Ian** (English): Baño (*Bathroom*)
>
> **Sra. Soto:** No, no vas al baño, Ian. Tú ya fuiste al baño. Ian, tú eres de la mesa 5. Tú tienes que prestar atención. Mira, Ian, necesitas medio papel, ponga el doble... (*No, you're not going to the bathroom. Ian. You already went to the bathroom. Ian, you are from Table 5. You have to pay attention. Look, Ian, you need a half sheet of paper, fold it in half...*)

Sra. Soto demands the children's undivided attention both directly (by insisting that Ian pay attention) and indirectly, by asking the children to call out the names of the colors, for which of course they must be watching the colored sheets of paper as she holds them up. As she continues to explain the project, she continues pausing to ask questions, and the children also continue to interrupt her with their own questions. Dorinda interrupts her explanation about folding the paper in half to check whether they will be asked to trace the paper:

> **Dorinda** (English): Trace it?
>
> **Sra. Soto:** Lo trazan con... (*You trace it with...*) [holds up a crayon and allows her voice to trail off expectantly, waiting for a volunteer to finish the sentence]
>
> **Joël** (Spanish): ¡Crayola! (*Crayon*)
>
> **Sra. Soto:** Con la crayola. (*With the crayon*)
>
> **Child:** Crayon?
>
> **Child:** ¿La crayola? (*Crayon?*)

Sra. Soto: [ignores both children and addresses Kathleen, who has been talking to me] Kathleen, tú estas supuesta a estar prestándome apunte a mi, no a la Sra. DePalma. (*Kathleen, you are supposed to be paying attention to me, not to Ms. DePalma*)

Note that she attends to Dorinda's question, although it is in English, and simply responds in Spanish. In this activity, Sra. Soto accepts interruptions that are addressed to her (such as Ian's request to go to the bathroom and Dorinda's tracing question), but she does not tolerate Kathleen's lack of attention. Characteristic of Kathleen (as described in Chapter 6), she has ceased to pay attention to Sra. Soto during this highly teacher-centered activity. She is, according to my field notes, speaking to me in Spanish.

After attempting to attract Kathleen's attention, Sra. Soto returns to her explanation of how they are to complete the project, eventually producing a book:

Sra. Soto: Mira. Yo voy a poder abrir esto como un... (*Look. I am going to be able to open this like a...*) [Places her palms together, opening them outward, and her voice trails off expectantly]
Emily (English): ¡Libro! (*Book*)
Sra. Soto: Libro. Porque yo quiero hacer agujeros acá... (*Because I want to make holes here...*)
Mark (English): [interrupting] You have to cut it
Sra. Soto: [ignoring Mark] Ustedes primero tienen que contester... (*First you have to answer...*)
Mark (English): [interrupting] You have to glue it. And get another piece of paper...
Sra. Soto: No... no vas a pegar. Espera. (*No, you're not going to glue. Wait.*) [Reaches down and pulls a chart with questions onto her lap]
Sandra (English): Maybe it's gonna be a lollipop or something. Or maybe it's gonna be our Valentine.
Sra. Soto: No... espera... Hay preguntas. (*No, wait. There are questions*)

Throughout her explanation, Sra. Soto maintains the children's attention by explicitly demanding it (in Ian's and Kathleen's cases), by inviting participation (encouraging them to finish her sentences) and by tolerating the children's interruptions for speculations. She welcomes these speculations even though the children don't raise their hands, even when the speculations are incorrect (in Mark's case) or even far-fetched (in the case of Sandra's lollipop), and even when they are in English, the unsanctioned language.

Sra. Soto continues to explain the project, which requires the children to select the design of their project based on answering a series of personal questions. She holds up the chart with pictures and simple words. By asking questions that can be answered by looking at the chart, she involves the children as co-participants in her explanation:

> **Sra. Soto:** [pointing to a blue circle in the diagram] Si soy un niño, ¿qué voy a cortar? (*If I am a boy, what am I going to cut?*)
> **Dorinda** (English): ¿Azul? (*Blue?*)
> **Sra. Soto:** [adding to Dorinda's description in an affirmative tone of voice] ...círculo. (*circle*) [points to a red triangle in the diagram] Si soy una niña, ¿qué voy... (*If I'm a girl what am I going...*)
> **Dorinda** (English): [interrupting] ¡Rojo! (*Red*)
> **Sra. Soto:** [continuing over Dorinda]...a cortar? (*...to cut?*)
> **Dorinda** (English): ¡Triángulo! (*Triangle*)
> **Sra. Soto:** [in an affirming voice, looking at Dorinda] Triángulo rojo. (*Red triangle*) [pointing to the corresponding icon in the diagram as she names each] Niño es un círculo azul. Niña es un triángulo rojo. (*Boy is a blue circle. Girl is a red triangle*)

Recall from Chapter 5 that Dorinda tended to participate enthusiastically in more structured Spanish language activities, although she was hesitant to use Spanish in less structured activities. Here, Dorinda participates willingly and with apparent confidence. She calls out the answers, providing key words in Sra. Soto's explanatory narrative, thereby participating in an interaction that actually requires very little vocabulary on her part. The vocabulary is familiar (they have been studying colors and shapes) and reinforced visually (the chart has the shapes and colors with the corresponding words written in Spanish).

As the segment continues, Sra. Soto invites Kathleen to participate. Unlike Dorinda, who has enthusiastically volunteered, Kathleen is not paying attention. Sra. Soto's pointed invitation to Kathleen may be interpreted as a strategy to involve the disengaged girl, who is standing with her back to the group and writing on the chalkboard:

> **Sra. Soto:** [looks over at Kathleen] Kathleen, ¡ven acá! (*Kathleen, come here!*) [directly addressing Kathleen and pointing to the diagram] Dice, '¿qué te gusta?' (*It says, 'what do you like?'*)
> **Dorinda** (English): ¡Rectángulo! (*Rectangle*)
> **Sra. Soto:** [ignores Dorinda and continues, still directly addressing

Kathleen] Si te gusta la nieve... (*If you like snow...*)
Dorinda (English): ¡Morado! (*Purple*)
Sra. Soto: [ignoring her] ¿Qué voy a usar? (*What am I going to use?*)
Kathleen (English): ¡Morado! (*Purple*)
A few children: [along with Kathleen] ¡Morado! (*Purple*)

At this point Sra. Soto seems to shift her strategy: ignoring Dorinda, whose attention seems to show no sign of wandering, she chooses to focus on the disconnected Kathleen. Having received some response from Kathleen, indicating that Kathleen is now paying attention, Sra. Soto shifts back to her previous technique of acknowledging the volunteered responses from the group:

> **Sra. Soto:** [addressing the group] Si no les gusta la nieve, ¿qué voy a usar? (*If you don't like snow, what am I going to use?*)
> **Sandra** (English): Verde (*Green*)
> **Sra. Soto:** Un cuadrado verde. ¿Qué forma es ésta? (*A green square. What shape is this?*)
> **Dorinda** (English): Rectángulo. (*Rectangle*)
> **Sra. Soto:** [looks at Dorinda] Sí, gracias, Dorinda. (Yes, thanks, Dorinda) [looks at the group] Si tienen mitones, ¿que voy a usar? (*If you have mittens, what am I going to use?*)
> **Dorinda** (English): Ro- [pausing, changing her mind mid-word] -amarillo. (*Re-yellow*)
> **Sra. Soto:** Un diamante amarillo. Si tengo guantes... (*A yellow diamond. If I have gloves...*)
> **Dorinda** (English): [interrupting] ¡Mano! (*Hand*)
> **Sra. Soto** [ignores Dorinda]
> **Dorinda** (English): [rapidly trying again] ¡Color café! (*Brown*)
> **Sra. Soto:** [in an affirmative tone] Un corazón café. (*A brown heart*)

Dorinda participates in Sra. Soto's narrative despite her obvious uncertainty. At the beginning of the segment, she offered a correct word (*azul*) but in a questioning tone of voice, and Sra. Soto accepted her contribution as if she were confident. Later, when Dorinda calls out a word that doesn't fit her narrative structure (*mano*), Sra. Soto ignores her and continues, accepting her second and more appropriate response seamlessly into her own narrative by repeating it approvingly. This rather subtle system of indicating correct and incorrect responses seems to encourage Dorinda not only to pay close attention, but also to keep trying to participate in Sra. Soto's overall narrative despite the fact that she does not always know what's going on.

Task-Completion: Problems Create Opportunities for Language Learning

After receiving their instructions, the children went to their assigned tables and began working on their projects. As mentioned earlier, these activities tended to proceed without much linguistic interaction, as each child focused more or less on the independent accomplishment of his/ her task. Sra. Soto circulated from table to table during Tables time, and the children frequently approached her, holding out their finished or partially finished projects for her appraisal. Children whose projects were completed and done well generally received some short approving comment, but children who were having problems with their project received more of her verbally mediated attention. For example, in the following segment, two children manage to receive some detailed instructions without needing to express themselves verbally. They have been working on a project where they have to paste together geometric shapes to form a bird:

> **Mark** (English): [holds out his partially finished bird for inspection]
> **Sra. Soto:** Tienes que pegar la cola. Tienes que pegar las alas… (*You have to paste the tail. You have to paste the wings…*) [holds her hands out to her sides and flaps them to imitate flying] …y el pelo. (*…and the hair*) [places hand on top of her head with fingers splayed to imitate a bird's top feathers]
> **Sandra** (English): [approaches Sra. Soto holding up the pieces of the bird all drawn on one piece of paper, she has not cut them out yet]
> **Sra. Soto:** Tienes que cortar… (*You have to cut…*) [cuts the paper in half with scissors] …porque esta parte va pegada acá. (*because this part gets pasted here*) [places the pieces together in the way they should be pasted]

These two children are both English speakers, and Sra. Soto uses gestures involving the physical objects to make her instruction clear. These children, who obviously did not understand the instructions as given earlier, had another opportunity as they approached Sra. Soto with their problems and heard her repeat her instructions in Spanish with gestural context.

While this example suggests that the majority of problem-based interactions during Tables time consisted of a series of private interactions between Sra. Soto and an individual child, other children often participated in these exchanges between Sra. Soto and the child with the problem. In the following example, Sra. Soto sits with Khamil, a Spanish speaker, who has failed to complete his assignment correctly. On this day, the children have been working on a worksheet that requires them to count the number of differently colored shapes on a piece of paper, and write the number on the paper. Sra. Soto kneels on the floor next to Khamil and guides him step by step through this activity. Mark, Oscar and Lucía, who are sitting at Khamil's table, participate in different ways during the exchange:

> **Sra. Soto:** ¿Qué color quieres hacer ahora? ¿Qué color te hace falta? (*What color do you want to do now? What color are you missing?*)
> **Khamil** (English): [inaudible response]
> **Sra. Soto:** [affirmingly] Azul. Cuenta los azules. (*Blue. Count the blues*)
> **Khamil** (English): [points to his paper, quietly counting 1 through 6 in Spanish]
> **Sra. Soto:** Seis. Busca el azul y pon seis. (*Six. Look for the blue and put 6*) [A few seconds pass and Khamil still hasn't written anything]
> **Sra. Soto:** Vamos a ver los números, muchacho. (*Let's look at the numbers, boy*) [begins to write numbers from one to ten on a piece of paper, saying them out loud in Spanish as she does] Uno, dos, tres, cuatro, cinco, seis, siete, ocho, nueve, diez. ¿Dónde está el seis? Cuéntalos hasta que llegues a seis. (*Where's the six? Count them until you get to six*) [leans over the paper, pointing to the numbers and counts out loud with him] Uno, dos... (*One, two...*) [falls silent, continuing to point as Khamil continues to count and point]
> **Khamil** (English): [counts the numbers out loud in Spanish as both he and Sra. Soto point to them]
> **Mark** (English): [has been watching them intently while working on his own paper, now leans over the table and points to Khamil's paper] Seis. (*Six*)
> **Sra. Soto:** [waves him away dismissively with a flick of her hand, looking at Khamil] Muéstrame seis. (*Show me six*)
> **Khamil** (English): [points to his paper]
> **Sra. Soto:** [nods affirmingly]
> **Khamil** (English): [writes on his paper]
> **Sra. Soto:** Seis, Khamil, está muy guapo. (*Six, Khamil. That's very nice*)

In this segment, Mark is observing closely the interaction between Sra. Soto and Khamil, and his participation suggests that he has been watching carefully enough to point out the correct answer to Sra. Soto's question. While she does not encourage him (gesturing dismissively), Mark continues to participate by silently watching. This participation enables him to benefit peripherally from the exchange, attending to and understanding the simple language Sra. Soto uses. Lucía (Spanish), sitting across the table from Khamil and working silently on her own paper, is also participating peripherally by listening and glancing occasionally over at Khamil and Sra. Soto. Similarly, Oscar, who is sitting next to Khamil, participates by silently listening and casting sideways glances at Khamil's paper. As the segment continues, both Oscar and Mark continue to watch the exchange and eventually participate verbally:

> **Sra. Soto:** [to Khamil] ¿Qué te falta contar? ¿Qué color? ¿Qué color es esto? (*What do you have left to count? What color? What color is this?*) [points to the paper]
> **Khamil** (English): Azul. (*Blue*)
> **Sra. Soto:** Eso no es azul (*That's not blue*)
> **Mark** (English): Verde. (*Green*)
> **Sra. Soto:** Verde. Cuenta los verdes. (*Green. Count the greens*)
> **Khamil** (English): [points to his paper, quietly counting 1 through 9 in Spanish]
> **Sra. Soto:** Nueve. Busca el nueve. ¿Dónde está el nueve? (*Nine. Look for the 9. Where's the 9?*)
> **Khamil** (English): [Points to the wrong number on the paper]
> **Sra. Soto:** Eso no es nueve. Tú pones cualquiera cosa. ¿Qué dice aquí? (*That's not nine. You're just putting anything. What does it say here?*)
> **Khamil** (English): [points to the numbers on Sra. Soto's paper as he counts to 9 in Spanish]
> **Oscar** (Spanish): [counts out loud in Spanish along with Rashid]
> **Sra. Soto:** Nueve. Allí está el nueve. Pon nueve. (*Nine. There's the nine. Put nine*) [pointing to another color] ¿Qué color te falta hacer ahora? (*What color do you have left to do now?*)

The exchange continues as Sra. Soto guides Khamil through counting the brown shapes (there were two and he has to write two) and the red shapes (there were none and he has to put zero).

During the time that Sra. Soto was working individually with Khamil, Emilio (Spanish) and Dorinda (English) approached Sra. Soto and stood quietly for a few seconds waiting for her to notice them so they could ask a question about their own projects. While they waited, they were also watching the exchange between Sra. Soto and Khamil. Toward the end of the segment, four other children gathered around the table, quietly watching the exchange. It is interesting to note that there was no verbal interaction among the other three children at the table during this exchange (Oscar, Mark and Lucía), nor among the children standing around watching. Even the children sitting and working at a nearby table worked silently. This suggests that the only interaction inspired by this Tables time activity was that of Sra. Soto helping Khamil with his problem.

Fostering (Spanish) Language Interactions: Sra. Soto as the 'Eye of the Hurricane'

Sra. Soto assigned the children to their tables, and each table consisted of a carefully mixed group of English and Spanish speakers. Nevertheless, even when some conversation arose, the tendency was to shift to English. At the end of Chapter 4, I focused on Berto, a native Spanish speaker who, despite his relative lack of English proficiency seemed to prefer to speak in English. Even under the conditions that might seem to most strongly favor the use of Spanish (interactions with other Spanish natives during official Spanish time), Berto insisted on speaking Spanish. Here, I will revisit this exchange in more detail as an example of the kind of (minimal, English) language dynamic that tended to emerge during Tables time and illustrate Sra. Soto's efforts to shift this dynamic.

In the following excerpt, the conditions were ideal to promote Spanish conversation. There was a disagreement that required discussion. The children at the table were three native Spanish speakers (Joël, Wilma and Berto) and one English speaker, Sandra. As described in Chapter 4, Sandra lived with her Spanish-speaking father, and, although her parents spoke English to each other at home, Sra. Soto identified her as one of the classroom's Spanish 'role models'. Therefore, seated around this particular table were three native Spanish speakers and one English speaker who was highly motivated to speak Spanish and had demonstrated some basic proficiency by the time of this exchange, which took place toward the end of January.

The children are working on a project where they need to cut out and arrange geometric shapes into the form of a penguin. They begin silently, and work for several minutes silently on their projects until Wilma initiates an argument, in Spanish, about whether they need to color the penguin parts first (the beginning of this argument is detailed in Chapter 4). Berto vehemently disagrees, in English. After a few exchanges, Berto finally exclaims:

> **Berto** (Spanish): OK. I'm looking. But you don't have to talk... I should know what... everything what I'm doing, girl.

Although Wilma dutifully initiates this Tables time discussion in Spanish, the conversation drifts into English until Sra. Soto intervenes in

Spanish. Wilma has been gesturing at her own paper, trying to convince Berto that he should color his penguins as she has done, because Sra. Soto said to do it that way, and Berto has remained adamant that he knows what he is doing. Wilma then calls on Sra. Soto to come over and solve the dispute:

> **Wilma** (Spanish): [looks over to the other side of the room, where Sra. Soto is working with another child, and calls loudly] ¡Sra. Soto!
> **Sra. Soto:** ¿Sí? (*Yes?*)
> **Wilma** (Spanish): ¡Venga! (*Come here!*)
> **Berto** (Spanish): [turns to Sandra, who is working on the other side of him] Look, a penguin. You doin' it wrong!

Despite Wilma's use of Spanish, Berto continues his side of the conversation in English, even though he is not particularly fluent in English. He is still arguing with Sandra, criticizing her penguin in English, when Sra. Soto approaches the table:

> **Sra. Soto:** [looking at Berto's paper] Muy bien, Berto, y tú las coloreas, y las cuentas y las pones... (*Very good, Berto. And you color them, and count them, and put them...*)

Sra. Soto's response indicates that he has done some but not all of the work, and she describes the parts of the assignment that he has missed, not as commands but more as a simple list of activities. Berto has not colored his shapes, which is what Wilma was pointing out to him at the beginning of the exchange. Despite Sra. Soto's intervention in Spanish, Berto immediately addresses the two girls in English, only reverting to Spanish when Sra. Soto directly demands it:

> **Berto** (Spanish): [interrupting Sra. Soto and addressing Sandra] Look, look at mine, see... yellow yellow, red, red, green... [continues, naming all the colored shapes he has placed inside his penguin outline]
> **Wilma** (Spanish): [to Berto] Come on over here, help me.
> **Berto** (Spanish): You want me to do it for you?
> **Wilma** (Spanish): First you need to put the triangle...
> **Berto** (Spanish): [interrupting] First you need to put this, girl.
> **Sra. Soto:** Bien hecho, pero tienes que poner los números (*Well, done, but you have to put the numbers*)
> **Berto** (Spanish): [counts softly to himself in Spanish] uno, dos, tres, cuatro... (*one, two, three, four...*) Sra. Soto, I done it.

Sra. Soto: Yo no te entiendo. (*I don't understand you*)
Berto (Spanish): Lo terminé. (*I finished*)

Berto continues to speak in English, even with Sra. Soto, only speaking in Spanish when he counts out loud and when specifically demanded by Sra. Soto. As the segment continues, Sra. Soto asks him guiding questions entirely in Spanish as she did in the example with Khamil and Berto, while he provides simple one word responses concerning colors and numbers in Spanish, still uses English for the statements he generates without her prompting:

> **Sra. Soto:** [standing by Berto and looking down at his paper] Ahora. Vamos a ver. ¿Qué color es esto? (*Now. Let's see. What color is this?*)
> **Berto** (Spanish): Azul. (*Blue*)
> **Sra. Soto:** ¿Cuántos azules tienes? Cuéntalos. (*How many blues do you have? Count them*)
> **Berto** (Spanish): Dos. (*Two*)
> **Sra. Soto:** Dos. ¿Qué número es ese? (*Two. What number is that?*) [pointing to the place on his paper where he should have recorded the '2']
> **Berto** (Spanish): Ocho. (*Eight*)
> **Sra. Soto:** Ahh. Pero no es el ocho. ¿Qué número es? ¿Qué necesitas? (*Ahh. But that's not eight. What number is it? What do you need?*)
> **Berto** (Spanish): Dos. (*Two*) [pauses, then adds in an irritated voice] But somebody messed it up! [turns to Sandra] Sandra, do like me!
> **Sandra** (English): I don't want to.

As described earlier in this chapter, the ideal of the TWI classroom, where children learn a second language through interaction with children for whom their second language is a native language, is not evident in this segment. The native Spanish speakers, as illustrated by Berto above, are often reluctant to speak Spanish even with other Spanish natives, even during official Spanish time and even, as in Berto's case, when their English is not highly developed. This tendency seemed to substantiate Sra. Soto's concern, as expressed in Chapter 4, that the Spanish-speaking children have 'given away' their Spanish.

Most Spanish conversation during Tables time could be heard centering on Sra. Soto, as she circulated among the children and helped them solve their problems. Otherwise, the children conversed mainly in English, or not at all. As Sra. Soto circulated throughout the room, only those children who asked her for help, or whom she singled out to help, had the opportunity to interact with her, as well as the few children who happened to be standing or sitting nearby, as illustrated in this chapter. Therefore, contrary to Sra. Soto's expectation that working together on tasks would result in cross-linguistic language-learning opportunities, this activity structure seemed to provide few opportunities for language learning, and those few tended to require Sra. Soto's direct participation. I suspect that this was due not only to the preference some Spanish speakers had for English, but also to the activity structure of Tables time, which consisted of activities that were to be completed individually by physical means (cutting, coloring, pasting, writing), which did not require much verbal communication. Merely sharing a table and materials did not seem enough to provoke much interaction, verbal or otherwise, among the children.

Sra. Soto noticed this phenomenon and referred to herself as 'the eye of the hurricane', observing that as she moved through the room, conversation seemed to follow her, while the children she was not engaging with tended to remain quiet. As the children worked during Tables time, those with problems completing their activities tended to attract Sra. Soto's attention, while others whose projects were proceeding without problems, worked quietly. In summary, the Tables time task-completion phase, while intended to generate conversation, generated conversation mainly when problems arose, and these verbal exchanges were mainly in English unless Sra. Soto intervened.

Focus on Rashid: From Legitimate to Illegitimate Participation

Rashid was an African-American child who had not had any experience with Spanish before he entered this classroom. Sra. Soto described him as a very bright child with a strong English foundation that allowed him to pick up Spanish skills such as 'alphabet, letters sounds, writing, etc.' quickly. Nevertheless, she reported that his mother and step-father, with whom he lived at the beginning of the year, had some problems that eventually resulted in Rashid moving in with his biological father, whom Sra. Soto described as very nice but 'lax about maintaining a school routine'. She reported that Rashid's performance dropped toward the end of the school year as a result of his changing family situation. I noticed that Rashid was quite popular with the other children and that he generally participated enthusiastically and well in class activities. He was not, however, quite as enthusiastic about speaking Spanish as some of the other English speakers (such as the twins Emily and Sandra, and Kathleen). As illustrated at the beginning of this book, Rashid was quite aware of the Spanish-only rule in the mornings, but was not averse to breaking it in the interest of easy communication:

> **Rashid** (English): [in a whisper to researcher] Why was Sra. Soto laughing?
> **Researcher:** [shakes head, shrugs shoulders] Why are you speaking to me in English?
> **Rashid** (Spanish): Because I don't know Spanish.
> **Researcher** [glances over at Sra. Soto]
> **Rashid** (English): [smiles, tilts heads, touches researcher's arm] No no no. Don't tell her. I was only tricking you.

While Rashid was fully aware that he was meant to speak in Spanish during official Spanish time, he also seemed aware that there were situations where he could participate in Spanish conversations with Sra. Soto without needing to express himself in Spanish.

In the following excerpt, Rashid participates almost entirely in English, as Sra. Soto continues to address him in Spanish. The children are working on a project where a flower person is represented by a stem-based body and a flower-based face. Rashid has completed the stem part, but seems unsure how to add the flower part, where a white piece of paper representing a face is decorated with flower petals all around. He approaches Sra. Soto, holding up his stem, and initiates the exchange in English:

> **Rashid** (English): [holding up his flower stem for Sra. Soto to see] How do I do like a face?
> **Sra. Soto:** ¿Pegaste la cabeza? ¿Dónde está tu cabeza? (*Did you paste the head? Where is your head?*)
> **Rashid** (English): [ignoring the questions] How do I do it?
> **Sra. Soto** [turns to talk with another child who has asked for help]
> **Rashid** (English): [walks off and returns with a white piece of paper and holds it out to Sra. Soto]
> **Sra. Soto:** [taking the paper] Tienes que cortar esto acá... (*You have to cut this here*) [indicating on the paper with a circular motion that the pattern of petals on the outside need to be removed] ...Y pegar los pétalos acá. (*And paste the petals here*) [indicating with gesture where the cut petals need to be individually glued back]
> **Rashid** (English): You have to cut all these off... [taking the paper and repeating her hand motions as he speaks]
> **Sra. Soto:** [interrupting] Dímelo en español. (*Say it to me in Spanish*)

Rashid (English): [looks at her, silently]
Sra. Soto: Corto... (*I cut*)
Rashid (English): [in a weak voice] Corto... (*I cut*)
Sra. Soto: ¿Sabes qué? Necesitas una cara nueva. (*You know what? You need a new face*)
Rashid (English): [steps back, imitating again her previous hand motions on the paper]

Sra. Soto never finished the sentence she wanted Rashid to repeat, but instead finished the interaction with him by instructing him to start over again with a new paper flower face. Perhaps this was because she was attending to several other children at the same time and was distracted. It was certainly unusual behavior for Sra. Soto, who often required children to repeat words and phrases until they said them correctly (as illustrated by her painstaking exchange with Khamil described earlier in this chapter). Nevertheless, this seemed to be a valuable learning moment for Rashid, who was able to participate in the officially Spanish exchange.

It was not clear from this exchange how much of Sra. Soto's Spanish instructions Rashid understood, but it was apparent that he was reluctant to speak in Spanish, clearly preferring to address his problem to Sra. Soto in English. He seemed to be attending to Sra. Soto's non-verbal gestural cues, imitating her hand motions, and he even repeated her Spanish instructions in English (you have to cut it here), indicating that he understood at least some of her instructions.

Rashid's legitimate participation in this Tables time exchange contrasts sharply with his participation in the following segment. In this case, Sra. Soto's insistence on checking to make sure that Rashid has understood her (and has paid attention) transforms his actions into illegitimate participation, resulting in a more adversarial relationship.

In the Housekeeping Center, Sra. Soto, Rashid and Sandra are sitting around a low table that is covered with plastic food, plates and cups. Sra. Soto has been pretending to eat and drink while asking Sandra to name the items that she is eating and drinking. Sandra has been dutifully doing so, while Rashid has been silently pretending to prepare himself a tea using the plastic tea set. Judging by her tone of voice, Sra. Soto is annoyed with Rashid because he has not been paying attention to her exchange with Sandra:

Sra. Soto: [turns to Rashid] ¿Tú me estas escuchando, Rashid? Mira, Rashid. ¿Qué es esto que me voy a comer(sic)? (*Are you listening to me, Rashid? Look, Rashid. What's this, what am I going to eat?*) [brings a glass of orange juice to her lips]

Rashid (English): [looks at her without answering]

Sra. Soto: [forming the first syllable of the word and waiting for Rashid to finish it] ju-... ju-...

Rashid (English): Jugo (*Juice*)

Sra. Soto: Jugo. ¿Jugo de qué? (*Juice. What kind of juice?*)

Rashid (English): [looks at Sra. Soto but does not respond)

Sra. Soto: De na-... [waits for him to finish the word for her]

Rashid (English): [continues to look at her silently]

Sra. Soto: [takes Rashid's hand] Estoy hablando contigo. Jugo de naranja. Dilo. (*I am talking to you. Orange juice. Say it*)

Rashid (English): [reaches out to pick up a glass of orange juice from the table]

Sra. Soto: [catches his hand and guides it firmly to the table, forcing him to put the glass back down] Mírame. Mira. Tú estás jugando. No estás prestándome tu atención. (*Look at me. Look. You are playing. You aren't paying attention to me*) [begins to repeat the first syllable of the word, again for him to finish] Ju-...

Rashid (English): [slowly finishes the full phrase] Jugo de naranja. (*Orange juice*)

Rashid's confusion here may very well have been due to an inability to guess correctly the nature of Sra. Soto's request, since he reached for the orange juice rather than simply repeating the word, but he did eventually repeat the phrase correctly (see DePalma, 2006 for a more detailed examination of this exchange). Unlike in their Tables time exchange above, where both Sra. Soto and Rashid were focused on the flower-making activity, Sra. Soto focused here on making sure that Rashid 'learned', that is, making sure that he demonstrated that he paid proper attention and could successfully repeat her phrases in English. Rashid was focusing on other aspects of the activity. Not unreasonably, since it was a play Center, he played at making tea, and then started to play at drinking orange juice until he was firmly redirected. By continuing to focus on the play activity at hand when Sra. Soto had shifted the activity from a play context to a more school-like vocabulary exercise, Rashid became an illegitimate participant, and was chastised for it.

Analysis: Defining Legitimate Participation through Activity Structures

Tables time activities were originally planned as activity Centers that would foster language interactions among the group; recall from Chapter 3 that Sra. Soto was critical of one science teacher at Calvary whose science centers were too strongly directed by the teacher and did not allow children to explore sufficiently on their own. Nevertheless, in these Tables time activities, the children were expected to follow the instructions carefully and use the materials properly, which did not require much interaction among the children or between the children and Sra. Soto. I have argued elsewhere that children who meticulously follow instructions for independent cutting, pasting and drawing/writing activities can actually miss out on opportunities for language interaction (DePalma, 2008). I argue here that, despite the fact that they were carefully connected to other curricular activities and completed around group tables rather than individual desks, these Tables time projects were inherently individualized physical tasks and so they were not as conducive to language interactions as Sra. Soto had hoped.

On the other hand, while not especially successful in generating target-language conversation, Tables time did offer the children the opportunity to participate in Spanish language exchanges with Sra. Soto. The fact that the children did not need to be able to produce much complex language did not prohibit them from communicating with her. Sra. Soto employed a variety of strategies to make the language comprehensible, including linguistic redundancy and gestures. She provided highly contextualized instructions that supported comprehension. She allowed the children to participate with her in Spanish interactions while they were still relatively non-fluent, by allowing them to respond in English or non-verbally.

Recall from Chapter 3 that Sra. Soto explicitly described her pedagogical technique as scaffolding, or 'forms of support... to help students bridge the gap between their current abilities and the intended goal' (Rosenshine, 1992: 26). This definition parallels Vygotsky's (1978: 86) notion of teaching within the zone of proximal development (ZPD), defined as 'the distance between actual developmental level as determined by independent problem solving and the level of potential development as determined through problem solving under adult guidance or in collaboration with more capable peers'. Nevertheless, while the notion of scaffolding assumes learner and teacher roles to be clearly defined and established prior to the relationship, some interpretations of the ZPD take into account the distribution of power in classrooms and the ways in which new meanings and social relationships are negotiated within these contexts (Lee & Smagorinsky, 2000).

Vygotsky's emphasis on the social contexts of learning has inspired sociocultural and activity theory approaches to learning that treat learning as a shared and culturally mediated practice (Moll, 1990). Going beyond notions of comprehensible input and opportunities for output, which are based on the concept that language is a container in which ideas as objects are sent from one individual to another (Lantolf & Thorne, 2006), a sociocultural approach sees communication and learning as jointly constructed. This understanding shifts the focus from the learner's head as the site of learning to new meanings co-constructed within communities of learners. Language is not separable from the social contexts within which it exists, 'Every social language communicates in use, as it creates and reflects specific social contexts, socially-situated identities that are integrally connected to social groups, cultures, and historical formations' (Hawkins, 2004: 3).

Classrooms whose organization and practices are based on an understanding of the child as an individual learner can impede language-learning processes and marginalize those who most rely on community processes (Toohey, 1998). The cultural and historical analysis of social relationships that form among participants allows us to bring certain questions to bear on Roseshine's definition of scaffolding: What kind of relationships constitute (and detract from) support for learning? How are learning goals defined? Who defines these goals, and how do cultural understandings and institutional contexts mediate these definitions? How are learners themselves socially constructed through their participation in learning communities, of which a classroom is just one example?

From a sociocultural perspective, Sra. Soto's conversations in Spanish with the children might be considered an example of legitimate peripheral participation (Lave & Wenger, 1991), that is, a form of participation that does not require learners to be experts in order to participate in the activities of the community. In this case, the activity in question is participating in Spanish communication (while various other activities, such as producing a paper bird and monitoring peer progress, are concurrent and interconnecting). Members of the community of learners range from highly expert Spanish speakers (Sra. Soto) to barely competent ones (English natives who have just recently been introduced to the language). Sra. Soto, in collaboration with the children, creates contexts in which the child need not carry equal responsibility for maintaining the conversation in order to participate in the conversation. In these Tables time examples, the children barely speak, but participate in less verbal ways, i.e. holding out an unfinished project.

Rashid's behavior during Tables time constituted learning through peripheral participation. Even though his participation at this point can be considered very peripheral, he was learning aspects of the language that may gradually allow him to be able to participate more fully. Rashid's learning as he asked for help making a flower during Tables time was almost undetectable, since he did not perform the kind of easily identified and quantifiable learning that might be more satisfying to the teacher (as might be the case, for example, if he simply repeated a word correctly in Spanish). Yet Sra. Soto treats his participation as legitimate, even though he speaks almost entirely in English, which provides him with an opportunity to learn within the activity.

This learning community provides opportunities for moving from peripheral to full participation (many learners will eventually become more fully bilingual), and the questions raised earlier about the nature of scaffolding apply here, as they do to any social context in which learning takes place. We need to look at how the legitimacy of legitimate peripheral participation is defined and how this, in turn, defines learners. We have already seen how Dorinda was characterized as both an enthusiastic learner (in terms of chants) and a reluctant learner (in terms of less structured learning activities). We have seen that Emily and Sandra were constructed as successful learners at least in part because they were able to follow and even anticipate the teacher's thematic planning structure. We have seen that Emily and Sandra were constructed as Spanish role models, even though they were not particularly proficient in Spanish, while Berto failed to be constructed as a Spanish role model, despite the fact that he was a proficient Spanish speaker. In this chapter, we see how Rashid, a reluctant Spanish learner, tended to hover on the brink of legitimate participation, at times benefiting from the chance to participate despite his limitations and at times failing to participate in ways defined in this classroom as legitimate.

As the teacher, Sra. Soto defined legitimate participation by referring to her multiple institutional mandates (district curriculum guidelines, the expectations of first grade teachers) as well as her own professional understandings and personal values (as described in Chapter 3). These multiple goals and values interacted in various, sometimes conflicting ways, and made guessing the rules for legitimate participation tricky at times. While in the more strongly teacher-directed activities, it was up to the children to determine whether they should raise their hands, call out answers, sit still or walk over to point something out, Sra. Soto was faced with the task of figuring out how to participate when, as in the Housekeeping and Play Centers, the activities were supposed to be structured by the children.

When she was the center of the activity, the children could participate in all sorts of ways, including by simply observing from a distance. Language learning, as well as other forms of learning, took place in various quiet ways, although it was not always easily measurable. This is particularly apparent in the task-explanation phase of Tables time activities. As Sra. Soto explained the activity, the children did not speak much, but were usually highly engaged. They listened as Sra. Soto spoke and tended to participate eagerly, albeit often in rather brief Spanish utterances or English phrases. Nevertheless, they were participating fully in a predominantly Spanish interaction with the teacher, using Spanish as a medium through which they received, at times, rather complex instructions. Sra. Soto facilitated this comprehension with repetition of certain key phrases (*¿Qué color es esto?*), physical gestures (opening her hands to imitate a book) and graphic representations (the chart with pictures and words). Generally, the children voluntarily attended and participated (along the lines of Dorinda's enthusiastic contribution here). When they didn't attend and participate, she explicitly requested that they do so, which, as in the case of Kathleen, might mean more directly involving them in the exchange.

In this particular activity structure, Sra. Soto's techniques of demanding attention while providing input and asking known-answer questions to check for comprehension, perhaps stemming from her expertise in direct teaching methodology, provided valuable comprehensible input (Krashen, 1985) and permitted a range of strategies for legitimate peripheral participation. Sra. Soto was highly skilled at maintaining this participation when she was, in her words, the eye of the hurricane, but the children were not as likely to remain engaged in ways the teacher deemed legitimate when she was expected to take a less central role. This was evident even when she had designed the activity specifically to work without her, as in the Tables time task-completion phase and the even less structured play Centers. As her brief exchange with Rashid in the Housekeeping play Center illustrates, her participation tended to transform her designed child-centered activities into something very different. By transforming the rules of the activity, she de-legitimized a form of participation that might have been perfectly legitimate in a genuine play activity. In the following chapter, I will examine more closely the nature of the children's interactions in these play Centers, which were designed to be informal, child-centered spaces for promoting Spanish conversation, as well as the ways in which these activity structures changed when Sra. Soto participated in them.

Chapter 8

Housekeeping and Blocks Centers: Keeping them Talking

Recall from Chapter 3 that during our tour of Calvary School, Sra. Soto identified the overall principle of two-way immersion (TWI) program design as 'designing instructional activities to promote desired interactions among the children'. While this was not particularly evident in any of the classroom activity structures described in the preceding three chapters, this perspective was reflected in her design of the Housekeeping and Blocks Centers. It is also useful to keep in mind Sra. Soto's criticism of the Calvary teacher's science lesson, 'Her Centers were very teacher-oriented, without enough exploration on the part of the kids. She was guiding them, and I was disturbed by that'. These reflections suggest that, at least in terms of Centers design, Sra. Soto considered interactions among children to be crucial and to be fostered by indirect design rather than by the kind of direct teacher–student interactions characteristic of the other classroom activities.

The Centers always took place in the morning, during Spanish time. Two large sections of the classroom were designated as play Centers, Blocks (*La Zona de Construcción*) and Housekeeping (*La Casa*). The Centers were side by side, occupying about one third of the classroom space, and the name of each Center was written clearly in both Spanish and English, displayed prominently on the wall within each Center. Center play was a voluntary activity; when the children finished their work at the tables, they were allowed to choose which of these Centers they wished to play in, and their wish was usually granted as long as they were able to make the request in Spanish. Both Centers seemed highly popular. Sra. Soto eventually decreed that no more than four children at a time could participate in each Center, but this rule was only occasionally invoked. Usually, the Centers were fully occupied by children moving freely between the two Centers, creating an atmosphere of rather chaotic enjoyment.

The Blocks Center emphasized construction activities and was fully stocked with relevant materials including plastic and wooden building blocks and a snap-together plastic highway with toy cars, trucks and

149

buildings. In January, Sra. Soto added a workshop (*taller*), a large plastic work station with plastic tools hanging from the sides, around which children gathered, banging and pounding enthusiastically with the plastic tools. Sra. Soto was pleased that the children were having so much fun with the *taller* and she was particularly pleased that girls were happily hammering and sawing away there, since one of her classroom goals was to encourage children to stretch themselves beyond gender stereotypical behaviors (construction for boys and playing house for girls). Nevertheless, the *taller* was extremely noisy and actually made conversation impossible, not that the children even tried. The *taller* in the Blocks Center was a good illustration of how Sra. Soto's multiple classroom goals sometimes conflicted, a theme that will be taken up again later in this chapter.

The Housekeeping Center was characterized by role-playing domestic activity. Toys provided consisted of household furniture, including a low, round, wooden table and several child-sized plastic chairs; appliances, including a play sink, stove, cabinets; and a tall cupboard with doors and shelves, part of which was designated the refrigerator/freezer. A wide selection of baby dolls and a crib was designed to nurture family play; additionally, there were household utensils, including small pots and pans, plastic plates, glasses, cups and silverware. A mirror and a toy chest filled with clothes and hats provided materials for dressing up. As in the Blocks Center, Sra. Soto eventually designed a particular themed play station in Housekeeping. Toward the middle of the year a store was set up, complete with two cash registers, a conveyer belt, a scale, baskets and play money. As described in Chapter 4, during official Spanish time this was designed as a Mexican *tienda* (where customers would naturally be expected to speak only Spanish).

Sra. Soto made several comments to me throughout the year, defining the 'desired interactions' that children should have while playing in the Centers as 'conversation', which meant practicing Spanish by talking to each other as they played. Toward the end of January, she initiated a policy where children had to pick a language partner who spoke a different language to play with in the Centers. On the blackboard in the front of the room, she taped two columns of the children's photos, one column for children who spoke English at home, and the other for children who spoke Spanish at home. She reported to me that this was in response to her observation that the children were not talking with each other in the Centers and that Spanish speakers and English speakers did not tend to play with each other. Recall from Chapter 3 that Sra. Soto saw this language partner practice as embedded in the broader classroom theme of helping each other, which was also reflected in the classroom stories:

> I said (to the children) "how are we going to get better at speaking Spanish?" And I said it to them during English time. I said by practicing more Spanish. When do we do that? During Spanish time. Well, who can we do that with? With our friends. Because our friends are here to help us. I tried to tie it all together... and we've been doing it with the concept of our African tales... a lot of them were about helping one another, that cooperative spirit.

This policy is reflected in the following exchange, where Sra. Soto directs Dorinda (English) to select a Spanish-speaking language partner before entering Housekeeping. Dorinda (English speaker) approaches Sra. Soto in the Tables area, as usual, to ask permission to enter Housekeeping, and Sra. Soto directs her to identify a partner:

> **Dorinda** (English): [approaches Sra. Soto] ¿Yo pue (sic) jugar? (*I can play?*)
>
> **Sra. Soto:** ¿Con quién, quién es tu compañera? ¿Quién? (*With whom, who is your partner? Who?*)
>
> **Dorinda** (English): Alicia [using English pronunciation]
>
> **Sra. Soto:** [turning toward Alicia and repeating her name with the Spanish pronunciation] Alicia. Alicia. ¿Terminaste? (*Alicia. Alicia, did you finish?*) [turning back to Dorinda] Anda. ¿Qué le pides? Dorinda, ¿qué le pides a ella? ¿Qué le dices? (*Go ahead. What do you ask her? Dorinda, what do you ask her? What do you say to her?*)
>
> **Dorinda** (English): [silence]
>
> **Sra. Soto:** [slowly] ¿Puedes... jugar... conmigo? (*Can you play with me?*)
>
> **Dorinda** (English): [joining in to say the last two words together with her, with a split second delay] ¿... jugar... conmigo? (*play... with me?*)

Once Dorinda has identified her Spanish language partner and has invited her in Spanish to play with her, the two girls are permitted to enter Housekeeping.

However, despite Sra. Soto's efforts to establish a play dynamic that would encourage Spanish interaction during play, the girls hardly spoke together as they played together. They happily bustled around, moving objects from the stove area to the table and back again, but there was very little linguistic interaction in any language. As I will illustrate in the following section, both Sra. Soto and I noticed that the Centers play did not meet Sra. Soto's curriculum goal of promoting language development, despite her conviction that play would lead to conversation in the target language. In Chapter 4, we saw that the children tended to speak in English with each other even during official Spanish time. While this tendency extended to the play Centers as well, both of us observed that the children's play interactions often didn't involve very much linguistic interaction of any kind.

Sra. Soto explained at the end of the year, as she reflected on her Centers design, 'I wanted them to practice the language I was teaching them, there in the Centers'. She explicitly connected conversation to play, 'We as adults, we banter with each other and we talk and we, you know, we play. We are actually having a play right now, conversing with each other'. Nevertheless, to her disappointment, the play Centers did not seem to support this goal of generating conversation among the children through play.

The Failure of Centers Play to Promote Conversation

The tendency of the children to play in the Centers with very little language interaction is exemplified by the following incident in the Blocks Centers. Rashid and Sandra, both English natives, are playing together during official Spanish time. They are making a train by snapping the plastic cars together:

> **Rashid** (English): [silently snaps another plastic car onto the growing train]
> **Sandra** (English): [silently hands Rashid a train car she finds in the plastic bin]
> **Rashid** (English): [takes it and silently snaps it onto the train]
> **Sandra** (English): [reaches toward the train and reverses the direction of one of the cars]
> **Rashid** (English): [snaps the reversed car into place]
> **Sandra** (English): I'll put people in the car. [moves off to the plastic bin in the corner to search for the little plastic people that fit into the cars] Here. [hands Rashid a plastic person]

The play described in this segment involved very little verbal interaction, and no interaction in Spanish, the officially designated language. The silences were long: as I watched this video clip, I counted 23 seconds of silence from the beginning of the segment to Sandra's first utterance, an English declaration that she will find people to put into their train. Another period of 19 seconds silence ensued while she searched through the plastic bin, broken finally by the single English word 'here' as she handed the people to her play partner, Rashid. As the segment continues, the children speak a bit more, still in English, when a conflict emerges that must be negotiated:

Sandra (English): [unsnaps a piece of the train and, making a motor noise, rolls it over to the corner]
Rashid (English): Don't do it!
Sandra (English): I'm gonna put the people in the car.
Rashid (English): [follows her to the corner] No, you gotta put the wheels on.
Sandra (English): No, I'm gonna put the people in first.
Rashid (English): [grabs the car from Sandra] It goes here first, look! It goes on that car.
Sandra (English): [as Rashid is pulling the toy car from her grasp] No, I didn't... [pauses, then lets go of the toy] You got it.

This silent play only became verbal interaction when the play needed to be negotiated. In the beginning, Rashid and Sandra were happily playing together with little need to speak, since their play was smoothly coordinated (Sandra found the cars and Rashid snapped them on). When a difference of opinion emerged (whether to snap together the trains before or after adding the people), language was used as a means of negotiating, convincing, explaining one's view.

In Housekeeping, the children engaged in very different activities as afforded by the different play items provided. Nevertheless, as in Blocks, the play was often characterized by nearly silent physical activity, as illustrated by the following segment. As the segment begins, Amalia is silently bustling around, setting the table with plastic plates, cups and utensils. First Sandra and then Alberta enter the play scenario, and each child simply observes what is going on and moves to take up her place in the collective but silent play scenario of preparing a meal:

Amalia (Spanish): [setting the table silently and alone]
Sandra (English): [enters, does not acknowledge Amalia but goes directly to the cupboard and takes out a plastic bin full of pots, pans, plates, etc. and puts it on the counter]
Alberta (Spanish): [enters and goes directly to the stove, looks inside, turns the plastic dial to 'on'. Walks over and takes a plastic bin full of plastic food from the cupboard, carries it to the counter by the sink, reaches under the cupboard by the sink to retrieve some plastic pots and pans, and begins to cook]

Sandra (English): [goes to the cupboard to get a bin of plastic glasses and begins to set the table with them]
Amalia (Spanish): [pretends to eat a plastic ice cream cone as she sets the table, steps back and licks the ice cream cone thoughtfully as she looks at the table, and then runs to the cupboard to get something]
Alberta (Spanish): [runs over from the sink to the table and looks intently at the table for a few seconds, than runs back to the sink and continues cooking]

Not a word is exchanged among the girls throughout this entire play scenario, even when the two girls each enter for the first time.

My own interpretation of this phenomenon was that the girls were playing at work, at the serious and familiar business of running a household. The girls were silent and apparently unengaged with each other because, like at the beginning of the train-building play between Sandra and Rashid, everyone understood and agreed on what needed to be done. The play roles were integrated smoothly into the whole play scenario, in this case probably because each girl was very familiar with the way cooking, washing up and setting a table are coordinated household activities. There was no need for conversation because the girls shared a cultural framework for understanding the overall activity and the parts they played in it, and because each seemed to be content with her role. There was, quite simply, nothing to talk about, and the girls proceeded silently as they may well have done, and/or seen others do, at home.

However, Sra. Soto and I discussed these kinds of relatively silent Centers play scenarios throughout the year, and it became clear that our interpretations of this phenomenon were different. To begin with, Sra. Soto understandably reflected on this silence through the lens of her teaching goals. She had hoped to design the Centers to promote conversation, and so, not surprisingly, she interpreted the Centers activity in terms of its lack, 'There was no conversation going on there'.

Sra. Soto's ongoing commentary on the children's play further revealed her definition of play as not simply an activity engaged in by children, but one that required certain skills, suggesting that a child could be a relatively skilled or unskilled player. During one of our conversations, which I paraphrased in my journal, she explained her belief that children today are fundamentally different from the children she remembers growing up with, and lamented the lost skills of play. Later, during an interview, she returned to this theme, 'Kids today do not have the same imaginative capabilities. They don't know how to play'.

Sra. Soto also blamed herself for the failure of the Centers to generate conversation-based play, specifically citing her lack of attention to design: 'I would change things in there to try to make them apply the language they were learning . . . I should have brought more stuff in, but I ran out of money, energy, so I just gave up'.

These comments reveal that Sra. Soto and I held very different perspectives on play. My interpretation of the children's silent play was that the children were in fact playing, but my definition of valid play included not only verbal but also non-verbal interactions, for example, where one child offers a piece of toy train and another child accepts it. My definition of play also included individual actions coordinated into a shared play scenario, for example where children participate jointly in the global task of preparing a meal by individually carrying out specific isolated tasks (arranging plates, bringing food to the table). The goals of the activity will determine the nature of the play; therefore, the fact that the children's play was not rich in conversation was not due to the inability of the children to play properly, nor to a lack of attention or planning on the part of the teacher. Conversation generation was a goal of the teacher, not the children, and conversation did not arise in this play because it was neither a goal of the children nor perceived by the children as an effective means to achieve their play goals.

When, despite the careful design of the Centers, the children's play failed to meet her curriculum goal of producing Spanish conversation, Sra. Soto located the source of this failure in the children (they were inadequate players) and in herself (she was an inadequate play designer). In this manner, failure emerged systemically in this classroom and was immediately assigned to people, reflecting the fundamental assumption typical of American schooling that failure must be rooted within individuals (McDermott, 1993; Varenne & McDermott, 1998). Sra. Soto's interpretation of the children's lack of conversation was based on a deficit model, postulating that children did not converse while playing because they lacked specific (learnable and teachable) skills, as expressed in the following quote, 'How did you learn to converse? At school. Somebody taught you how to converse. Some people are inept speakers, they never learned how, nobody ever showed them'.

A corollary of this deficit assumption is that, since failure results from an individual's lack of discrete skills, failure can be remediated by teaching these skills. Despite the child-centered philosophy she initially expressed, as described above, when faced with the relative failure of her teaching goals, Sra. Soto's actions and comments became increasingly rooted in a more teacher-centered transmission-of-skills approach. Having decided that the children lacked play skills, she remediated this deficit by directly teaching the children the skills of conversation while they played.

Remediation Strategies: Teaching Play

I first observed Sra. Soto participating in Centers play in January, about halfway through the academic year, although she had been intervening in the children's play more and more frequently by calling out instructions from outside the Centers. At this point, she began to enter the play as a participant, for example sitting on the floor in Blocks and building plastic houses with the children or sitting at the table in Housekeeping while children served her and each other plastic food. She explained these entries into the Centers as attempts to 'teach' the children to play. She explicitly linked this concept of teaching play skills to the technique of play with purpose (Einon *et al.*, 1986), 'Play with purpose is where you teach them to play, because they don't know how to play'.

However, a closer analysis of Sra. Soto's participation in the children's play reveals an interesting dynamic, one which I doubt Sra. Soto was consciously aware of. Although the play Center was an area that Sra. Soto herself specifically designed to afford conversation, her own interactions with the children resembled not so much conversation as the teacher-directed dynamic typical of classrooms. Her interactions with the children consisted mainly of the teacher asking the sort of 'known answer' questions characteristic of classroom discourse, following the pattern of question-response-evaluation (Lemke, 1990; Wells & Chang-Wells, 1992). Rather than generate conversation, these kinds of pseudo-questions simply stimulate children to offer simple answers, hoping to guess what the teacher wants to hear and to receive a positive evaluation.

In the following example, Sra. Soto has just sat down at the table where several children are sitting and pretending to eat plastic fruits and vegetables. As soon as Sra. Soto enters, she sits down and begins quizzing the children about the names of the food items, concentrating on Dorinda, an English speaker:

> **Sra. Soto:** [holding up a plastic carrot] ¿Qué es esto? (*What's this?*)
> **Dorinda** (English): [in a questioning tone of voice] It's a carrot?
> **Sra. Soto:** [in an affirming tone] Zanahoria (*carrot*) [holding up a stalk of celery] ¿Qué es esto? (*What's this?*)

Several children: [calling out together) ¡Apio! (*celery*)
Sra. Soto: [holds up a cucumber]
Several children: [calling out together] ¡Pepino! (*cucumber*)
Dorinda (English): [has not been paying attention to this activity, looking down at the table and pretending to eat some plastic food in front of her]
Sra. Soto: [taps Dorinda on the shoulder] Mira. Mira, que me escuches. Mira. (*Watch. Watch and listen to me. Watch*)
Dorinda (English): [looks expectantly at Sra. Soto]
Sra. Soto: [holds up the celery] Apio. (*celery*)
Dorinda (English): aplo (sic)

Apparently satisfied with Dorinda's approximation, Sra. Soto continues to hold up vegetables, this time saying the name herself as she holds them up, and some of the children name the vegetable with her. She holds up a pepper, saying '*pimiento*', then a tomato, saying '*tomate*' and then an ear of corn, saying '*choclo*'. When she gets to the banana (*plátano*), she holds the banana up and waits for a child to say the name before she says it. She then continues in this style with a head of lettuce (*lechuga*) and finally a pear (*pera*).

This kind of teacher-led naming activity seemed characteristic of Sra. Soto's involvement in the play in both Housekeeping and Blocks Centers. In this excerpt from the Blocks Center, recorded just two days later, Berto, Mark, Ian, Oscar, Joël and Khamil are playing in the Blocks area. Each boy is taking tiny plastic figures from the same bin of plastic pieces, but each seems to be working on an individual project. The children are not collaborating and there is very little interaction as they select and pursue their own projects, occasionally noticing and commenting on the projects of others. When she enters, Sra. Soto does not simply participate in the ongoing play, but she invites the children to 'play' something different with her:

Sra. Soto: Saben que hoy, hoy yo quiero jugar con ustedes. ¿Podemos hacer un pueblo? ¿Una ciudad? (*You know, today, today I want to play with you. Can we make a town? A city?*)[None of the children respond to this invitation, but continue their individual activities]
Joël (Spanish): Sra. Soto, he broke my thing!
Sra. Soto: [ignoring his comment] Quiero hacer una ciudad con ustedes (*I want to make a city with you*)
Mark (English): We're making something.
Sra. Soto: [changing her invitation slightly] ¿Podemos hacer una

casa? (*Can we make a house?*)
Several children: [together] Yeah.

In this exchange, it is apparent that Sra. Soto enters the play with her own agenda. Sra. Soto announces her agenda (building a city together) as she enters, thus signaling a shift in play, centering the focus on herself. While she explicitly refers to the city-building activity she proposes as 'play', it eventually becomes clear that her agenda is actually a different kind of activity, that of accurately naming things in Spanish. She invites the children to engage in her new activity, and when Mark resists by asserting that they are already doing something (working on their individual projects) she ignores him and changes the nature of her proposed play to making a house instead of a city. Her offer is finally accepted, and eventually Sra. Soto does manage to engage the children in the activity of building a house. Later, we see that Sra. Soto has finished her house and holds up each item for the children to name:

> **Sra. Soto:** Yo tengo en mi casa… (*I have in my house…*) [pauses, inviting the children to finish the sentence]
> **Several children:** [call out together the names of various items]
> **Sra. Soto:** [holding up each item of the house one by one, and repeating each time] ¿Qué es esto? (*What is this*?)
> **Children:** [calling out together, name the items correctly]
> **Khamil** (English): [walking over to Ian] Excuse me, Ian. Excuse me, Ian. Will you play with me?
> **Ian** (English): Yes.
> **Sra. Soto:** Ian. Ian. Dile 'Sí' (*Ian. Ian. Tell him, 'Yes'*)
> **Ian** (English): Sí. (*Yes*)
> **Sra. Soto:** Khamil, pregunta en español. '¿Puedes jugar?' (*Khamil, ask in Spanish. 'Can you play?'*)
> **Khamil** (English): [draws a breath but then pauses]
> **Sra. Soto:** Puedes… (can you…) [pauses expectantly]
> **Khamil** (English): [finishing the phrase] …jugar (*play*)
> **Ian** (English): [responds again, this time in Spanish] Sí. (*Yes*)

In this excerpt, Sra. Soto succeeded in engaging the children in naming the parts of a house in Spanish, as well as translating an invitation to play into Spanish, using the same kind of strategies described in earlier chapters: demanding repetition in Spanish, and modeling and repeating the Spanish phrases. Although the context of the children's initial Blocks play, building things, was quite different from the Housekeeping play with plastic food described in the preceding episode, Sra. Soto's agenda of naming objects became clearly visible soon after she entered the play on both occasions. In other words, while the two play contexts began as very different activities, they became strikingly similar once Sra. Soto entered the play scenario.

Sra. Soto's entry into the Centers often involved some degree of chastisement. Frequently, the children were chastised for failing to provide expected answers when this failure was attributed to a lack of attention, as exemplified by the exchange with Rashid at the end of Chapter 7. Sra. Soto's frustration with Rashid for failing to pay attention to her transformed Rashid's legitimate play participation into illegitimate classroom participation. Unlike in play, where participants shift attention among themselves according to the progression of the activity, the direct teaching classroom norm that Sra. Soto imposes on the children's play requires that all participants attend to the teacher at all times (see DePalma, 2006 for further analysis of ways in which implicit classroom norms can conflict with language learning). The children were also chastised for arguing with each other and for behavior that did not conform to certain conventions of custom and of realism. For example, Sandra was chided for feeding a baby with a plastic carrot, pretending it was a bottle, Norma was chastised for placing a baby wrapped in a blanket on a chair instead of the cradle, and Wilma was told she could not hold a baby while she was playing the role of store cashier.

As the excerpts depicting Sra. Soto's participation in the House-keeping and Blocks Centers demonstrate, what she considered to be direct modeling of good play ceased to look very much like play at all in that it was extremely orderly. Roles were clear: the teacher asks a question, the students respond and the teacher evaluates. The children were expected to pay attention to the teacher and respond when they were asked a question. There were no shifting roles, and no ambiguous or debatable realities; a plastic carrot is always a carrot and never a baby's bottle.

As demonstrated in Chapter 3, Sra. Soto had many goals for the classroom, including that they learn to 'speak without yelling' and to be 'kind and gentle' while playing with dolls. In Chapter 5, we saw that Sra. Soto's interest in maintaining an orderly classroom resulted in many opportunities for the children to follow clear and highly contextualized instructions for cleaning up. Nevertheless, my observations in the play Centers suggested that Sra. Soto's goal of maintaining classroom order, especially in terms of polite behavior, quietness and following norms of social convention and reality, conflicted with her goals of producing conversation through play. Conversation is afforded by uncertainty and ambiguity, when roles must be negotiated, realities debated and interests defended.

It seemed to me that while Sra. Soto recognized that free play Centers were the least successful part of the classroom design, failing to produce the conversations she expected, her attempts to rectify the situation actually made matters worse. When Sra. Soto tried to teach the children to play more effectively, she tended to co-opt the play activity initiated by the children and change the activity structure to a teacher-centered activity consisting of the children providing brief responses to known-answer questions. As we have seen, this kind of interaction pattern may have been effective in the more highly structured activities where attention to the teacher afforded listening comprehension and supported the production of predictable, formulaic responses. Nevertheless, this interaction pattern did not support, but actually seemed to short circuit, improvisation and sustained conversation.

Fostering (or Inhibiting) Conversation

In order to check these overall impressions, I decided to analyze more closely the language produced in the Centers to determine to what extent conversations emerged, what kinds of conversations emerged and under what conditions, and how Sra. Soto's interventions in the Centers affected the Centers dynamic. As a methodological note, it is important to keep in mind that the numerical tabulation was performed on the existing corpus of narrative data and not as an independent quantitative analysis. As explained in Chapter 2, the two forms of data included in this chapter – the narrative analysis and numerical tabulation – are linked to each other and to the data presented in previous chapters as a means of validity reinforcement.

Because Sra. Soto was concerned with the children's failure to have conversation with each other during play, I coded for conversation in terms of dialogic length, measured in terms of thematically linked conversational turns. These conversational turns are delineated by a change in speaker and/or a clear change in addressee, therefore grounding the coding in terms of speaker interaction. This focus on interaction, rather than, for example, the utterance length as measured by number of words, is based on Sra. Soto's assumption that it is interaction among children that will foster conversation, which will, in turn, foster language development.

For the purposes of measuring the extent of this interactivity, I code conversation in terms of dialogic length, measured as the number of thematically related conversational turns. Bakhtin (1986) argues that a conversational utterance goes beyond simply the signifying units of a language and is defined by mutual engagement in terms of both the author and the addressee, related to both the preceding and following utterances by means of the speakers' awareness of each other. Drawing on Bakhtin's dialogic understanding of utterance, I defined the basic unit of measure to be the conversational 'turn'. I counted as one turn each time a person speaks to another, regardless of the length of the speech unit. Turns, therefore, are defined by a change in speaker or addressee (for further discussion of mutual engagement and the establishment of intersubjectivity in these classroom conversations, see Hayes & Matusov, 2005).

The extent of the conversation is determined as the number of thematically linked turns. Using an analysis scheme originally devised for an earlier investigation into web-based discussions (Matusov *et al.*, 1998), I coded each group of thematically related turns as a conversational thread and defined conversational length as the number of speaker turns in each thread. For example, in the following excerpt, Sra. Soto and Kathleen begin a conversation about a stain on Kathleen's shirt, and Sra. Soto shifts the topic in the middle of one of her speech turns to focus on what the children ate for lunch earlier in the day:

> **Sra. Soto:** [points to a large stain on Kathleen's t-shirt] Mira lo que pasó con tu camiseta nueva. (*Look what happened to you new t-shirt*)
> **Kathleen** (English): [smiles, clutches the shirt, and looks down at it]
> **Sra. Soto:** ¡Ayyy! [an exaggerated exclamation of dismay]
> **Kathleen** (English): [making scrubbing motions with her hands] Mi mamá voy (sic) a duchar. (*My mom I'm going to shower*)
> **Sra. Soto:** Aahh. Está bien. ¿Qué comiste abajo? ¿Qué comiste hoy? (*That's fine. What did you eat downstairs? What did you eat today?*)

I coded this fragment as one conversational thread ('the stain') consisting of two turns, and a second thread ('lunch') consisting of 20 turns,[1] beginning with Sra. Soto's comment (Aahh. Está bien. ¿Qué comiste abajo? ¿Qué comiste hoy?). Although this turn belongs to two threads, it is uttered by one speaker and directed at the same person, therefore I coded as one turn to avoid redundancy and inflated values for the thread length.[2]

When speakers clearly shifted their addressee when speaking, I coded this as two turns, even though the speaker remained the same, because mutual engagement involves the addressee as well as the speaker. For example, in the following excerpt from Housekeeping, Ian is trying to explain to Sra. Soto that his toy transformer, from the popular television show *Street Sharks*, has wings, which are included in the packaging box. During their conversation, Sra. Soto turns to Oscar and asks him a specific question:

> **Ian** (English): [tracing a square in the air with both arms] They have them in the box.
> **Sra. Soto:** En la caja. (*In the box*)
> **Ian** (English): En la caja. (*In the box*)
> **Sra. Soto:** Las tienen en la caja. (*They have them in the box*) [looks over at Oscar] ¿Tú sabes este programa de que está hablando? (*Do you know this program that he's talking about?*)
> **Oscar** (Spanish): [nods and smiles]
> **Sra. Soto:** ¿Y a ti te gusta también? (*And you like it, too?*)
> **Oscar** (Spanish): [still smiling, nods again]
> **Sra. Soto:** ¿Y cómo se llama este programa, Oscar? (*And what is this program called, Oscar?*)

I coded this exchange as five turns (Ian–Sra. Soto, Sra. Soto–Ian, Ian–Sra. Soto, Sra. Soto–Ian, Sra. Soto–Oscar). Further, Oscar's response, which is non-verbal, I did not code as a conversational turn. While he clearly responded, and Sra. Soto's continued as if he had verbally responded in the affirmative, I did not code non-verbal utterances as conversational turns because Sra. Soto's goal was to use conversation to develop language skills. This ability and tendency of children to use non-verbal means of communication was a crucial aspect of the problem with Sra. Soto's Center design that she had not anticipated: the children used non-linguistic strategies to advance their own play and communication agendas.

I also thematically analyzed the conversational threads. It had become evident to me as I viewed and transcribed videotaped data that the most productive themes in terms of language production seemed to involve negotiation (recall, for example, that Rashid and Emily spoke together when they had to negotiate the procedure for making their train in the Blocks Center). Negotiation is a central process in play, and involves terms of entry, nature and distribution of roles, the nature of the shared imaginary world and repair of disagreements (Sutterby, 2002). To test this emerging hypothesis, I coded all thread themes in terms of whether they involved negotiation. I found negotiation of two varieties: negotiation of conflict (where children have incompatible goals and struggle to win the right to satisfy their own goals at the expense of others' goals) and negotiation of ambiguous play scenarios. I later collapsed both types of negotiation into one negotiation category, since I was more interested in negotiation than the details of the nature of the negotiation, and also because there was not always a clear delineation between the two. The common defining denominator, which is most interesting in terms of classroom design, is that in order for negotiation to occur, the curriculum needs to be flexible enough for either conflicting agendas or ambiguous play situations to emerge.

Since Sra. Soto originally designed the Centers to promote extended conversations among children, I factored conversational threads initiated by Sra. Soto out of this analysis, initially to get a sense of what the children managed without her. I found the total number of conversational turns in play themes involving negotiation to be almost double the number of conversational turns involving non-negotiation themes. The mean conversational thread length of negotiation-based themes was greater than that of non-negotiation-based themes by 15.75 turns. This analysis demonstrates that, during Centers play, the most extended conversational interactions seemed to emerge from the children's play when the routine was disrupted and the children found themselves in the position of negotiating an ambiguous reality or conflicting agendas. The children were compelled to employ language to express their agendas, sometimes invoking classroom norms to defend these agendas and/or attempting to ally the teacher and/or peers in the negotiation.

For example, the longest conversational thread (91 turns) emerged as a conflict between two girls playing with dolls in Housekeeping, concerning who could be the mother of which doll. This conflict situation required negotiation because each girl was able to articulate a separate and conflicting agenda, and each attempted to win the support of other children and eventually the teacher. The stage is set for conflict right from the beginning, as Kathleen (English) attempts to enter Housekeeping where Ian (Spanish), Alberta (Spanish), Wilma (Spanish) and Sandra (English) are already playing. In an apparent attempt to exclude her, Wilma immediately invokes Sra. Soto's rule that only four children at a time can play in Housekeeping:

> **Kathleen** (English): [approaches the Housekeeping area]
> **Wilma** (Spanish): [stops brushing her doll's hair, holds out her hand, palm out] There's four people. You can't come in here.
> **Sandra** (English): [sitting nearby with her own doll, points to Wilma, herself, Ian and Alberta as she counts] Uno, dos, tres, cuatro (*One, two, three, four*)
> **Wilma** (Spanish): Uno, dos, tres, y cuatro, no puedes (*One, two, three, four, you can't*)

Since this rule is typically ignored, Kathleen considers it to be negotiable. She defends herself by involving Sra. Soto, who is outside the Center. In a move that is probably crucial to the extension of this conversation, Sra. Soto does in fact override her own rule. This allows Kathleen to continue negotiating entry into the Center and then rights of doll possession with the children inside. As the segment continues, it becomes apparent that Wilma is trying to defend the scarce resource of the highly prized dolls, since as soon as Kathleen enters and picks up a doll that is lying unattended in the corner, Wilma protests loudly and is supported by Alberta, who is sitting nearby:

> **Kathleen** (English): [bends to pick up a doll lying in the corner]
> **Wilma** (Spanish): [rushes over] ¡No, no!
> **Alberta** (Spanish): [sitting nearby in a chair with her own doll, reaches over and grabs the doll from Kathleen] Es de ella. Es de Sandra (*It's hers. It's Sandra's*)
> **Sandra** (English): [walks over and takes the doll from Alberta] Sí. Es las mía. Ella las mía (sic) (*Yes. It's the mines. She the mines*)
> **Alberta** (Spanish): Está hecha... (*It's made...*)
> **Kathleen** (English): [crouching in the corner, interrupts loudly] ¡Quiero un bebé! (*I want a baby!*)
> **Wilma** (Spanish): Esta es de Sandra (*This one is Sandra's*)
> **Kathleen** (English): [wailing] ¡Quiero jugarlo! (*I want to play it!*)
> **Sandra** (English): [motions for Kathleen to follow her] Uno minuto (sic) (*One minute*)
> **Wilma** (Spanish): ¡No puedes! ¡No puedes! ¡No puedes! (*You can't! You can't! You can't!*)
> **Sandra** (English): [addressing her sister, who is playing with another doll outside the Center] Emily, Kathleen quiere jugar con tu bebé (*Emily, Kathleen wants to play with your baby*)

While some of the language is basic and repetitious, the conversation does continue, and both English speakers and Spanish speakers are using predominantly Spanish. This elevated use of Spanish during negotiation may reflect the children's attempt to validate their arguments. By using the established official language, they can more effectively lobby for the teacher's approval and support of their positions. The children do invoke Sra. Soto's intervention several times during this exchange. When she does intervene, however, she attempts to minimize the conflict, effectively shutting down the language-productive negotiation. In fact, the negotiations finally come to a conclusion when Sra. Soto enters the Center, sits down and begins to chide the children for disorderliness, fighting and complaining, but without any mention of the doll conflict negotiation:

> **Sra. Soto:** ¿Qué decimos cuando jugamos? (*What do we say when we play?*)
> **Several children:** [calling out together] ¡Español! (*Spanish*)
> **Sra. Soto:** Sí, pero no sólo esto... ¿qué dijimos? que tenemos que ¿qué? (*Yes, but not only this, what did we say, that we have to what?*)
> **Several children:** [calling out together] ¡Hablar! (*talk*)
> **Sra. Soto:** Que tenemos que hablar, uno con el otro. (*That we have to talk with each other*) ¿Ustedes están hablando? (*Are you talking?*)
> **Several children:** [calling out together] ¡No!
> **Sra. Soto:** ¿O peleando? (*Or fighting?*) [pause, no children respond to this apparently rhetorical question] ¿Y quejándose? (*and complaining?*) [another pause, then she continues in an affirming tone, as if they had responded] Ahhh, peleando y quejándose. (*Ahhh, fighting and complaining*)

In these instructions, Sra. Soto sets up a clear dichotomy between what they should be doing (talking with each other in Spanish) and what they are doing (fighting and complaining). Clearly, fighting and good playing are not compatible, in her opinion. While Sra. Soto played a crucial role in requiring the children, especially Sandra and Kathleen, to speak Spanish, she lost the opportunity to engage the children in a meaningful and complicated negotiation (in Spanish) by resisting their attempts to draw her into the negotiation and by insisting on viewing their conflict as inhibiting, rather than generating, meaningful conversation (see Hayes, 2005 for a fuller explication of this extended conversation).

Initiating Conversations: An Unexpected Result

In order to analyze Sra. Soto's participation in the Centers, I also coded her Centers conversation in order to measure her success in initiating extended conversational threads. An initiating turn is one that begins or proposes a conversational thread, and the success of this initiation is measured by thread length, or the number of thematically related turns it elicits. This analysis allowed me to investigate the effectiveness of Sra. Soto's participation in the Center toward her own goal of promoting conversation. As I was mainly interested in Sra. Soto's effect on the Centers interactions, I eliminated instructions, discipline, etc. that she called out to children who were outside the Center. However, for the same reason, I did code Sra. Soto's utterances directed to the children in the Center when she was outside the Center, again, because this counted as an attempt to affect the Center dynamic even though she was not physically in the Center space.

According to the data analysis, Sra. Soto's participation in the play Centers was, overall, not a successful strategy in eliciting sustained conversation during play (bearing in mind that she probably entered the play Centers while I was not present, and so my analysis is not exhaustive). I recorded a total of 227 initiating turns on the part of Sra. Soto, and only 10 (4.4%) were successful in initiating conversational threads that lasted for more than three turns. I used this minimum to see how often she was able to go beyond the classic three-turn dynamic of the teacher-directed exchanges (teacher question, student response, teacher evaluation) described earlier in this chapter.

I further analyzed Sra. Soto's initiating utterances to determine if there was a pattern in the type of initiation that seemed most successful. I coded all her initiating utterances as either 'known-answer', 'language management', 'classroom management' or 'other'. To avoid artificially inflating the number of Sra. Soto's initiating utterances, I coded these utterances as if these categories were mutually exclusive, although they were not.

Of Sra. Soto's total initiating utterances, 82 (36%) were known-answer questions. These questions differ from genuine questions in that the teacher knows the answer and is expecting a certain 'correct' answer. A common known-answer question, as we have already seen, was '¿Qué es esto?' (*What is this?*), generally accompanied by holding up the object in question and asking the children to name it in the target language. This type of turn was generally unsuccessful in initiating sustained conversation, as only 1 (0.4%) of these statements elicited conversation that was sustained beyond three turns.

Another type of utterance that Sra. Soto characteristically directed at children playing in the Center was language management, which characterized 14.9% of her initiating turns and initiated sustained conversation only 2.9% of the time. Sometimes language management consisted of a command to speak the designated language or to stop speaking the non-designated language, for example, '¿Qué es este idioma que estoy escuchando?' (*What is this language that I am hearing?*). Although this is a rhetorical question and the answer is obviously known, and it might even be considered a disciplinary action (which I coded under the category of classroom management), I coded this as a language management utterance, since that seemed to be the primary function.

The most common of Sra. Soto's initiating turn types was classroom management, comprising 37.9% of all initiating turns. Nevertheless, these turns were successful in eliciting a sustained conversational thread only 1.8% of the time. These included commands to clean and organize the play area (orders to place things in their proper place or to stop placing things in the wrong place). These took the form of direct statements such as 'No juguemos más y guardan las cosas' (*Let's not play anymore, and put away the things*), as well as indirect, rhetorical questions such as '¿Por qué hay dentro de la heladera una caja de panecillos?' (*Why is there a box of muffins inside the refrigerator?*). Classroom management utterances also included commands aimed at behavior management (orders to stop arguing, hitting or yelling). Like commands to clean up, these commands also sometimes took the form of rhetorical questions, for example '¿Por qué están gritando cuando la gente está hablando? ¿Eso es justo? ¿Sí o no?' (*Why are you yelling when people are talking? Is that fair? Yes or no?*).

I coded as 'other' any questions that did not seem to have a known answer and statements and questions that did not seem to be intended to modify either the language or behavior of the children. These included genuine questions eliciting either the children's opinion or information that Sra. Soto was not privy to, for example, 'Estabas enfermo?' (*Were you sick?*). They also included statements that seemed to be designed to convey information, for example, '¿Sabes que voy a hacer mañana, Kathleen? Tengo una cuna en casa que voy a traer' (*You know what I'm going to do tomorrow, Kathleen? I have a crib at home that I'm going to bring in*). Turns categorized as 'other' comprised 39.2% of Sra. Soto's total initiating turns, and initiated sustained conversation 1.76% of the time.

This analysis indicates that not only were Sra. Soto's utterances not particularly successful in eliciting conversation, but that there was not much difference in success among the different types of utterances. Based on my initial observations of the short and simple responses they tended to elicit (as described earlier), I had predicted that known-answer and management questions would be less successful than others, and had assumed that genuine questions (such as questions about personal preferences that did not have an expected answer or statements that conveyed new information) would be most successful of all. In fact, my analysis did not support this prediction. In order to explain this unexpected result, I decided to examine in more detail cases where my prediction did not hold up, in order to understand more fully the factors that led to extended conversation under unexpected conditions.

Keeping the Conversation Going: Coordinating Goals

In order to investigate the failure of my own prediction, I analyzed two cases in which Sra. Soto began an exchange with a type of utterance that I would not have expected to elicit a long conversation, but which did exactly that. In both cases, she asked a simple known-answer question, the sort of question that usually elicited a very brief answer, the exchange ending quickly with the teacher's evaluation. Both these conversations occurred on the same day, a coincidence that suggests that perhaps Sra. Soto was having an unusual day. Both conversations took place in Housekeeping, but with different children. Close analysis of these two cases suggests that conversational success depends not so much on the nature of the initiating utterance, but on the coordination of goals between the teacher and children, each of whom has a different reason for advancing the conversation, reasons that may not be the same but are compatible.

In the first extended conversation, Sra. Soto discusses *Street Sharks*, a popular television show, with two boys, Oscar and Ian. She is sitting at the table with the two boys. Oscar is playing with a toy car, which is not related to the program, and Ian is playing with a Street Sharks transformer, a shark with wings that can transform itself into a car. Sra. Soto begins the exchange by asking Ian to name his transformer, which is currently in shark mode:

> **Sra. Soto:** [indicating Ian's transformer] ¿Y eso? ¿Qué es eso? (*And this? What is this?*) [begins to pronounce the Spanish word for shark (*tiburón*) pausing in the middle for Ian to finish the word] Tibur...
> **Ian** (English): [pronouncing the last syllable, but incorrectly] ...-rai.
> **Sra. Soto:** [correcting him] ...-ron.
> **Oscar** (Spanish): [standing nearby, playing with his car] Y es un carro. (*And it's a car*)
> **Sra. Soto:** Es un carro también, pero es un tiburón también. (*It's a car, too, but it's a shark, too*)
> **Ian** (English): It's from *Street Sharks*.
> **Sra. Soto:** [turning back to Oscar] Pero ves, esta palabra en español, ¿qué? (*But see, this word in Spanish, what?*)

At first, her initiating question might have seemed to be a genuine question, but as she begins to pronounce the word for shark (*tiburón*), waiting for Ian to finish the word, it becomes clear that she knows exactly what she wants him to say. Her interest in language remains apparent as she continues by asking Oscar, a native Spanish speaker, to provide the word as well. The boys, however, seem eager to participate in the conversation, as evidenced above by both Oscar and Ian volunteering information about the toy (It's a car; It's from *Street Sharks*). Clearly, they want to share their views on Street Sharks transformers with Sra. Soto.

As the conversation continued, the boys obliged Sra. Soto by continuing to name items at Sra. Soto's request, and she obliged them by allowing them to further describe their out of school interests. Ian, for example, was willing to answer Sra. Soto's language-specific questions (correctly labeling not only the shark, but its teeth, *dientes*, and what it can do with them, *morder*). In exchange for his attention, he demanded that she listen to his description of his brother's flying sharks (also transformers, apparently).

All three of them seemed highly engaged in the rather jovial debate that ensued about whether or not sharks, which live in water, can have wings. Smiling and laughing, Sra. Soto was able to advance her agenda of vocabulary building (making sure the boys knew the Spanish word for water and wings), while the boys seemed eager to convince her that sharks can indeed fly in their fantasy world. This conversation, which lasted for 30 turns, started inauspiciously with the classic known answer question ¿Qué es eso? (*What is this?*), which, as we have seen earlier, usually resulted in Sra. Soto holding up a series of objects and waiting for the children to call out names. Nevertheless, in this unusual case, the teacher and children were able to maintain a shared focus on the conversation by coordinating their disparate goals: by advancing the children's goal of explaining their fantasy, the teacher's goal of vocabulary practice is advanced as well (see Hayes & Matusov, 2005 for an extended analysis of this conversation).

The second unexpectedly long conversation initiated by Sra. Soto was with Kathleen and Norma, also in the Housekeeping. Like the Street Sharks conversation, this conversation had inauspicious beginnings. Sra. Soto and Kathleen are talking about a stain on Kathleen's shirt, when Sra. Soto suddenly changes the topic, asking her what she had to eat for lunch:

Sra. Soto: ¿Qué comiste abajo? ¿Qué comiste hoy? (*What did you eat downstairs? What did you eat today?*)
Kathleen (English): [hugs Sra. Soto around her neck] French toast.
Sra. Soto: Ooh, no era French toast. (*Ooh, it wasn't French toast*)
Kathleen (English): [nodding emphatically] ¡Sí! (*Yes!*)
Sra. Soto: ¿Era tostada francesa? (*Was it French toast?*)
Kathleen (English): [no response]

Sra. Soto: No, me parece que era... (*No, it seems to me that it was...*) [trails off, looking over at Norma, who is playing nearby]
Norma (Spanish): [calls over something partially unintelligible, but which includes the word 'hamburguesa'] (*hamburger*)
Kathleen (English): [looking down at Norma] No. Era French toast también. (*No, it was French toast, too*]

As it turns out, Sra. Soto's question about what Kathleen ate for lunch was in fact a known-answer question, since she rejects Kathleen's answer when it isn't what she is expecting. Sra. Soto corrects Kathleen's statement that she ate French toast for lunch, checking with Norma to verify her belief that it was, in fact, hamburgers. A crucial step in the continuity of this conversation is Kathleen's rejection of Sra. Soto's evaluative response. In the three-step pattern typical of Sra. Soto's known-answer questions, as described earlier (question-response-evaluation), the children normally accept Sra. Soto's final evaluative turn. In this case, Kathleen chooses to reject Sra. Soto's negative evaluation of her response, which leads Sra. Soto to continue her argument, seeking out Norma as an ally. Another important step is Kathleen's insistence that she ate French toast, even after Sra. Soto has presented her with Norma's corroborating evidence to the contrary. Equally important, however, is Sra. Soto's willingness to entertain an alternative response, to continue the argument with Kathleen even though she is convinced that Kathleen is wrong:

Sra. Soto: ¿También? Yo pensé que había hamburguesas hechas con pollo. (*Also? I though there were hamburgers made with chicken*)
Kathleen (English): Era también hecho... (*It was also made...*) [pauses, apparently searching for the words]
Sra. Soto: ¿Y también tostada francesa? (*And also French toast?*)
Kathleen (English): [nods]
Sra. Soto: ¡Muchas cosas! (*A lot of things!*) [looks over at Norma] ¿Cómo había tantas cosas abajo? ¿Había tostada francesa? (*How were there so many things downstairs? Was there French toast?*)
Norma (Spanish): [response is unintelligible]
Sra. Soto: ¿O eran papas fritas? (*Or were they French fries?*)
Norma (Spanish): [response is unintelligible]
Sra. Soto: [turning back to Kathleen] Eran papas fritas. (*They were French fries*)
Kathleen (English): [stands silently for a few seconds, watching Norma]
Sra. Soto: [to Kathleen] ¿Era tostada o eran papas? (*Was it toast or*

were they potatoes?)
Kathleen (English): Tostada. (*Toast*)
Sra. Soto: Me parece que eran unas papas. Unas papas fritas. (*It seems to me that they were potatoes. Some French fries*)
Kathleen (English): Tostada, verdad. (*Toast, really*)
Sra. Soto: [looks puzzled] No, ¿te parece? (*No, do you think?*)

This conversation seems to be at a standstill, at least in terms of arriving at mutual agreement. They seem to be, after several turns, exactly in the same state of disagreement as when they started. Nevertheless, nobody seems particularly frustrated or annoyed, nor does Sra. Soto exercise her power in the classroom by simply closing the discussion and declaring Kathleen wrong. This may be because Sra. Soto has decided that her goal is not to ensure that Kathleen report the correct lunch menu, but to extend the conversation as a vehicle for language practice. This interpretation is further supported by Sra. Soto's reaction when Kathleen switches to English, as the segment continues:

Kathleen (English): They gave us French toast.
Sra. Soto: Ay, pero lo sabes en español (*Ay, but you know it in Spanish*) [begins the phrase, then allowing her voice to trail off, indicating that Kathleen should finish] Me...
Kathleen (English): [with a questioning intonation] ¿Dió tostada? (*Gave me toast?*)
Sra. Soto: Te dieron tostada (*They gave you toast*) [smilingly widely] Te creo. Si tú me lo dices, debe ser. (*I believe you. If you tell me that, it must be*)
Kathleen (English): Y papas fritas también. (*And French fries, too*)
Sra. Soto: Ay, que [unintelligible]
Kathleen and Sra. Soto: [laugh together]

This conversation, like the earlier *Street Sharks* one, seemed to emerge from the ability of the participants to coordinate their different goals. Kathleen clearly wished to engage Sra. Soto in conversation about a topic of interest to her, as in the case of Ian above. She was also apparently motivated to be recognized as correct, as she repeatedly insisted on her interpretation, despite Sra. Soto's repeated insistence that she was wrong. Sra. Soto, on the other hand, apparently decided to suspend her teacher's rights to define the correct interpretation and to allow Kathleen to pursue her own interpretation, probably motivated by the opportunity to practice vocabulary in context.

These sustained conversations highlight the importance of recognizing the role played by the children's goals in maintaining a mutual engagement. While the utterances in both cases tended to be basic and repetitive, they did afford the monolingual children opportunities to construct basic grammatical structures in Spanish that went beyond the usual single-word translation: Ian struggled to explain that his brother's winged shark came in a box, and Kathleen needed to clarify the difference between singular and plural verb forms in order to explain that 'they' gave her French toast for lunch. Most importantly, the children are forced to think quickly, listening to Sra. Soto's comments in Spanish and constructing an immediate, meaningful response, even when it is not completely correct. This approximates more closely the kind of functional language learning that happens in immersion settings, which is different from memorization and recitation of isolated vocabulary items.

Focus on Kathleen: From Problem Child to Effective Language Learner

Recall from Chapter 6 that Kathleen was quickly constructed in this classroom as a generally unsuccessful learner. In the more teacher-directed activities (such as the Language Arts activities described in Chapter 6), her inability or refusal to adhere to the norms for social engagement implicit in these activity structures resulted in frequent clashes with the teacher. In the Centers, by contrast, Kathleen shone. In fact, Sra. Soto identified her as a 'good role model' because, despite the fact that she was a monolingual English speaker, she tended to try to speak Spanish, particularly in her play Center interactions.

My observations suggested that it was more than just her willingness to speak Spanish that made her a model (play Center) learner. Perhaps she was most effective as a learner in the play Centers for the same reason that Sra. Soto was least effective as a teacher: while Sra. Soto seemed uncomfortable with ambiguity and conflict, Kathleen seemed to thrive on it. In the exchanges described in this chapter, we see Kathleen doggedly negotiating her agenda of playing with the dolls in the Housekeeping Center with other children who wanted to exclude her. We see her actively contradicting Sra. Soto's (and Norma's) recollection of the lunch menu and insisting on her point until the teacher, laughingly, concedes.

Furthermore, while most children failed to conform to Sra. Soto's ideal of good imaginative play, which involved a great deal of self-narration and verbal interaction, Kathleen seemed to most closely approximate that ideal. Sometimes she even talked to her dolls in Spanish when she played with them during Spanish time Housekeeping. In the following Housekeeping segment, for example, Kathleen and Emily are sitting at the table, which is piled high with doll clothes. Emily is standing and putting clothes on her doll, while Kathleen is sitting with her doll on her lap, also dressing the doll:

> **Emily** (English): [holding up a pair of pants] ¡Mira! (*Look*)
> **Kathleen** (English): [taking an article of clothing from the pile] Esto para mi bebé. (*This for my baby*)
> **Researcher:** [walks in to the play Center and places the microphone on the table]
> **Kathleen** (English): ¡Hola! (*Hello*)
> **Researcher:** Hola, Kathleen (*Hello, Kathleen*)
> **Kathleen** (English): [moving the microphone to the shelf] Yo lo pongo aquí. (*I'm putting it here*)
> **Emily** (English): [holds up a shirt] Mira, Kathleen (*Look, Kathleen*)
> **Kathleen** (English): ¡Qué lindo! Eso es el mismo que mi bebé. (*How nice! That's the same that my baby*) [holds up a shirt] Para mi bebé. Mañana es la (sic) cumpleaños de mi bebé. (*For my baby. Tomorrow is my baby's birthday*)
> **Emily** (English): [holding up another article of clothing] Esto es para tu bebé cumpleaños. (*This is for you baby birthday*)
> **Kathleen** (English): Pretend that today is my baby's birthday. Hoy es mi bebé cumpleaños. (*Today is my baby birthday*) [a few seconds later] Pretend you came to visit me, OK? [A few seconds later] Pretend (unintelligible) that you let her play with mi bebé, ¿OK? (*Pretend... that you let her play with my baby OK?*)
> **Emily** (English): What?
> **Kathleen** (English): Cuando termines esto, déjalo jugar con mi bebe, ¿OK? (*When you finish this, let him play with my baby, OK?*)
> **Alicia** (Spanish) [silently enters the Housekeeping Center]
> **Emily** (English): Hola, Alicia. (*Hello, Alicia*)
> **Kathleen** (English): Hoy es mi bebé cumpleaños. (*Today is my baby birthday*)[a few seconds of silent play]
> **Kathleen** (English): [trying to put a shirt on her doll] Esto no me sirve. Es muy grande. (*This one doesn't suit me. It's very big*) [grabs another shirt from the table] Mira, esta camisa. (*Look, this shirt*)
> **Emily** (English): [picks up a shirt from the table] Voy a poner esto, es muy chiquita. (*I'm going to put this one, it's very tiny*)

Despite some grammatical problems, Kathleen and Emily, two monolingual speakers, manage to interact largely in Spanish during their doll play. Interestingly, the eventual entrance of Alicia, a Spanish speaker, does not support the interactional dynamic at all and, in fact, it almost seems like her silence is contagious, as the girls all play silently for a few seconds when she enters.

Kathleen seemed to be guiding the play, announcing the play scenario (selecting clothes for her baby) and then changing it periodically (her baby's birthday is tomorrow, then it is today) and even dictating Emily's role (she has come to visit, and will let her baby play with Kathleen's baby). She even felt confident enough to move my microphone when I put it down in its usual place. This was not the first or last time that she did this, and she was the only child to do so.

Kathleen's creativity and desire to direct others in the activity structures she designed resulted here in the kind of language-rich imaginative play that Sra. Soto expected. Nevertheless, in the more strongly teacher-directed areas of the classroom, where she was meant to follow the lead of a higher authority rather than take the lead, Kathleen was constructed as a problem learner. Sra. Soto worried that as Kathleen made her way through school grades that would be decreasingly flexible, her 'disruptive' behaviors would become an increasing problem. I wonder whether in future classrooms, where there will be no activity structures like play Centers that support this degree of creativity, independence and confidence, Kathleen's strengths will disappear and she will come to be defined entirely by her (institutionally constructed) failure (McDermott, 1993).

Centers: A Clash of Philosophies

The play Centers were the only areas of the classroom where the children were initially expected to participate without direct teacher guidance. The guidance in these Centers was indirect, mediated by design. The Centers, both Housekeeping and Blocks, were filled with toys, which Sra. Soto changed throughout the year. As Sra. Soto explained in her final interview, 'I set them up for a reason... I would change things in there to try to make them apply the language they were learning'. However, while she was able to consistently guide the children's language choices throughout the more teacher-directed activity structures in the classroom, as described in Chapter 4, the children rarely chose to interact in Spanish while playing. This is consistent with other studies that have shown, for example, that even children who use Spanish with the teacher tend to use English in free Centers play (Sutterby, 2002).

Recall from Chapter 3 that Sra. Soto advocated teaching by indirect design in the Centers while at the same time she defined herself as a 'Madeline Hunter direct instruction teacher'. While Sra. Soto tended to use 'conversation' to describe her goal for the Centers, in the above quote she restates this goal as application of language learned in the classroom. This is different from genuine social conversation, which tends to be short-circuited by traditional classroom discourse patterns:

> (t)raditional classroom environments do not lend themselves very well to conversation: by definition the classroom is a formal, institutional, and asymmetrical setting... paradoxically, in this setting the informal, unpredictable, spontaneous "conversational" interactions which should lead to communicative competence of learners somehow have to be accommodated. (Bannink, 2002: 267)

While she used the term 'conversation', a closer look at Sra. Soto's comments, as well as her actions, suggests that she did not share Bannink's understanding of the term. Unlike genuine conversation, which is spontaneous and unpredictable, Sra. Soto's definition of conversation as applied targeted language practice can more easily be reconciled with a direct teaching model. In Madeline Hunter's model of direct teaching, after providing input, monitoring and checking for understanding, the teacher is expected to provide the children with the opportunity for 'independent practice':

> Once pupils have mastered the content or skill, it is time to provide for reinforcement practice. It is provided on a repeating schedule so that the learning is not forgotten. It may be home work or group or individual work in class. It can be utilized as an element in a subsequent project. It should provide for decontextualization: enough different contexts so that the skill/concept may be applied to any relevant situation... not only the context in which it was originally learned. **The failure to do this is responsible for most student failure to be able to apply something learned.** (Allen, 1998, bold in original)

Sra. Soto's comments suggest that she imagined the Centers to be places where children, having learned certain vocabulary and linguistic structures in the more structured classroom activities, might 'apply the language they were learning' in a form of independent practice. To this end, she designed the Centers, ostensibly places where the children could play, as a place where their play was expected to meet a particular curriculum goal. She described this practice of using play to achieve curriculum goals as 'play with purpose', and explained, 'I don't just send them in there for the play, like it's free time to go and do whatever you want. No, it's really time for you to practice. It's not just free play; it's play with a purpose in mind'.

When her indirect design methodology of stocking the Centers with toys related to the broader curriculum (such as farmer clothes, plastic food and a fire truck) failed to produce much practice of the target vocabulary, Sra. Soto's pedagogical strategies began to approximate more closely those associated with direct instruction, the approach with which Sra. Soto was clearly familiar and comfortable. She shifted to the classic traditional teacher discourse of question-response-evaluation (Lemke, 1990; Wells & Chang-Wells, 1992), an efficient way of finding out what children know, but less effective for advancing dialogue. This discourse pattern not only limits the complexity of language use, but also reinforces power asymmetries, '(reinforcing) the roles played by the teacher, as knower and imparter of knowledge, and by the student as the recipient of such knowledge' (Pérez & Torres-Guzmán, 1996: 56).

Sra. Soto's direct teaching approach might be described as an objectivist, or transmission, approach, 'which views the teacher as the source of knowledge and students as passive receptacles of this knowledge... (which) emphasizes learning by *receiving* information, especially from the teacher and from textbooks, to help students encounter facts and learn well-defined concepts' (B.C. Howard *et al.*, 2000: 456). In an open-ended activity such as play, the children define their own goals and the chances that the play will result in the planned goals of the teacher are relatively low. In this sense, Sra. Soto's attempt to implement a classroom practice inconsistent with her fundamental objectivist philosophy resulted in a retreat to more familiar territory, where the target behavior of the children was concrete and easily identifiable (practicing specific target vocabulary). This pattern is consistent with similar patterns found in the literature, instances where teachers ultimately reject teaching practices that are inconsistent with their fundamental epistemologies (B.C. Howard *et al.*, 2000).

One social studies teacher described her own personal struggle as she consciously tried to change her teaching approach from one that she described as 'teacher-centered' (lecture-based) to one that she described as 'children-centered' (based on children's inquiry and research and, at times, allowing for children's mistakes):

> I think most people who go into teaching are not risk-takers. We had positive experiences with school. We are pleasers; we play the game.

We like controlled situations and are not comfortable making mistakes. We do the right thing so that we have stellar evaluations from administrators. (Glamser, 1998)

My impression is that Sra. Soto experienced a similar struggle, but was not explicitly aware of it. Her interventions in the children's play present Sra. Soto, generally a confident and capable teacher, in her worst light. Nevertheless, the analysis of the few extended conversations that did arise demonstrates that she was at her best in this unfamiliar territory when she relaxed her control and followed the children's lead, coordinating her goals with theirs and allowing enough ambiguity and conflict so that the children were forced to use language as a tool for negotiation. This is perhaps the most difficult thing for teachers to do, particularly veteran teachers like Sra. Soto who have perfected the skills of maintaining control and reducing conflict that generally result in what is recognized as a successful classroom.

Nevertheless, genuine conversation is not something that can be pre-planned and carefully controlled, as it is fundamentally based on uncertainty, suggesting that the role of the teacher is in responding effectively as fledgling conversations emerge (Bannink, 2002). The two instances described in this chapter where Sra. Soto stepped out of her usual direct teaching role and permitted the children to temporarily co-define legitimate participation suggest that she was able to make the kind of in-flight decisions that could sustain conversation, although to her these moments might have felt 'off-task'. TWI programs are unique in the possibilities they afford for bilingual language development, but to fully access their potential, we need to carefully reconsider our assumptions about successful classroom design and classroom management.

Notes

1. This conversation continued for some time, and is discussed in more detail later in this chapter.
2. Sra. Soto had a tendency to shift themes within her speech turns, so coding different themes within each turn as separate turns would have led to the impression that a rather extended teacher monolog was actually a conversation.

Chapter 9

Implications: Real Practices behind the Ideal Model

This study, as an extensive case study, offers a detailed analysis of practice rooted in daily realities and pedagogical decisions made by one particular teacher. I chose Sra. Soto not because she was somehow typical or representative, but because she was generally recognized as an excellent teacher. Based on her strong reputation and years of experience as an English as a second language (ESL) teacher, she had been selected to teach this new and high profile two-way immersion (TWI) classroom. Far from being a 'representative sample' of a typical teacher, Sra. Soto was an exemplary teacher who was working in response to social realities that, indeed, data suggest are generalizable to other classrooms. Her practices should not be seen to represent practice characteristic or typical of TWI teachers, but as possibilities to be analyzed, discussed and disseminated.

In this chapter, I will share my own interpretations of the main findings of this study and how they are relevant beyond this particular classroom. I want this research to contribute to an ongoing dialogic process of deepening understanding. This chapter examines how this study might fit into this process, explaining how my observations might be useful to members of various communities: researchers, teachers and educational administrators.

Recognizing that New Methodologies Involve New Philosophies

Freeman argues that teachers should be understood as architects of learning rather than transmitters of content, as 'someone whose thinking about and understanding of what she (is) teaching allow(s) for a range of learning possibilities (whether extensive or limited)' (Freeman, 2004: 179). Sra. Soto described herself as an expert in direct teaching methodologies, but she also felt that children would learn language most effectively through interactions with each other. While the new TWI classroom that she designed was coherent with some of her underlying teaching and learning philosophies, its inconsistency with others contributed to tensions and frustrations that she attributed to failure in the students, in the school administration and in herself.

Sra. Soto did not share my interpretation of why children's play failed to produce language interactions, or that her attempts to teach children to play more effectively were ineffective. In fact, when I asked her what was the most important factor in producing conversation in the Centers, she responded that the most effective strategy was her direct modeling of 'good' play in the Centers, 'I think my going in there and showing them what I expected. And kids are emulators. They emulate what they see. They mimic'. She only seemed to regret that she could not spend more time with the children there: 'I don't think that I participated with them enough... I'm like the (eye) of the hurricane. And whenever they're around me, there's Spanish, and as you move further away, the less you hear Spanish... I should have been there more'.

She seemed to see the ideal learning situation as involving more individualized attention, and expressed frustration that she was unable to provide this kind of attention due to classroom constraints, 'But that's because I also had kids who needed me academically, they needed me to be sitting there with them, to help'. She felt that the classroom was understaffed, 'We did not have enough assistance at all. And I could talk until I was blue about getting an assistant, and I didn't get it. I was supposed to get more than what I did'. She was also disappointed in the Spanish speakers, whom she had hoped would fill the role of proxy teachers, 'I thought I had enough role models to carry me through. But then some of my role models were not as good as I had hoped'.

In her identification of these constraints, Sra. Soto revealed her ultimate adherence to a direct-teaching philosophy, where the teacher is central to the learning process. While, initially, Sra. Soto expressed the belief, more in line with the TWI underlying philosophy, that the teacher should take a more indirect role of 'designing instructional activities to promote desired interactions among the children', it seems that, faced with the failure of these instructional activities to promote the expected conversational interactions, Sra. Soto began to look for sources of this failure in individuals, reverting to a more traditional teacher-centered approach where skills, including play skills, were remediated by direct instruction.

This finding indicates that implementing a TWI program means more than just following a new recipe: it requires a clear understanding of the teaching and learning philosophies implicit in the model and an honest ongoing interrogation of how these might relate to our existing philosophies. The fact that Sra. Soto found the least teacher-directed areas of the classroom, the Centers, to be particularly challenging does not mean that she was a poor teacher or that she should not have been teaching in this classroom. Another teacher might have had difficulties in other areas where Sra. Soto excelled, for example, in enforcing the official language policy, encouraging children to take risks, or in designing thematic links. This research suggests that even experienced and skilled teachers need to be supported in critically reflecting on their practice, particularly when teaching in unfamiliar contexts.

My own observations supported Sra. Soto's reputation as a skilled teacher: she seemed resourceful, confident and devoted to the children she taught. In this sense, the analysis of Sra. Soto's philosophies and their relation to her teaching, first presented in Chapter 3 and discussed through the book, illustrates the ways in which even an exemplary and successful teacher might struggle to reconcile her existing set of beliefs with the philosophies underlying a new methodology, even one that she passionately supports.

This case analysis suggests that, while not necessarily in the same ways, other good teachers might face similar challenges that would be difficult to anticipate and perhaps even difficult to identify. Administrators and researchers should expect teachers to be like Sra. Soto, with contextualized, complex and contradictory beliefs. The concept of a teaching philosophy suggests a static and isolated concept of mind, which is an overly simplistic and mentalistic explanation for the actions of humans within the complex settings (such as a school environment) of our everyday lives. This finding should be of interest to teachers and administrators who wish to engage in new practices, and suggests that:

(1) Frustrations in the face of new teaching approaches may be the result of systemic and philosophical conflicts rather than simply failure(s) of the participants (teacher, students, parents, society and administration).

(2) While there is no silver bullet solution to such a complex problem, a collegial and supportive atmosphere that supports open discussion and reflective practice may serve to facilitate alternatives to frustration, such as compromise and personal growth.

Rethinking Symmetry: Can the Two-Way Immersion Program be Counter-Hegemonic?

While the theory of the TWI program, especially the 50:50 model exemplified by this classroom, assumes a balanced and complete immersion in each language, the realities expressed in this study suggest that this assumption is extremely optimistic. In Chapter 4, we examined some of the factors that tip this theoretical balance dramatically in favor of English: the intrusive nature of the broader monolingual English school culture and the children's preference for speaking English, even on the part of many of the designated Spanish speakers. The realities depicted in this study call for an examination and reevaluation of the theoretical framework of the 'balanced' TWI program.

As described in Chapter 4, Sra. Soto's decision to increase her instructional time in Spanish as a compensatory measure, accounting for the prevalence of English in the broader school context, was not supported by the school administration. Nevertheless, this practice of allocating more time to the minority language is common in TWI classroom design. A classroom can either allocate language time evenly to English and Spanish (50-50) or allocate more time to the minority language (known as 80-20 or 90-10). In these latter programs, 80–90% of instruction in Kindergarten is devoted to the minority language, and this balance is gradually shifted each year until instruction time is divided evenly between majority and minority languages (Lindholm-Leary, 2004/2005).

Interestingly, there is a regional pattern to language allocation in the USA. In California, the majority of programs favor the minority language, in Texas there are roughly equal numbers of programs favoring the minority language and allocating languages equally, and in New York the majority of programs allocate equal time to languages (Howard & Sugarman, 2001). Children in these programs that favor minority languages in the earlier grades tend to become more fully bilingual than those in 50-50 programs, yet their English proficiency is not compromised (Lindholm-Leary, 2001). Furthermore, these students are more likely to report that they enjoy reading in Spanish, an affective response that is closely tied with reading proficiency (Lindholm-Leary, 2005).

The Monteverde school in California, described in Chapter 1 as highly successful in terms of both academic proficiency and language proficiency, uses the 90:10 model with the explicit goal of balancing the fact that children engage in a wide variety of English-speaking activities (computer games, TV, etc.) outside school (Quintanar-Sarellana, 2004). At the Davis school in Arizona, where Spanish is the exclusive language of instruction for Kindergarten and Grade 1 and only a 70:30 Spanish to English ratio is reached by the fifth and final year, fifth graders scored above national and district averages in English Language Arts and reading proficiency tests (Smith & Arnot-Hopffer, 1998). Sra. Soto's decision to increase Spanish time might have been supported had she been teaching in a different school, and it would have been supported by research and the experience of other programs.

Sra. Soto's informal investigation of the language proficiencies of her students through her own classroom observations, observations of her students outside the classroom and conversations with parents provided a valuable insight into the realities behind the children's assigned language dominance. Her pedagogical strategies to ensure that the children spoke Spanish during Spanish time emerged from the reality that her classroom lacked the language constraints that might be found in a genuine Spanish immersion setting, where speakers are forced to communicate in the environmental language as best they can. Sra. Soto's strategies to create this illusory 'immersion' in a minority language required a great deal of perseverance and imagination. The children learned that they were to participate in a sort of game where, despite the fact that almost everyone spoke English as well as or better than Spanish, they were to pretend to speak and understand only Spanish during Spanish time.

It is also important to note that there may well be some sacrifices made in maintaining this artificial sense of Spanish immersion. Some of Sra. Soto's techniques, such as chiding Spanish speakers for speaking English (inadvertently recasting bilingualism as a deficit) and easily praising English speakers for minor achievements in Spanish, might serve to exacerbate the inequity that already exists between majority and minority language speakers (Valdés, 1997).

However, it is also important to keep in mind that some of the Spanish speakers who were initially reluctant to speak Spanish, thereby being constructed as poor role models, eventually shifted their language attitudes and therefore their positioning within the classroom. According to Sra. Soto's written evaluation at the end of the year, Joël was a good example of this phenomenon:

> I know you often heard me tell him that I refused to speak English with him. I wanted him to realize that Spanish was a language of power, a power that he possessed... I was pleased, however, that as the year progressed, that he opted to speak more and more his mother's tongue, and a power language in our classroom.

The role of educational and other institutions in maintaining hegemonic processes calls for consciously counter-hegemonic teaching; 'teachers are challenged to recognize their responsibility to critique and transform these classroom conditions tied to hegemonic processes that perpetuate the economic and cultural marginalization of subordinate groups' (Darder *et al.*, 2003: 13). The Center for Applied Linguistics (CAL) recommends that teachers explicitly address with children the unequal status of the two languages; one of their criteria for exemplary practice is that 'issues of language status are frequently discussed, and particular consideration is given to elevating the status of the (minority) language' (E.R. Howard *et al.*, 2007: 84).

Jaffe's (2002) study of a Corsican bilingual school describes how children were invited to share teachers' understandings of the value of reclaiming Corsican through visits from politicians, students, teachers, journalists, and even a television film crew, all of which sent children the clear message that learning Corsican made them special and subject to positive attention. Sra. Soto's classroom was visited by a local journalist who interviewed the children about why they thought speaking Spanish was important. This journalist was himself of Latino origin, and made it clear to the children that he personally valued their efforts to learn Spanish. Sra. Soto also explained to the children that my own presence as a researcher during Spanish time was related to the importance of learning Spanish. She also explained to me that she tended to speak Spanish with the children during field trips in order to reinforce that Spanish was a powerful and legitimate community language. There might have been further opportunities to reinforce this message by encouraging Spanish-speaking members of the local community, including parents, to visit the classroom and share particular skills and experiences that might be relevant to the classroom themes.

In general, my observations of the language asymmetry in Sra. Soto's classroom and her attempts to redress this asymmetry suggest that:

(1) Administrators must consider the social realities of language and power when they design TWI schools and consider the need to support the minority language in the overall school and classroom design.

(2) Teachers need to plan carefully how they will foster the development of both languages, but in particular, how they will make sure that the minority language is used and valued in the classroom.

(3) The need to speak the minority language must be artificially created, for example, by creating game-like rules of language restriction, by fostering communication with minority language speakers outside the classroom or by inviting these speakers into the classroom.

Understanding Language as a Means to an End

Based on a communicative approach to language learning, Sra. Soto considered conversation to be a crucial component in fostering language development. To this end, she designed a space, the play Centers, to facilitate conversation. However, her attempts to afford conversation production by indirect design failed to produce the degree of conversation she expected, as did her subsequent attempts to 'teach' children to converse while playing.

This finding provides some insight into the nature of language and the limitations involved in attempting to create or enforce it. First, it seems that children do not necessarily need conversation to advance play. The segments illustrated in Chapter 8 reveal that children are perfectly capable of playing together with the same toys, even engaging in a shared loosely structured pretend reality (building a train, playing house) with very little sustained conversation. This reflects a crucial flaw in Sra. Soto's Centers design: she considered language as the end, rather than as a means to an end. Language is a tool; words develop meaning only in action (Wittgenstein & Anscombe, 2001). Rather than designing environments to foster language production, teachers need to design tasks for which language serves as a means to achieve goals. The fact that more extended linguistic interactions emerged when conflicts had to be negotiated and ambiguities needed to be resolved supports this pragmatic view of language.

The design of free play Centers may not be the best way to stimulate language interactions. In this classroom, the notion of play with purpose involved appropriating the children's play for the teacher's purpose of stimulating language, a goal that was not shared by the children. Children's play is itself a cultural activity with its own norms and goals, which makes trying to interpret play through adult lenses a misguided effort (Hakkareinen, 2005). Rather than designing free-play zones and then hoping children will play with our (adult) purposes in mind, it might be more productive to design collaborative problem-solving activities around particular tasks. This shifts the metaphor, common in language acquisition, of learners as computers (in terms of input and output) to that of learners as apprentices in a community of practice, where 'Language is not seen as input, but as a tool for getting other things done' (Kramsch, 2002: 2).

Since negotiation of conflict and ambiguity seemed to most effectively achieve the intersubjectivity required to maintain conversation, these activities should be flexible enough to inspire this sort of language-based negotiation. Children might be asked to build together a dream house or model city, for example, which would require them to come to some consensus of what this house or city will contain. They might be asked to prepare and perform a skit for the class that draws on and extends the story of one of the books read during Language Arts. This might include, for example, retelling familiar stories in pairs or small groups and encouraging creativity and improvisation over accuracy (Iddings & McCafferty, 2007). As long as group negotiation is needed to complete the task, language is cast as the means to an end, as the vehicle by which the activity will be carried to its successful conclusion. This shifts the teacher's role to that of stage director, who will 'inspire and direct the student-actors' (Bannink, 2002: 285) and shifts the student's decision making and creativity to a more central role.

Sra. Soto's attempts to engage in conversational 'play' with the children tended to yield mainly the 'question, short response, evaluation' teacher-talk pattern characteristic of traditional teacher-student class-room dynamics, which failed to result in extended conversations. This was partly due to her expertise in a direct teaching methodology that is explicitly based on this discourse pattern. Furthermore, this discourse pattern and the learning and teaching philosophies implicit in it are embedded in a broader school culture that considers paying attention to the teacher and demonstrating one's learning by responding to teacher's questions to be unquestioned norms for a successful and orderly classroom (Kennedy, 2005). For most teachers, ambiguity and conflict signify failure, not progress. Yet anyone who has successfully learned a second language (L2) knows that there is a good deal of uncertainty and discomfort involved, and that it takes a strong desire to communicate to override our natural tendency to take the path of least resistance.

An analysis of Sra. Soto's most productive conversations with the children in the play Centers suggested that when she allowed the children to talk about their interests and lives outside the classroom, she was able to engage them in extended meaningful conversation. Drawing on Bakhtin's notion of carnival, fostering interactions that momentarily disrupt power hierarchies through humor and a sense of mutual transgression can lead to rich and creative L2 language interactions; these carnivalistic moments must be 'nurtured as a legitimate activity of the classroom instead of being punished or dismissed as off-task behavior' (Iddings & McCafferty, 2007: 42–43). It seems that Sra. Soto momentarily stumbled on this technique as she temporarily suspended classroom discourse rules to engage with the children in conversations about their 'off-topic' concerns. However, she still managed to coordinate her goals with theirs as the conversations progressed, suggesting that this was more a matter of adapting to an emerging situation than of conscious planning.

By engaging the children in explaining how their favorite toys worked, for example, she provided them with the chance to take the expert role and explain something that had special meaning in their lives. Some research has suggested that teachers can help children learn language by engaging them in particular kinds of dialogic interactions (Hayes & Matusov, 2005; Lindholm-Leary, 2005); there must be more research in order to understand just what that might entail and how it might relate to other kinds of classroom talk (Hayes, 2005; Takahashi-Breines, 2002). Referring to Gee's (1996) distinction between natural settings for language acquisition and classroom settings, Miller (2004: 119) points out that 'a site where students spend at least 1600 hours a year can hardly be termed "unnatural" or "inauthentic"'. She argues that while it may be a difficult task, teachers can draw on sociocultural understandings of apprenticeship into practice communities to create social contexts for language acquisition. I argue that this difficult task requires designing contexts for purposeful language use and a high degree of flexibility and tolerance for uncertainty.

In summary, my observations about conversation and play suggest that:

(1) Conversation is dependent on the need to negotiate meaning. This suggests that teachers who want to stimulate conversation might consider incorporating into the curriculum open-ended activities that have implicit goals attractive to children.
(2) Teachers should work together with each other or with researchers to examine interactional patterns in the classroom. These patterns need to be made explicit in order to find out when they conflict with our objectives, but also to identify those moments when we achieve the sorts of interactions that advance our classroom goals.
(3) Further research should focus on the nature of children's interactions with each other and with the teacher, in terms of linguistic richness and complexity, with an emphasis on what types of classroom activities seem to be most productive in this regard.

Taking a Close Look at Activity Structures and how they Construct Us as Learners

School is a cultural institution; its physical structures and routines have been shaped by and shape understandings of what it means to teach and learn (Stigler & Hiebert, 1998). These structures and routines are inherently power-laden, although we tend not to see the underlying power dynamic as anything but routine and normal:

> What meanings can one decode with the spatial production of perfect student lines marching in unison down the hallways in total silence? Is there a power differential produced between the teacher and student as they march? Yet, if this behavior is enacted on an everyday basis, do the classroom subjects lose consciousness of the underlying, hidden meanings within such synchronized routines? (Hadi-Tabassum, 2006: 70)

While teachers and students alike may be unable to articulate these power dynamics, children perform in school in response to an institutional culture of constant surveillance and sorting. Becoming aware of these unconscious, culturally embedded practices and their significance should be one of the benefits of careful classroom ethnography.

As much as we would like to imagine that all children might succeed, failure is an inevitable by-product of success in a competitive schooling system (DePalma *et al.*, 2009; Varenne & McDermott, 1998). While we tend to think of failure and success as rooted in the individual, the result of something that students do (or don't do), they are in fact socially constructed. Different kinds of learners, enthusiastic or reluctant, gifted or disabled, come to be constructed in different kinds of schooling contexts (Matusov *et al.*, 2007; McDermott, 1993). This is not to say that learners are passive, but that they participate in the co-construction of these learner identities as they manage their performance in light of their own partial and situated understandings of the context (DePalma, 2008). More and more attention is paid to identifying and sorting children according to fixed problem categories, such as language delays, learning disabilities and behavior disorders, yet perhaps more attention should be paid to how these conditions are co-constructed through school practices, 'American schools are not always better off for their careful attention to kinds of children, but they do relentlessly create conditions under which rumors of disability and disadvantaged background are attended to and their persons counted, theorized, explained, and remediated' (McDermott *et al.*, 2006: 16).

Sra. Soto's classroom, typical of most US Kindergarten classrooms, was divided into various daily activities that differed not only in terms of the nature of the activity itself, but also in terms of the definition of legitimate and illegitimate participation. One might be expected to sing loudly and even jump up and dance a bit during a chant, but this same behavior was quickly chastized during a vocabulary exercise; within certain activity structures one might be expected to engage the teacher in a discussion about what was served for lunch that day, but definitely not if the teacher happened to be reading a book out loud at that moment.

Learning the different norms for discourse and physical behavior in these different activity systems was part of the business of learning school for these Kindergarten children, and some of them caught on more quickly than others. Some, like Sandra and Emily, quickly learned to excel across several activity structures, while others, like Rashid and Kathleen, seemed less adept at interpreting and contextualizing these norms. Different activity structures constructed the children in very different ways. Dorinda, for example, was a competent and confident Spanish speaker in highly ritualized and collective activities, such as chants and songs, even though she was hesitant and incompetent when asked to perform independently. Kathleen simultaneously developed a reputation as a serious behavior problem and a positive role model, as she participated with varying degrees of success in different activity structures.

Sometimes learners were constructed in unexpected ways: Sandra, Emily and Kathleen were constructed as good role models of a language in which they were far from proficient while Berto, a native speaker of this language, was not. These roles might have shifted quickly if the same children were introduced into different activity settings, for example, at a family dinner, a playground soccer game or a church social in Berto's neighborhood.

This situation presents the teacher with a quandary: on the one hand it is important that truly monolingual English speakers quickly develop confidence and rudimentary language skills in Spanish in order to catch up with their Spanish-speaking peers, most of whom are already well on the way to becoming bilingual by the time they enter school. If not, the quality and complexity of Spanish language used in the classroom might be compromised to facilitate comprehension and the Spanish speakers might not have a chance to develop academic proficiency in their native language (Valdés, 1997). On the other hand, when children like Berto become constructed as failed role models for speaking their own language, what message are we sending them?

This might seem like a no-win situation for Spanish speakers, but I am in no way suggesting that it is a reason to abandon TWI programs. I do suggest that teachers, program designers and researchers recognize the complex ways in which the construction of failure and success in these classrooms might reinforce existing inequities across language, ethnicity and social class, and consider ways to counter these effects. While most researchers and policy makers seem to assume that the English-speaking children in TWI programs will be from middle-class White families, many of the children in this Kindergarten classroom came from African-American families who may have had relatively little experience themselves with what is considered to be the standard variety of English in the USA (Valdés, 2002).

At the same time, the potential for certain activity structures to work against traditional lines of inequity should be examined. Dorinda, for example, was an African-American girl from what Sra. Soto described as a relatively unstable home background. Particularly through her performance in the more structured activity settings, she was constructed as a gifted language learner in this classroom, as reflected in her final evaluation, 'Dorinda...was extremely language-oriented. She had an affinity toward auditory skills which helped her acquire Spanish skills easily'. In most classrooms, Dorinda's language-based success would probably never have existed, while assumptions based on her race, gender, neighborhood and family structure might have facilitated her construction as a different kind of learner. Kathleen, similarly, seemed able to transcend class-based assumptions through her remarkable performance in the less structured activity settings, even while she was constructed as a failure in other areas.

These finding suggest that:

(1) We need to become aware of the power dynamics inherent in all school contexts, including those of TWI programs. Some of these might facilitate, and some might inhibit, social equity-based goals underpinning TWI programs.
(2) A broad range of carefully designed activity structures will not only provide opportunities for various aspects of language development, but can also provide opportunities for success to emerge for different children.

Finally, it is important to recognize that these implications have been formed within my own particular conceptual frameworks. I do not pretend to have found all the possible interpretations and implications of this study, but I hope to begin a discussion that will engage negotiations and reinterpretations of meanings, and stimulate and provide some direction for further research.

Conscious of the ultimate importance of interpretation as the essential practice of research, I present this final chapter as something more than a conclusion, since it is here more than at any other point that the reader is invited into the interpretive research dialog. The reader's participation is part of the research process:

> Readers of qualitative research must... constantly question the text to explore the authors' responses to these issues and to see where they themselves stand. Among the questions we as readers could ask are: What assumptions might the author not acknowledge? (Brizuela *et al.*, 2000: xvi)

At the end of Chapter 2, I explained how my own interpretations, like those of the teacher in this study, are situated within the framework of my own personal and professional values and experiences. As I was not as deeply immersed in the institutional context of the school and classroom as Sra. Soto, I do not pretend that my interpretations are somehow more pure and objective. Since Sra. Soto was not able to continue to work with me as I analyzed the data and formed my interpretations, it is important that readers keep in mind that her views, which often diverge from my own, are also those of an experienced and educated professional. Similarly, I hope that I have managed to provide rich and detailed enough data so that readers can actively contribute to this process of interpretation.

Appendix:
Data coding template

Segment #:   Date: Location:
Summary:
Children involved:
Maximum number of children: Minimum number of children:
Total duration:
More than one participant: Yes/No
Teacher present: Yes/No
Spanish language turns: English language turns:
Mixed language turns: Unknown language turns:

Threads with more than three turns:
Theme: Theme:
Initiating utterance: Initiating utterance:
Number of turns: Number of turns:
Theme: Theme:
Initiating utterance: Initiating utterance:
Number of turns: Number of turns:
Theme: Theme:
Initiating utterance: Initiating utterance:
Number of turns: Number of turns:

Teacher initiating utterances:
Known-answer   Language control   Discipline-order   Other

References

Aguirre, A. (1988) Code switching, intuitive knowledge, and the bilingual classroom. In H.S. Garcia and R. Chavez (eds) *Ethnolinguistic Issues in Education* (pp. 28–38). Lubbock, TX: Director of Bilingual Education, Texas Tech University.

Alanís, I. (2000) A Texas two-way bilingual program: Its effects on linguistic and academic achievement. *Bilingual Research Journal* 24 (3), 225–248.

Alanís, I. (2007) Dual language education: Answering the Texas challenge. *The National Association of African American Studies and Affiliates, Fall*. On WWW at http://www.utpa.edu/colleges/coe/orgs/naaas/duallanguage.html.

Alba, R. (2007) Bilingualism persists, but English still dominates. On WWW at http://www.migrationinformation.org/Feature/display.cfm?id = 282. Accessed 21.12.07.

Allen, T. (1998) Some basic lesson presentation elements. 30 September. On WWW at http://www.humboldt.edu/ ~ tha1/index.html.

Amrein, A. and Peña, R.A. (2000) Asymmetry in dual language practice: Assessing imbalance in a program promoting equality. *Education Policy Analysis Archives* 8 (8), 1–17.

Anderson, J.R., Reder, L.M. and Simon, H.A. (1997) Situated versus cognitive perspective: Form versus substance. *Educational Researcher* 26 (1), 18–21.

Arnold, J. (1999) *Affect in Language Learning*. Cambridge: Cambridge University Press.

Arriaza, G. and Arias, A. (1998) Claiming collective memory: Maya languages and civil rights. *Social Justice* 25 (3), 70.

Asher, J. (1982) *Learning Another Language through Actions: The Complete Teacher's Guidebook* (2nd edn). Los Gatos, CA: Sky Oaks Productions.

Asher, J. (1984) Language by command: The total physical response approach to learning language. On WWW at http://www.context.org/ICLIB/IC06/Asher.htm. Accessed 20.7.02.

Avalos, C. and Caminos, J. (1992) *Chana y su rana*. New York: Scholastic.

Bahruth, R.E. (2000) Bilingual education. In D. Gabbard (ed.) *Knowledge and Power in the Global Economy : Politics and the Rhetoric of School Reform* (pp. 203–209). Mahwah, NJ: Lawrence Erlbaum Associates.

Baines, L. and Stankey, G.K. (2000) 'We want to see the teacher': Constructivism and the rage against expertise. *Phi Delta Kappan* 82 (4), 327–330.

Baker, C. (2006) *Foundations of Bilingual Education and Bilingualism* (4th edn). Clevedon, Buffalo: Multilingual Matters.

Bakhtin, M.M. (1986) *Speech Genres and Other Late Essays*. Austin, TX: University of Texas Press.

Bakhtin, M.M. (1999) *Problems of Dostoevsky's Poetics*. Minneapolis, MN: University of Minnesota Press.

Bannink, A. (2002) Negotiating the paradoxes of spontaneous talk in advanced L2 classes. In C.J. Kramsch (ed.) *Language Acquisition and Language Socialization: Ecological Perspectives* (pp. 266–289). London, New York: Continuum.

Bellin, H.F. and Singer, D.G. (2006) *My magic story car*: Video-based play intervention to strengthen emergent literacy of at-risk preschoolers. In D.G. Singer, R.M. Golinkoff and K. Hirsh-Pasek (eds) *Play =learning: How Play Motivates and Enhances Children's Cognitive and Social-Emotional Growth* (pp. 101–123). New York: Oxford University Press.

Bialystok, E. (2006) Second-language acquisition and bilingualism at an early age and the impact on early cognitive development. In R.E. Tremblay, R.G. Barr and RDeV Peters (eds) *Encyclopedia on Early Childhood Development* [online] (pp. 1–4). Montreal: Centre of Excellence for Early Childhood Development.

Bickle, K., Billings, E.S. and Hakuta, K. (2004) Trends in two-way immersion research. In J.A. Banks and C.A.M. Banks (eds) *Handbook of Research on Multicultural Education* (2nd edn, pp. 589–604). San Francisco, CA: Jossey-Bass.

Bigus, O.E., Hadden, S.C. and Glaser, B.G. (1994) The study of basic social processes. In B.G. Glaser (ed.) *More Grounded Theory Methodology: A Reader* (pp. 38–64). Mill Valley, CA: Sociology Press.

Blas-Arroyo, J.L. (2002) The languages of the Valencian educational system: The results of two decades of language policy. *International Journal of Bilingual Education and Bilingualism* 5 (6), 318–339.

Bourdieu, P. (1986) The forms of capital. In J.G. Richardson (ed.) *Handbook of Theory and Research for the Sociology of Education* (pp. 241–260). New York: Greenwood Press.

Brice Heath, S. (2000) Linguistics in the study of language education. In B. Brizuela, J.P. Stewart and R.G. Berger (eds) *Acts of Inquiry in Qualitative Research* (Vol. 34). Cambridge, MA: Harvard Educational Review.

Brint, S., Contreras, M.F. and Matthews, M.T. (2001) Socialization messages in primary schools: An organizational analysis. *Sociology of Education* 74 (3), 157–180.

Brizuela, B., Stewart, J.P. and Berger, R.G. (eds) (2000) *Acts of Inquiry in Qualitative Research* (Vol. 34). Cambridge, MA: Harvard Educational Review.

Bruner, J. (1983) *Child's Talk: Learning to Use Language*. New York: Norton.

Carson, T.R. and Sumara, D.J. (1997) *Action Research as a Living Practice*. New York: P. Lang.

Cazabon, M.T., Nicolaidis, E. and Lambert, W.E. (1998) *Becoming Bilingual in the Amigos Two-Way Immersion Program*. Santa Cruz, CA: CREDE Center for Research on Education Diversity & Excellence.

Center for Applied Linguistics (2009) Directory of two-way bilingual immersion programs in the US. 2 June. On WWW at http://www.cal.org/twi/directory. Accessed 6.10.09.

Center for Research on Education Diversity & Excellence (2001) Some program alternatives for English language learners (Practitioner Brief #3). *Online Resources: Digests*. On WWW at http://www.cal.org/resources/digest/PracBrief3.html. Accessed 24.12.07.

Collier, V.P. and Thomas, W.P. (2004) The astounding effectiveness of dual language education for all. *NABE Journal of Research and Practice* 2 (1), 1–20.

Collins, J. (2007) Language interactions in the classroom: From coercive to collaborative relations of power. In O. García and C. Baker (eds) *Bilingual Education: An Introductory Reader* (pp. 108–136). Clevedon, Philadelphia: Multilingual Matters.

Collins, T.M. (1993) Why Juanito is bilingual and Jane is not: A third grade ethnography. Unpublished Master of Art, San Diego State University.

Collins, T.M. (1998) Two-way bilingual education: Strong and weak models. Unpublished manuscript, San Diego, CA.

Cziko, G.A. (1992) The evaluation of bilingual education: From necessity and probability to possibility. *Education Reseacher* 21 (2), 10–15.

Chen-Hayes, S.F., Chen, M.-W. and Athar, N. (2001) Challenging linguicism: Action strategies for counselors and client-colleagues. On WWW at http://www.counseling.org/conference/advocacy1.htm. Accessed 2.8.99.

Christian, D. (1994) *Two-Way Bilingual Education: Students Learning Through Two Languages* (Educational Practice Report No. 12): National Center for Research on Cultural Diversity and Second Language Learning.

Christian, D. (1996) Two-way immersion education: Students learning through two languages. *Modern Language Journal* 80, 66–76.

Christian, D. and Genesee, F. (2001) Two-way immersion. 25 November. On WWW at http://www.cal.org/crede/twoway.htm.

Christian, D., Montone, C.L., Lindholm, K.J. and Carranza, I. (1997) *Profiles in Two-Way Immersion Education*. McHenry, IL: Delta Ststems, Inc.

Darder, A., Baltodano, M. and Torres, R.D. (eds) (2003) *The Critical Pedagogy Reader*. New York: Routledge Farmer.

De Jong, E.J. (2002) Effective bilingual education: From theory to academic achievement in a two-way bilingual program. *Bilingual Research Journal* 26 (1), 65–84.

DePalma, R. (2006) 'There wasn't a conversation going on': How implicit classroom norms can short-circuit language learning. *International Journal of Learning* 12 (6), 197–206.

DePalma, R. (2008) When success makes me fail: (De)constructing failure and success in a conventional American classroom. *Mind, Culture, and Activity* 15 (2), 141–164.

DePalma, R., Matusov, E. and Smith, M.P. (2009) Smuggling authentic learning into the school context: Transitioning from an innovative elementary to a conventional high school. *Teachers College Record* 111 (4), 934–972.

Dick, B. (2000, November 29) Grounded theory: A thumbnail sketch. On WWW at http://www.scu.edu.au/schools/gcm/ar/arp/grounded.html#a_gt_memo.

Donato, R. (1993) Segregation, desegregation, and integration of Chicano students: Problems and prospects. In R.R. Valencia (ed.) *Chicago School Failure and Success: Research and Policy Agendas for the 1990s* (pp. 20–59). New York: Falmer Press.

Doyle, W. (1981) Research on classroom contexts. *Journal of Teacher Education* 32 (6), 3–6.

Ebsworth, M. (2002) Comment. *International Journal of the Sociology of Language* 155–156, 101–114.

Einon, D., Farndon, J. and Betsy, A. (1986) *Play with a Purpose: Learning Games for Children Six Weeks to Ten Years*. New York: Random House Trade Paperbacks.

Ellis, R. (2008) *Principles of Instructed Second Language Acquisition*. Washington, DC: Center for Applied Linguistics (CAL).

Erickson, F. (1982) Classroom discourse as improvisation: Relationships between academic task structure and social participation structure in lessons. In L.C. Wilkinson (ed.) *Communicating in the Classroom* (pp. 153–181). New York: Academic Press.

Erickson, F. (1986) Qualitiative methods in research on teaching. In M.C. Wittrock (ed.) *Handbook of Research in Teaching* (3rd edn, pp. 119–161). New York: Macmillan.

Escamilla, K. (1994) The sociolinguistic environment of a bilingual school. *Bilingual Research Journal* 18 (1 and 2), 21–47.

Fassler, R. (2003) *Room for Talk: Teaching and Learning in a Multilingual Kindergarten*. New York: Teachers College Press.

Foley, D. (2004) Ogbu's theory of academic disengagement: Its evolution and its critics. *Intercultural Education* 15 (4), 384–397.

Foreman, J. (2002) Health sense; The evidence speaks well of bilingualism's effect on kids. *The Los Angeles Times*, 7 October.

Freeman, D. (2004) Language, sociocultural theory, and L2 teacher education: Examining the technology of subject matter and the architecture of instruction. In M.R. Hawkins (ed.) *Language Learning and Teacher Education: A Sociocultural Approach* (pp. 169–197). Clevedon: Multilingual Matters.

Freeman, R.D. (1998) *Bilingual Education and Social Change*. Clevedon: Multilingual Matters.

Garcia, E.E. (2002) Bilingualism and schooling in the United States. *International Journal of the Sociology of Language* 155–156, 1–92.

García, E.E. (2005) *Teaching and Learning in Two Languages : Bilingualism & Schooling in the United States*. New York: Teachers College Press.

Gatbonton, E. and Segalowitz, N. (1988) Creative automatization: Principles for promoting fluency within a communicative framework. *TESOL Quarterly* 22 (3), 473–492.

Gee, J.P. (1996) *Social Linguistics and Literacies : Ideology in Discourses* (2nd edn). London: Taylor & Francis.

Gerardo, S. (1994) *The Bojabi Tree: A Folktale from Gabon*. New York: Scholastic.

Ginsburg, H.P. (2006) Mathematical play and playful mathematics: A guide for early education. In D.G. Singer, R.M. Golinkoff and K. Hirsh-Pasek (eds) *Play = learning: How Play Motivates and Enhances Children's Cognitive and Social-emotional Growth* (pp. 145–167). New York: Oxford University Press.

Glamser, M.C. (1998) Notes from a teacher/soldier in the learning revolution. *Houston Chronicle*, 19 April.

Godina, H. (2004) Contradictory literacy practices of Mexican-background students: An ethnography from the rural midwest. *Bilingual Research Journal* 28 (2), 153–180.

Gómez, L., Freeman, D. and Freeman, Y. (2005) Dual language education: A promising 50–50 model. *Bilingual Research Journal* 29 (1), 145–164.

Gonzalez-Jensen, M. (1997) The status of children's fiction literature written in Spanish by US authors. *Bilingual Research Journal* 21 (2 & 3), 103–112.

Graham, C.R. and Brown, C. (1996) The effects of acculturation on second language proficiency in a community with a two-way bilingual program. *The Bilingual Research Journal* 20 (2), 235–260.

Gramsci, A., Hoare, Q. and Nowell-Smith, G. (1972) *Selections from the Prison Notebooks of Antonio Gramsci* (1st edn). New York: International Publishers.

Gunn, C., Lavelle, T. and Lirette, C. (2002) Boggle's World ESL worksheets and lesson plans. On WWW at from http://bogglesworld.com. Accessed 17.7.02.

Gurza, A. (1999) A language is a terrible thing to lose. *Los Angeles Times*, 18 May.

Gutiérrez, K., Rymes, B. and Larson, J. (1995) Script, counterscript, and underlife in the classroom: James Brown vs. Board of Education. *Harvard Education Review* 65 (3), 445–472.

Hadi-Tabassum, S. (2005) The balancing act of bilingual immersion. *Educational Researcher* 62 (4), 50–54.

Hadi-Tabassum, S. (2006) *Language, Space and Power: A Critical Look at Bilingual Education*. Clevedon: Multilingual Matters.

Hakkareinen, P. (2005) Cultural development in play. Paper presented at the International Society for Cultural and Activity Research (ISCAR).

Hakuta, K. and Garcia, E.E. (1989) Bilingualism and education. *American Psychologist* 44 (2), 374–379.

Han Chung, H. (2006) Code switching as a communicative strategy: A case study of Korean–English bilinguals. *Bilingual Research Journal* 30 (2), 293–307.

Hawkins, M.R. (2004) *Language Learning and Teacher Education: A Sociocultural Approach*. Clevedon: Multilingual Matters.

Hayes, R. (2004) Dual Language Pedagogy: Compensating for Asymmetry. *Academic Exchange Quarterly* 8 (3), 41–46.

Hayes, R. (2005) Conversation, negotiation, and the word as deed: Linguistic interaction in a dual language program. *Linguistics and Education* 16, 93–112.

Hayes, R. and Matusov, E. (2005) Designing for dialogue in place of teacher talk and student silence. *Culture and Psychology* 11 (3), 339–357.

Heath, S.B. (1983) *Ways with Words: Language, Life, and Work in Communities and Classrooms*. Cambridge: Cambridge University Press.

Holl, A. and Duvoisin, R. (1968) *The Rain Puddle*. New York: William Morrow.

Howard, B.C., McGee, S. and Schwartz, N. (2000) The experience of constructivism: Transforming teacher epistemology. *Journal of Research on Computing in Education* 32 (4), 355–365.

Howard, E.R. and Christian, D. (2002) Two-way immersion 101: Designing and implementing a two-way immersion education program at the elementary level. On WWW at http://www.cal.org/crede/pubs/edpractice/EPR9.htm. Accessed 3.2.04.

Howard, E.R., Christian, D. and Genesee, F. (2003a) *The Development of Bilingualism and Biliteracy from Grade 3 to 5: A Summary of Findings from the CAL/CREDE Study of Two-Way Immersion Education* (No. 13). Santa Cruz, CA and Washington, DC: Center for Research on Education, Diversity & Excellence.

Howard, E.R. and Loeb, M.I. (1998) In their own words: Two-way immersion teachers talk about their professional experiences. On WWW at http://www.cal.org/resources/digest/intheirownwords.html. Accessed 1.11.05.

Howard, E.R., Olague, N. and Rogers, D. (2003b) *The Dual Language Program Planner: A Guide for Designing and Implementing Dual Language Programs*. Santa

Cruz, CA and Washington, DC: Center for Research on Education, Diversity & Excellence.

Howard, E.R. and Sugarman, J. (2001) Two-way immersion programs: Features and statistics. March. On WWW at http://www.cal.org/ericcll/digest/0101twi.html.

Howard, E.R., Sugarman, J. and Christian, D. (2003c) *Trends in Two-Way Immersion Research: A Review of the Research* (No. 63). Center for Research on the Education of Students Placed At Risk (CRESPAR).

Howard, E.R., Sugarman, J., Christian, D., Lindholm-Leary, K.J. and Rogers, D. (2007) *Guiding Principles for Dual Language Education* (2nd edn). Washington, DC: Center for Applied Linguistics.

Howe, A.C. and Jones, L. (1998) *Engaging Children in Science* (2nd edn). Columbus, OH: Prentice Hall.

Hunter, M. (1971) *Teach for Transfer*. Thousand Oaks, CA: Corwin Press.

Iddings, A. and McCafferty, S. (2007) Carnival in a mainstream Kindergarten classroom: A Bakhtinian analysis of second language learners' off-task behaviors. *The Modern Language Journal* 91 (1), 31–44.

Jaffe, A. (2002) Cooperative learning in a Corsican bilingual classroom. Paper presented at the Fifth Congress of the International society for Cultural Research and Activity Theory, Vrje University, Amsterdam, The Netherlands, 18–22 June.

Kennedy, M.M. (2005) *Inside Teaching: How Classroom Life Undermines Reform*. Cambridge, MA: Harvard University Press.

Kirk Senesac, B.V. (2002) Two-way bilingual immersion: A portrait of quality schooling. *Bilingual Research Journal 26* (1), 85–101.

Kleinsinger, S.B. (1992) *Learning Through Play: Science*. New York: Scholastic.

Knell, E., Haiyan, Q., Miao, P., Yanping, C., Siegel, L.S., Lin, Z. and Wei, Z. (2007) Early English immersion and literacy in Xi'an, China. *Modern Language Journal* 91 (3), 395–417.

Kramsch, C.J. (2002) Introduction: 'How can we tell the dancer from the dance?'. In C.J. Kramsch (ed.) *Language Acquisition and Language Socialization: Ecological Perspectives* (pp. 1–30). London, New York: Continuum.

Krashen, S.D. (1985) *The Input Hypothesis: Issues and Implications*. London, New York: Longman.

Kuhlman, N.A. (1993) Emerging literacy in a two-way bilingual first grade classroom. Paper presented at the National Association for Bilingual Education, Tucson, AZ, 1990; Washington, DC, 1991.

Labov, W. (1974) Academic ignorance and Black intelligence. In R.J. Mueller, D. Ary and C. McCormick (eds) *Readings in Classroom Learning and Perception* (pp. 328–345). New York: Praeger.

Lafford, B.A. and Salaberry, M.R. (2003) *Spanish Second Language Acquisition: State of the Science*. Washington, DC: Georgetown University Press.

Lambert, W.E. (1990) Issues in foreign language and second language education. Paper presented at the Research Symposium on Limited English Proficient Students' Issues, Washington, DC, 10–12 September.

Lantolf, J.P. and Thorne, S.L. (2006) *Sociocultural Theory and the Genesis of Second Language Development*. Oxford: Oxford University Press.

Lave, J. and Wenger, E.C. (1991) *Situated Learning: Legitimate Peripheral Participation*. Cambridge: Cambridge University Press.

Lazaruk, W. (2007) Linguistic, academic, and cognitive benefits of French immersion. *Canadian Modern Language Review* 63 (5), 605–627.

Lee, C.D. and Smagorinsky, P. (2000) *Vygotskian Perspectives on Literacy Research: Constructing Meaning through Collaborative Inquiry.* Cambridge, New York: Cambridge University Press.

Legarreta, D. (1977) Language choice in bilingual classrooms. *TESOL Quarterly* 11 (1), 9–15.

Lemke, J.L. (1990) *Talking Science.* Norwood, NJ: Ablex Publishing.

Lenker, A. and Rhodes, N. (2007) Foreign language immersion programs: Features and trends over 35 Years. *Online Resources: Digests.* On WWW at http://www.cal.org/resources/digest/flimmersion.html. Accessed 24.12.07.

Lindholm-Leary, K.J. (2001) *Dual Language Education.* Clevedon: Multilingual Matters.

Lindholm-Leary, K.J. (2004/2005) The rich promise of two-way immersion. *Educational Leadership* 62 (4), 56–59.

Lindholm-Leary, K.J. (2005) Review of research and best practices on effective features of dual language education programs. On WWW at http://www.lindholm-leary.com/resources/review_research.pdf. Accessed 8.9.05.

Lindholm-Leary, K.J. and Borsato, G. (2002) Impact of two-way bilingual elementary programs on students' attitudes toward school and college. On WWW at http://www.cal.org/ericcll/digest/0201lindholm.html. Accessed 12.7.02.

Lindholm, K.J. (1990) Bilingual immersion education: Criteria for program development. In H. Fairchild and C. Valadez (eds) *Bilingual Education: Issues and Strategies* (pp. 91–105). Newbury Park, CA: Sage.

Luo, S-H. and Wiseman, R.L. (2000) Ethnic language maintenance among Chinese immigrant children in the United States. *International Journal of Intercultural Relations* 24 (3), 307–324.

Maris, R. (1982) *Better Move On, Frog!* London: Franklin Watts.

Matusov, E., DePalma, R. and Drye, S. (2007) Whose development? Salvaging the concept of development within a sociocultural approach to education. *Educational Theory* 57 (4), 403–421.

Matusov, E., Hayes, R. and Pluta, M.J. (1998) Using discussion world wide webs to develop an academic community of learners. Paper presented at the International Conference on the Learning Sciences, Atlanta, Georgia, December.

Maykut, P.S. and Morehouse, R. (1994) *Beginning Qualitative Research: A Philosophic and Practical Guide.* London, Washington, DC: Falmer Press.

McDermott, R.P. (1993) The acquisition of a child by a learning disability. In S. Chaiklin and J. Lave (eds) *Understanding Practice. Perspectives on Activity and Context* (pp. 269–305). New York: Cambridge University Press.

McDermott, R.P., Goldman, S. and Varenne, H. (2006) The cultural work of learning disabilities. *Educational Researcher* 35 (6), 12–17.

Miller, J. (2004) Social languages and schooling: The uptake of sociocultural perspectives in school. In M.R. Hawkins (ed.) *Language Learning and Teacher Education: A Sociocultural Approach* (pp. 113–146). Clevedon: Multilingual Matters.

Miller, S. (2008) Como Se Dice? Obama clarifies comments over foreign languages. ABC News, 11 July.

Mishler, E.G. (2000) Validation in inquiry-guided research: The role of exemplars in narrative studies. In B. Brizuela, J.P. Stewart and R.G. Berger (eds) *Acts of Inquiry in Qualitative Research* (Vol. 34). Cambridge, MA: Harvard Educational Review.

Moll, L.C. (1990) *Vygotsky and Education: Instructional Implications and Applications of Socio-Historical Psychology.* Cambridge, New York: Cambridge University Press.

Mora, J.K., Wink, J. and Wink, D. (2001) Dueling models of dual language instruction: A critical review of the literature and program implementation guide. *Bilingual Research Journal* 25 (4), 417–442.

Moraes, M. (1996) *Bilingual Education: A Dialogue with the Bakhtin Circle.* Albany, NY: State University of New York Press.

Morison, S.H. (1990) A Spanish-English dual-language program in New York City. *Annals of the American Academy of Political and Social Science* 508, 160–169.

National Council of La Raza (2001) Beyond the census: Hispanics and an American agenda. On WWW at http://www.nclr.org/policy/census/census_report01_part_I.pdf.

Nieto, S. (1999) Identity, personhood, and Puerto Rican students: Challenging paradigms of assimilation and authenticity. Paper presented at the American Educational Research Association, Montreal, Canada.

Norton, B. (2000) *Identity and Language Learning: Gender, Ethnicity and Educational Change.* Harlow: Longman.

Nuñez-Janes, M. (2002a) Bilingual education and identity debates in New Mexico: Constructing and contesting nationalism and ethnicity. *Journal of the Southwest* 44 (11), 61–79.

Nuñez-Janes, M. (2002b) I'm Mexican, I'm Mexican-American: Conflicting and oppositional identities in a bilingual school. Paper presented at the 23rd Penn Ethnography Forum, University of Pennsylvania.

Olvera, J.E. (2004) Spanish language in midst of a 'cultural renaissance'. *Rocky Mountain News*, 1 May.

Orellana, M.F., Ek, L. and Hernandez, A. (1999) Bilingual education in an immigrant community: Proposition 227 in California. *International Journal of Bilingual Education and Bilingualism* 2 (2), 114–130.

Oxford, R.L. (1998) *Where is the United States headed with K-12 foreign language education?* (news report No. Vol. 22, No. 1) ERIC/CLL.

Parsons, E.C. (2000) Culturalizing science instruction: What is it, what does it look like and why do we need it? *Journal of Science Teacher Education* 11 (3), 207–219.

Pellerano, C., Fradd, S.H. and Rovira, L. (1998) Coral way elementary school: A success story in bilingualism and biliteracy. On WWW at www.ncbe.gwu.edu.

Pennycook, A. (1998) *English and the Discourses of Colonialism.* London, New York: Routledge.

Pennycook, A. (2001) *Critical Applied Linguistics: A Critical Introduction.* Mahwah, NJ: Lawrence Erlbaum Associates.

Peregoy, S.F. (1991) Environmental scaffolds and earner response in a two-way Spanish immersion kindergarten. *The Canadian Modern Language Review* 47 (3), 463–476.

Peregoy, S.F. and Boyle, O.F. (1999) Multiple embedded scaffolds: Support for English speakers in a two-way Spanish immersion Kindergarten. *Bilingual Research Journal* 23 (2&3), 135–146.

Pérez, B. (2004) *Becoming Biliterate: A Study of Two-Way Bilingual Immersion Education*. Mahwah, NJ: Lawrence Erlbaum Associates.

Pérez, B. and Torres-Guzmán, M.E. (1996) *Learning in Two Worlds: An Integrated Spanish/English Biliteracy Approach* (2nd edn). White Plains, NY: Longman.

Potowski, K. (2004) Student Spanish use and investment in a dual immersion classroom: Implications for second language acquisition and heritage language maintenance. *Modern Language Journal* 88, 75–101.

Pufahl, I., Rhodes, N.C. and Christian, D. (2001) Foreign language teaching: What the United States can learn from other countries. On WWW at http://www.cal.org/ericcll/digest/0106pufahl.html.

Quintanar-Sarellana, R. (2004) ¡Si Se Puede! Academic excellence and bilingual competency in a K-8 two-way dual immersion program. *Journal of Latinos and Education* 3 (2), 87–102.

Rickert, E. (1958) *The Bojabi Tree*. New York: Doubleday and Company.

Riley, R.W. (2000) Dual language grant announcement, 19 December. On WWW at http://www.connectlive.com.events/deptedu/duallangtran-script122000.html. Accessed 3.3.02.

Riojas-Clark, E. (1995) 'How did you learn to write in English when you haven't been taught in English?': The language experience approach in a dual language program. *Bilingual Research Journal* 19 (3&4), 611–627.

Riojas-Cortéz, M. (2001) Mexican-American preschoolers create stories: Socio-dramatic play in a dual language classroom. *Bilingual Research Journal* 24 (3), 295–308.

Rodriguez, R. (1983) *Hunger of Memory : The Education of Richard Rodriguez: An Autobiography*. New York, Toronto: Bantam Books.

Rogoff, B. (1990) *Apprenticeship in Thinking: Cognitive Development in Social Context*. New York: Oxford University Press.

Rogoff, B., Göncü, A., Mistry, J. and Mosier, C. (1993) *Guided participation in cultural activity by toddlers and caregivers. Monograph of the Society for Research in Child Development 236* 58 (8), i–179.

Rogoff, B., Turkanis, C.G. and Bartlett, L. (eds) (2001) *Learning Together: Children and Adults in a School Community*. New York: Oxford University Press.

Rosenshine, B. (1992) The use of scaffolds for teaching higher-level cognitive strategies. *Educational Leadership* 49 (7), 26–33.

Rumbaut, R.G., Massey, D.S. and Bean, F.D. (2006) Linguistic life expectancies: Immigrant language retention in southern California. *Population and Development Review* 32 (3), 447–460.

Sagasta-Errasti, M.P. (2003) Acquiring writing skills in a third language: The positive effects of bilingualism. *International Journal of Bilingualism* 7 (1), 27–43.

Sautter, R.C. (1994) Who are today's city kids? Beyond the 'deficit model'. On WWW at http://www.ncrel.org/sdrs/cityschl/city1_1a.htm. Accessed 28.7.03.

Shannon, S.M. (1995) The hegemony of English: A case study of one bilingual classroom as a site of resistance. *Linguistics and Education* 7, 175–200.

Shannon, S.M. and Milian, M. (2002) Parents choose dual language programs in Colorado: A survey. *Bilingual Research Journal* 26 (3), 681–696.

Silverman, D. (2000) *Doing Qualitative Research: A Practical Handbook.* London, Thousand Oaks, CA: Sage.

Simmons, P.E., Emory, A., Carter, T., Coker, T., Finnegan, B., Crockett, D., Richardson, L., Yager, R., Craven, J., Tillotson, J., Brunkhorst, H., Twiest, M., Hossain, K., Gallager, J., Duggan-Haas, D., Parker, J., Cajas, F., Alshannag, Q., McGlamery, S., Krockover, G., Adams, P., Spector, B., La Porta, T., James, B., Rearden, K. and Labuda, K. (1999) Beginning teachers: Beliefs and classroom practices. *Journal of Research in Science Teaching* 36 (8), 930–954.

Skutnabb-Kangas, T. (2007) Linguistic human rights in education? In O. García and C. Baker (eds) *Bilingual Education. An Introductory Reader* (pp. 137–144). Clevedon: Multilingual Matters.

Smith, P.H. and Arnot-Hopffer, E. (1998) Exito Bilingüe: Promoting Spanish literacy in a dual language immersion program. *Bilingual Research Journal* 22 (2–4), 103–119.

Smith, P.H., Arnot Hopffer, E. and Carmichael, C.M. (2002) Raise a child, not a test score: Perspectives on bilingual education at Davis Bilingual Magnet School. *Bilingual Research Journal* 26 (1), 1–19.

Stigler, J.W. and Hiebert, J. (1998) Teaching is a cultural activity. *American Educator* Winter 4–11.

Suarez-Orozco, M. (1987) Becoming somebody: Central American immigrants in U.S. inner-city schools. *Anthropology & Education Quarterly* 18 (4), 287–299.

Suarez, D. (2002) The paradox of linguistic hegemony and the maintenance of Spanish as a heritage language in the United States. *Journal of Multilingual and Multicultural Development* 23 (6), 512–530.

Sugarman, J. and Howard, E. (2001) Development and maintenance of two-way immersion programs: Advice from practitioners (Practitioner Brief 2). On WWW at http://www.cal.org/crede/pubs/PracBrief2.htm.

Sumara, D. and Carson, T.R. (1997) Reconceptualizing action research as a living practice. In T.R. Carson and D. Sumara (eds) *Action Research as a Living Practice* (pp. xii–xxi). New York: Peter Lang.

Sutterby, J. (2002) The language of children's play in a two-way immersion setting: The language of negotiation. Paper presented at the Annual meeting of the American Educational Research Association, New Orleans, April.

Swain, M. and Lapkin, S. (1998) Interaction and second language learning: Two adolescent French immersion students working together. *The Modern Language Journal* 82 (3), 320–337.

Tafuri, N. (1991) *¿Has visto a mi patito ?* New York: Scholastic.

Takahashi-Breines, H. (2002) The role of teacher-talk in a dual language immersion third grade classroom. *Bilingual Research Journal* 26 (2), 213.

Tannenbaum, M. and Howie, P. (2002) The association between language maintenance and family relations: Chinese immigrant children in Australia. *Journal of Multicultural and Multilingual Development* 23 (5), 408–424.

Terborg, R., Landa, L.G. and Moore, P. (2007) The language situation in Mexico. In R.B. Baldauf and R.B. Kaplan (eds) *Language Planning and Policy in Latin America: Ecuador, Mexico, and Paraguay* (pp. 115–217). Clevedon: Multilingual Matters.

The Associated Press (2005) Foreign languages not just for big kids. *Associated Press*, 15 August.

Thomas, W.P. and Collier, V. (1997) School effectiveness for language minority students. December. On WWW at http://www.ncbe.gwu.edu/ncbepubs/resource/effectiveness/thomas-collier97.pdf. Accessed 12.7.02.

Thomas, W.P. and Collier, V.P. (2003) The multiple benefits of dual language. *Educational Researcher* 61 (2), 61–64.

Tobin, J.J., Davidson, D.H. and Wu, D.Y.H. (1989) *Preschool in Three Cultures: Japan, China, and the United States*. New Haven, CT: Yale University Press.

Toohey, K. (1998) Breaking them up, taking them away: ESL students in Grade 1. *TESOL Quarterly* 32 (1), 61–84.

Torres-Guzmán, M.E. (2007) Dual language programs: Key features and results. In O. García and C. Baker (eds) *Bilignaul Education: An Introductory Reader* (pp. 50–63). Clevedon: Multilingual Matters.

Torres-Guzmán, M.E., Kleyn, T., Morales-Rodríguez, S. and Han, A. (2005) Self-designated dual-language programs: Is there a gap between labeling and implementation? *Bilingual Research Journal* 29 (2), 453–474.

Valdés, G. (1997) Dual-language immersion programs: A cautionary note concerning the education of language minority students. *Harvard Education Review* 67 (3), 391–429.

Valdés, G. (2001) *Learning and not Learning English : Latino Students in American Schools*. New York: Teachers College Press.

Valdés, G. (2002) Enlarging the pie: Another look at bilingualism and schooling in the US. *International Journal of the Sociology of Language* 155–156, 187–195.

Varenne, H. and McDermott, R. (1998) *Successful Failure: The School America Builds*. Boulder, CO: Westview Press.

Vygotsky, L.S. (1978) *Mind in Society: The Development of Higher Psychological Processes*. Cambridge, MA: Harvard University Press.

Wainwright, D. (1997) Can sociological research be qualitative, critical and valid? *The Qualitative Report 3* (2). http://www.nova.edu/ssss/QR/QR3-2/wain.html

Walker, C.L. and Tedick, D.J. (2000) The complexity of immersion education: Teachers address the issues. *The Modern Language Journal* 84 (1), 5–27.

Wells, C.G. and Chang-Wells, G.L. (1992) *Constructing Knowledge Together : Classrooms as Centers of Inquiry and Literacy*. Portsmouth, NH: Heinemann.

Wiese, A.M. (2004) Bilingualism and biliteracy for all? Unpacking two-way immersion at second grade. *Language and Education* 18 (1), 69–92.

Willis, P.E. (1981) *Learning to Labor: How Working Class Kids get Working Class Jobs* (Morningside edn). New York: Columbia University Press.

Windschitl, M. (1999) Challenges of sustaining a constructivist classroom culture. *Phi Delta Kappan* 80 (10), 751–768.

Wittgenstein, L. and Anscombe, G.E.M. (2001) *Philosophical Investigations: The German Text, with a Revised English Translation* (3rd edn). Oxford, Malden, MA: Blackwell.

Wong-Fillmore, L. (1991) When learning a second language means losing the first. *Early Childhood Research Quarterly* 6 (3), 323–347.

Wong-Fillmore, L. (2000) Loss of family languages: Should educators be concerned? *Theory into Practice* 39 (4), 203–210.

Wood, D., Bruner, J. and Ross, G. (1976) The role of tutoring in problem solving. *Journal of Child Psychology and Psychiatry* 17, 89–100.